Worse Than Death

WORSE
THAN
DEATH

*The Dallas Nightclub Murders
and the Texas Multiple Murder Law*

Gary M. Lavergne

Number Two:
North Texas Crime and Criminal Justice Series

University of North Texas Press
Denton, Texas

The paper in this book meets the minimum requirements of the
American National Standard for Permanence of Paper for Printed
Library Materials, Z39.48.1984

Permissions
University of North Texas Press
PO Box 311336
Denton, TX 76203-1336
940-565-2142

Library of Congress Cataloging-in-Publication Data
Lavergne, Gary M., 1955-
  Worse than death : the Dallas nightclub murders and the Texas
multiple murder law / Gary M. Lavergne.— 1st ed.
      p. cm. — (North Texas crime and criminal justice ; no. 2)
  ISBN 1-57441-167-5 (cloth : alk. paper)
  1. Serial murders—Texas—Dallas. 2. Homicide—Texas. 3. Life
imprisonment—Texas. I. Title. II. North Texas crime and criminal
justice series ; no. 2.
  HV6534.D2L28 2003
  364.6'09764—dc21
                                        2003007236

Jacket credit:
Artwork by Karen T. Taylor, Facial Images

Design by Angela Schmitt

For Richard and Kenneth Lavergne
(a.k.a. Black and Keno)

Contents

Acknowledgments

Anyone who knows my wife, Laura, can only be amazed at her patience and tolerance. The evil world of mass murder and serial killing is completely foreign to her interests. And yet, this is the third book on that subject she has proofed and edited. She is an expert writer and editor, who helped to craft a first-rate book. She has endured the same stories dozens of times—with grace.

Our four children, Charlie, Mark, Amy, and Anna remind me that the world has many more good people than bad. They, and my brothers, Black and Keno, save me from despair.

At The University of Texas at Austin I shamelessly exploited my friendships with Bruce Walker, Geoff Leavenworth, Kathie Fagan, Michael Washington, Mark Long, Maryann Ruddock, Arturo Mancha, and Gary Speer, all of whom looked over this work after the end of their long workdays. Deane Willis of the International Office gave me valuable assistance in the area of travel/business/tourist permits and visas.

I am truly indebted to each of the persons I interviewed (listed in Notes on Sources.) Some of them went beyond sacrificing their valuable time for an interview to helping me secure other forms of information. The Honorable Judge Gerry Holden Meier, who had never before granted a formal interview, patiently answered every single question I asked of her, including several I posed via e-mail after my interview. Her cooperation extended beyond her retirement at the end of 2002. Norman Kinne welcomed me to his home for most of an entire day, and subsequently endured my repeated phone calls. Bill Parker drove me to the Harvest Hill Shopping Center, where the building that was once Ianni's still stands.

Charles Butts, a renowned criminal defense attorney, and a former president and charter member of the Texas Criminal Defense Lawyers Association, reviewed this manuscript and gave me valuable advice and information from the perspective of defending the accused. Another friend, Crawford Long, the First Assistant District Attorney of McLennan County, Texas, did the same from a prosecutorial angle.

My collaborator for a forthcoming book, Karen T. Taylor, is the world's foremost forensic artist. Her drawing of the moment Abdelkrim Belachheb fired the first shot captured the horror of what was to come. While producing such a dramatic picture, her questions were tough and thought provoking. She and her spouse, David Griffith, a Commander of the Texas Department of Public Safety, engaged me in conversations that significantly contributed to the quality of this work.

Staff of the Texas Department of Criminal Justice was particularly helpful, including Larry Todd, Public Information Officer, John Moriarty, Inspector General, and Dr. Keith Price, Warden of the Clements Unit. Major Richard Duffy, also of the Clements Unit, escorted me throughout the maze of chain-link fences to every prison operation I wanted to see.

At the Dallas County District Attorney's Office, the staff of District Attorney Bill Hill was especially professional. Larissa Roeder, an Assistant DA in the Appeals Section, handled my repeated and determined open records requests with patience and professionalism. The DA's Office prosecutes tens of thousands of cases each year, so finding a specific, fully-adjudicated case prosecuted eighteen years earlier was not an easy task, but Jeff Shaw, Chief Investigator for the Dallas DA, kindly and diligently searched for the Belachheb Case file for weeks so that it could be made available for this book.

Stephanie Lavake, Carolyn Rice, and Rose Gatlin of the Texas Court of Appeals, Second District, located and made available the *Statement of Facts* and the exhibits of the Belachheb Case.

Justice Sharon Keller, Presiding Judge of the Texas Court of Criminal Appeals, kindly assisted my search for court records and answered questions I had regarding searches for cases involving the multiple murder statute.

Librarians from the Legislative Reference Library in the Texas State Capitol, the Barker History Center, and the Perry-Castañeda Libraries of The University of Texas were very helpful in locating materials necessary to produce this book. Rebecca Rich-Wulfmeyer of the Austin History Center is more than just a librarian—she is my good friend.

J. W. Thompson, now a retired homicide detective from the Austin Police Department, reviewed this work at my request and made valuable suggestions. So did A. P. Merillat, an Investigator for the Special Prosecutor's Unit with jurisdiction over the Texas Department of Criminal Justice. Also a gifted writer, A. P.'s suggestions transcended criminal justice.

I am fortunate to have a business relationship with James D. Hornfischer, my literary agent who is also a licensed attorney. Jim continues to reconcile my esoteric intellectual interests with the real world of publishing. (Not an easy task.) This is the third book we have worked on together.

I am also indebted to Ron Chrisman, Director of the University of North Texas Press, and his staff, Paula Oates, Mary Young, and Karen DeVinney, for their fine work on this project.

No doubt there are others. For those whose names I forgot, be assured it was due to a fatigued mind, and not my heart.

Author's Notes

This is a work of nonfiction; all of the characters are/were real people and all of the episodes are carefully documented through interviews, official records, sworn statements, or eyewitness testimony. I have tried to make clear those few instances where I have drawn conclusions, made assumptions, or reconstructed dialogue.

In producing *Worse Than Death,* I collected many thousands of pages of official and unofficial documents. In some cases, I viewed reports that are not yet public record. On other occasions, during interviews, sources gave me information on the condition that they not be identified. Since most of the major characters of this book are still alive, I accepted those conditions. Information from confidential documents and/or sources are hereafter cited as "Confidential Source."

In some instances I used only first names, altered first names, or nicknames of some individuals who deserve peace and privacy. An asterisk (*) follows my first use of those names.

Throughout the year 2002 I made repeated attempts to convince Abdelkrim Belachheb to allow me to interview him. First, I requested an interview through the Office of Public Information of the Texas Department of Criminal Justice. Officials at the William C. Clements Unit at Amarillo contacted him and he declined my request. Second, I wrote a series of letters to him directly. He responded cordially twice, but still declined to be interviewed in person. I repeated my requests throughout the process of writing, editing, and submitting a manuscript. He was also offered an opportunity to speak to me during my visit to the Clements Unit on September 13, 2002. Mr. Belachheb could not have been given more opportunities to express his version of the events that led to the murders he committed on June 29, 1984, his trial, and his incarceration. He declined.

It is my conclusion that as part of his defense Abdelkrim Belachheb shamelessly made attempts to exploit stereotypes and even fears some Americans have of Muslims and North Africans and peoples of the Middle East, especially of Berbers and Arabs. *I ask readers to remember that although I reported what Abdelkrim Belachheb said, it does not mean I believe it—quite the contrary.*

Finally, as with my previous books, my objective is to establish the facts of a case that has had a profound effect on the law, our perceptions of it, or law enforcement/criminal justice practices. Such crimes are usually monumentally offensive. Thus, providing context and establishing the facts requires detailed descriptions and analyses of gruesome scenes.

Gary M. Lavergne
Cedar Park, Texas
July 28, 2003

chapter one

Disconcerting Stares

> *"I want to get to that killer while the blood is still wet and while the adrenalin is still flowing."*
>
> —Bill Parker
> Retired Dallas Police Department

I

Bill Parker had just fallen asleep. He had been out to dinner that night and had even had a couple of drinks. The phone rang right after midnight. Many times he had gotten up in the middle of the night to rush off to a murder scene. But this time was different.

The dispatcher was excited and at times hard to understand. He told Bill that as many as a dozen people could be dead in a restaurant on the corner of Midway and Interstate 635 in the north section of Dallas.

"I'll call you right back," Bill said, before hanging up. He thought the best thing to do was to splash water on his face, wake up, and give the caller time to pull himself together.

"I had never heard of Ianni's," Bill recalled years later. But he would learn much about Ianni's Restaurant and Club. On the night of June 29, 1984, Bill would see the club for the first time—the site of the largest mass murder in the history of Dallas, Texas.

He drove directly to the scene from his home. A fairly large crowd had assembled outside of Cappuccino's, another nightclub nearby. There were plenty of policemen to hold them back, and the news of what had happened inside Ianni's was more than enough to subdue the crowd.[1]

It could have happened to them just as easily—the two clubs, separated only by a common parking lot in a small outdoor strip mall, were very close to one another. By the time Bill arrived, some of the onlookers may have known that the killer had been in Cappuccino's and another north Dallas nightspot earlier that evening.

Ianni's front doors were on either side of a glass foyer covered by a burgundy canopy embroidered with an "I." Bill walked in and turned left to a reception area where, earlier that evening, the head-waiter had greeted customers and kept track of what tables were occupied. Next to the headwaiter's stand hung an oil portrait of Joe Ianni, the restaurant's founder.[2]

Other police officers and medics were already there and busily at work. Two victims had been taken away in ambulances in desperate attempts to save their lives. One lived. The others were still on the floor in the bar, which was located down a hallway near the back of the building.

"When you are investigating a crime like this, you don't have the luxury of taking the time to look at the horror of it all," Bill later recalled. Intensely disciplined, Bill Parker wanted badly to arrest the man responsible for the grisly scene.[3]

As he entered the bar, to the left was a man, a mechanic, in blue work clothes lying on his back. His shirt had the word "Mercedes" embroidered on the pocket, and he had one of those retractable key chains that janitors wear, clipped to his wide, shiny black leather belt. The pool of blood surrounding his head was so thick that the dark blue carpet could not absorb any more. When the medics turned him over to be sure he could not be saved, they saw his eyes, now dull and set in a disconcerting stare.

A gruesome path of blood told the story of what had happened to the mechanic after he was shot. A large pool had formed on the bar in front of where he had been sitting, encircling the mixed drink he had been enjoying and two ashtrays positioned neatly within the pool. The blood soaked coaster was barely visible beneath the glass. Spatters and streaks ran down the beige barstool toward the floor where he had landed. Even the rich, oak panels of the bar near the floor had blood and tissue on them.

Next to the mechanic was a well-dressed blonde businesswoman in a white skirt and a purple sweater. Her skirt had a large bloodstain over her upper right leg, but that wound did not look to be fatal. She had landed, or crawled, a few feet from where she was sitting.

When the medics came to her, it was clear that she had died from a gunshot wound to her head that had shattered her skull. Her eyes were open as well, and she had that same disconcerting stare as the mechanic next to her.

Lying across her feet was another victim. She, too, was wearing a white skirt and was well-dressed though her attire was not as businesslike. Her tan blouse had been turned red by her blood.

When Sergeant Bill Parker entered Ianni's Restaurant and Club he immediately saw the pool of blood that had formed on the bar. (Dallas County District Attorney Files)

The medics had placed EKG electrodes on her chest to make sure she was beyond saving, but it had to have been as a precaution only. She had been shot twice in the head and was a bloody mess. One of the wounds entered her right cheek and had blown chunks of her dentures out of her mouth. Her bright blue eyes were now dull and lifeless as she lay on her back in death. They were fixed upon the ceiling—set in a disconcerting stare. Her badly damaged head rested on the right hand of yet another victim, a woman dressed for the evening in a white crocheted dress.

Even now, it was obvious that the woman in the crocheted dress had been stunningly beautiful. She had landed on the floor at the base of her barstool. Her head was turned to the right, her shoulders were flat against the floor, but her knees pointed to the right and her legs were crossed, almost as if delicately posed. The spike of one of her off-white high heels was hooked around the leg of another of those beige barstools. Her silver butane cigarette lighter was on the floor next to her lifeless body. Her eyes were closed.

To the right was a large pool of blood where another victim, the first to be shot, had fallen. The medics found her alive, but moaning and dying. When Bill reached that spot, he found evidence of how others had tried desperately to save her life, or at least make her comfortable. Her black silk belt and her tan shoes had been removed; they were left behind and were resting against the bar where she was sitting when her assailant shot her. She died en route to Dallas' infamous Parkland Hospital, where John F. Kennedy and Lee Harvey Oswald died in 1963.

Bill Parker didn't take time to "look at the horror of it all." He examined the bodies as he would pieces of evidence, clues to identify who might be responsible for this senseless slaughter. In an investigation like this, a slug or a shell, or even a strand of hair might make or break a case. Bill was looking everywhere for everything. He searched the floors to find spent ammunition. He talked to witnesses and the first cops to arrive and compared what they said to what he saw. He took the time to look at chairs, tables, and the bar.

Sergeant Bill Parker saw five murder victims as he viewed the scene. The four pictured here were seated along the bar. (1) a woman in the crochet dress, (2) an unemployed bartender, (3) a blonde businesswoman, and (4) a mechanic. (Dallas County District Attorney Files)

When Bill came upon the final victim, still on the floor by a potted plant near where the band played, he stopped in his tracks. He recognized the obese, gray-haired man wearing a tan leisure suit as someone he had arrested before. Years earlier Bill had worked vice. The dead man near the dance floor was a pimp. "What was he doing here?" Bill thought. He wondered if there could be a gang or organized crime connection to this mass murder, but that didn't fit with everything else he had seen and heard from the eyewitnesses. It was more likely that this poor fellow was in the wrong place at the wrong time. Just like all the others.[4]

II

Sadly, there have been other mass slayings with even greater body counts. Along the Interstate 35 central Texas corridor alone there have been much larger tragedies. Eighteen years earlier on August

1, 1966, Charles Whitman climbed the University of Texas Tower and gunned down nearly fifty people in about an hour and a half. Fifteen died as a result of his sniping. Two more victims, his wife and mother, killed at their homes earlier the same morning, brought the total to seventeen murders.[5]

On October 16, 1991, George Hennard drove his pickup through the window of a cafeteria in Killeen, Texas. He pulled out a gun similar to the one used in Ianni's and shot fifty-six people, killing twenty-three, which is still the largest simultaneous mass murder in American history.[6]

Episodic mass murders always make headlines, if for no other reason than because they surprise, shock, and sicken us. But for non-victims, they seldom bring about more than just momentary fear, anger, and grief. We read the newspapers, shake our heads, occasionally pray for people we do not know, and go about our lives.

Most mass murderers, like Whitman and Hennard, commit "suicide by cop" or do the job themselves, never to face a trial by jury. When that happens, the incidents are merely remembered on anniversaries divisible by five and ten. But the man who killed in Ianni's lived to face a jury.

Occasionally, an incident, like the Ianni's murders, transcends the act itself. Sometimes it is the descent of criminal proceedings into a memorable circus atmosphere of perverse entertainment, like the trials of O. J. Simpson and the Menendez Brothers. In spite of their high profiles, neither of those crimes brought about a significant change in how we deal with crime. Neither did the ultimate true crime story—the Charles Manson Family murders.

Murder becomes epiphanic when it causes us to change our institutions, perceptions, or behavior. Charles Whitman was the first to take his guns and go to school. He proved a boast he had made to several acquaintances that from his perch he could "hold off an army" of policemen for as long as he wanted. After Whitman, law enforcement agencies throughout the United States rushed to form Special Weapons and Tactics (SWAT) teams to handle similar "domestic terrorist" events.

Serial killers sometimes bring about change as well. In Texas, after serving twenty-three years in prison, including six years on death row, for the brutal and heartless murder of three high school students, Kenneth Allen McDuff was paroled. He walked out of prison. During the next three years he raped, tortured, and murdered at least five more women. His serial killing spree brought about radical changes in parole, called the McDuff Laws, and provided the catalyst for the construction of new prisons at the cost of billions of dollars.[7]

Outside of Texas, the "Tylenol poisonings" brought about the expenditure of many billions of dollars to repackage virtually every consumable product on store shelves throughout the world. Today, nearly everything we buy is grossly over-packaged and tamper-proof.[8]

In 1994, the parents and neighbors of seven-year-old Megan Kanka of New Jersey did not know their neighbor was a twice-convicted sex offender until after Megan had been brutally raped and murdered. Today, in all fifty states and the District of Columbia, laws requiring the registration of sex offenders and the disclosure of their location are collectively called "Megan's Laws."[9]

As isolated incidents, these crimes were tragically common. They are different because they were cases that forced us to look closely at our criminal justice system, what we do, and why we do it. Some crimes force us to look at our heritage, culture, and ourselves as a people—and they bring about change. They are few, but the Ianni's massacre was just such a crime for Texas.

Even before the dead could be buried, the bullet holes patched up, the shattered smoked mirrors replaced, and the carpet in Ianni's changed, prosecutors knew that it would not be possible for *this* killer to be prosecuted for *capital* murder. What he had done was not a capital crime in Texas!

Lawmakers supporting the death penalty, preparing for a legislative session that was to begin in a few months, raced to draft bills to rectify a gross "loophole" in the Penal Code the Ianni's murders had revealed. Current law favored property over a second human life. If the Ianni's murderer had killed one person and stolen a dime from her purse, he could have been sentenced to death. If he had dragged one of the dying victims to his car and taken her to a store next door, he could have been sentenced to death. If he had walked off with an ashtray or stolen a fork off a table, he could have been sentenced to death. He did none of those things. *All he did was kill six people and wound a seventh.* Thus, under Texas law at the time, the death penalty was not an option.[10]

Charles Whitman, for example, had he been taken alive, would have been eligible for the death penalty only because one of his victims was a policeman. So, the observation went, if he had missed the shot he fired at the policeman, and killed only sixteen instead of seventeen people, he could not have gotten the death penalty.

Following the murders in Ianni's, opponents of the death penalty had little hope of containing the emotion resulting from six dead bodies. Coupled with imagined scenarios of terrorists poisoning entire cities and all sorts of other multiple murderers who could not be put to death, the six bodies proved to be more than death penalty opponents could successfully combat.

Some death penalty opponents pointed out the obvious; surely the Ianni's killer, and the multiple murderers who strike fear into our hearts, could care less about whether or not what they do leads them to the death chamber. What does capital punishment mean to a man who would wipe out an entire community if he could? People who do these things are not considering the law while loading their semi-automatic pistols—quite the opposite. And most of them, like Whitman and Hennard, do not intend to live anyway. A new capital murder statute for multiple murderers, they argued, was merely an expansion of a policy we should not have in the first place. It exacerbated inequity and injustice by covering another group under its umbrella. It did nothing more than add to the body count of already tragic events.

But some believe that deterrence is not the issue; some believe death is justice, an appropriate response to a monstrous crime. Maybe, as old-time Texas Rangers say, "Some people just need killing."

III

But what if the murderer was crazy at the time? Surely someone who guns down seven people in full view of a bar half full of patrons has to be crazy? Almost all other people handle anger, even when provoked, without resorting to murder, much less *mass* murder. Does this mean he was insane? Some say, "yes." Others, using the same argument and looking at the same case, say, "no." Cases like the Ianni's murders, and that of Andrea Yates, convicted in 2002 of the drowning deaths of her five children in her suburban Houston home, bring forth a debate we *should* have over what we, as a state and nation, are willing to accept as an excuse for killing.

But debate without facts becomes a meaningless, emotional, and irrational exercise. The relevant facts come from the murder cases, like Ianni's, after a period sufficient to allow for a dispassionate historical review. History is the source of wisdom; to believe otherwise is to believe the wise are psychic.

The man responsible for the carnage of June 29, 1984, was a Moroccan national named Abdelkrim Belachheb. He never denied the fact that he gunned down those innocent people. During his trial his defense did not challenge a significant statement of fact or piece of evidence. Accepting *in toto* the prosecution's version of events, the first sentence of the defense attorney's opening statement was, "You know now what happened at Ianni's on June 29, 1984, and now the defense is going to tell you *why* it happened."[11] (Italics added)

Should *why* matter? The Belachheb plea was "not guilty by reason of insanity." In most states, Texas included, insanity essentially means that at the time of the crime, the perpetrator did not know the difference between right and wrong. It is always a controversial defense. It is also a misconception that the insanity defense is used often and successfully by the guilty to "cheat" prison, or the death chamber.

The Belachheb insanity defense was unique in that it included the notion that he suffered from "culture shock," or the inability to adjust to life from where he had been raised to where he was at the time of the killings. His trial was largely a parade of doctors, each with impressive credentials, all examining the same person and looking at the same data and coming to opposite conclusions.

But doctors do not decide what is an excuse for murder, i.e., insanity. Democratically-elected representatives on the state level who, during what we hope is a deliberative process, do more than read headlines, count dead bodies, and look at crime scene photos, give juries a precise definition. And even when a state decides with certainty and clarity when killing is murder or a manifestation of mental illness, what is to be done with the creatures that have committed either? Some say "life" and others say "death." The people decide not only what is murder but also what is justice.

IV

And finally, sometimes crimes like the Ianni's murders present us with warnings of things to come, and thus, with opportunities to take action and even avoid catastrophe. Consider this opening by Barbara Walters from a segment of the ABC News Program *20/20:*

> *The killer . . . came here as a tourist, and his past foretold the violence. . . . He came in to America with no questions asked. Bob Brown reveals how easy it is*—Passport for Murder. *Up Front tonight, a mass murder. It's a frightening tale heightened by this fact: The killer came through American customs on a tourist visa.*[12]

The segment aired, not after the terrorist attacks of September 11, 2001, but sixteen years earlier on August 22, 1985. The story was not about Al Qaeda but about Abdelkrim Belachheb and how he easily bluffed his way into the United States. Afterwards, the FBI, State Department, CIA, and the Immigration and Naturalization Service pointed fingers of blame at one another. It turns out Belachheb's records had been destroyed (along with all other visa applications) after only a year and while he was in the United States illegally. It could not be determined exactly how he got in, or who let him in, or if he had help to get here. All the Consulate in Morocco knew was that he lied on his application. If he had *volunteered* the truth, the fact that he was a criminal, an ex-con from a Kuwaiti prison, and wanted for violent crimes in Belgium, he could never have gotten his visa.

Instead of instituting any serious reform, the agencies decided that screening, and thus detecting, visa applicants for criminal records was "impractical" and nothing could be done to stop people like Belachheb from entering the United States. In short, nothing changed.[13]

Belachheb showed us how easy it was for a common criminal with minimal abilities to flaunt our open society and do us harm. We preferred to believe that uncommon, thoughtful, cunning criminals—terrorists, with much greater resources and grander designs for murder—could not do the same thing.

In the surreal world of mass murder, the body count in Ianni's, six dead and one wounded, is rather small. The crime itself lasted only a few minutes and there was never any mystery about who did the killing. However, few crimes and even fewer criminals are as mysterious. At the center of it all is Texas Department of Criminal Justice inmate #387133—Abdelkrim Belachheb.

---

[1] Bill Parker, interviewed by the author on June 22, 2002. Interviews will be cited first by name and date and then subsequently by name only.

[2] Descriptions of the restaurant and the crime scene are from crime scene photos in the files of the Dallas County District Attorney's Office and the Dallas Police Department.

[3] Bill Parker quote from interview.

[4] Bill Parker.

[5] See Gary M. Lavergne, *A Sniper in the Tower: The Charles Whitman Murders* (Denton: University of North Texas Press, 1997) in hardcover/trade paperback, and (New York: Bantam Books, 1998) in mass market paperback.

[6] Elinor Karpf, *Anatomy of a Massacre* (New York: WRS Group, 1994), is the only book about the Luby's Cafeteria tragedy listed in the Amazon.com database.

[7] See Gary M. Lavergne, *Bad Boy from Rosebud: The Murderous Life of Kenneth Allen McDuff,* (Denton: University of North Texas Press, 1999) in hardcover and *Bad Boy* (New York: St. Martin's Press, 2001) in paperback.

[8] An excellent overview of the Tylenol poisonings is presented in John Douglas and Mark Olshaker, *Anatomy of Motive* (New York: Scribner, 1999), 103-22.

[9] *Washington Post,* May 21, 2002.

[10] Norman Kinne, interviewed by the author on June 14, 2002.

[11] Frank Jackson quoted in *Texas* v *Belachheb,* 291st Judicial District, Case no. F84-75078-SU, et. al., V, 1234-36.

[12] Barbara Walters quote from ABC News: *20/20,* first broadcast on August 22, 1985.

[13] *Dallas Morning News,* August 5, 7, 8, 1984, and January 17, 1985; *Dallas Times Herald,* August 7, 12, 1984.

chapter two

Morocco

> *"He simply responds to women according to the script, the code, the prescription, the values that his culture has given him regarding women."*
> —Dr. Harrell Gill-King
> Anthropologist and Defense Expert Witness

I

There is an area of northwest Africa, between the Atlas and the Rif Ranges called the Maghreb, where at the height of its power and prestige, the mighty Roman Empire discovered it could go no farther. The Atlas Mountains form a diagonal range traversing Morocco from the southwest to the northeast, separating Morocco's Atlantic coastal plains to the north and west from the expansive Sahara Desert to the south. A smaller range, the Rif, runs parallel to the Mediterranean coast. Between the two ranges, which almost merge near the eastern urban center of Taza, a passage connects Algeria and the rest of North Africa to the Moroccan interior and the Atlantic Ocean.

From Taza, the fan-shaped plain of the Maghreb opens westward toward the Moroccan political capital of Rabat and the business capital of Casablanca. Though geographically close to the Strait of Gibraltar, this area is surprisingly isolated. On a political map, it appears ideally situated to be a portal from the Middle East, through

North Africa, to the New World. But topographically the region's proximity to the mountains, the dearth of natural harbors on both the Atlantic and Mediterranean coasts, and the monstrous Sahara Desert form an anatomy of isolation.[1]

Although not quite the "splendid isolation" the British enjoy, the region's seclusion has helped to protect its indigenous people, especially those in small agrarian communities, from sustained subjugation. Through the ages, conquering armies have marched through the area, only to discover how difficult it would be to govern such "defenseless" people. At one time or another, the Carthaginians, Vandals, Byzantines, Turks, Spanish, French, Germans, and the Allied Powers of World War II marched through the countryside with overpowering military force—only to march right back out, maybe not right away, but eventually—as the Romans did.

Located here along the northern slopes of the Middle Atlas Mountains are the Fes and Meknes Provinces. They are a mosaic of hills, plateaus, valleys, and rich plains. The foothills contain extensive areas of forest where oak, juniper, cedar, fir, and pine trees carpet large areas blending into plains, which if left uncultivated, are covered with brush and short grasses. Temperatures here are more extreme than on Morocco's coasts.[2]

In the Meknes Province, very near the border with Fes, is the village of Nzala Beni Ammar (Beni Ammar), along with other villages where the Berber dialect of Tamazight is spoken. Looking south from the grassy plains, Beni Ammar is visible on the slope of one of the mountains of the Middle Atlas. The area is an incongruous mixture of deceiving, mesmerizing beauty and harsh geography.[3]

During the 1940s, Beni Ammar was the home of Mohamed Ben Mohamed and Tahra Abdeslam—later known as the Belachhebs (pronounced BELL ah CHEB).[4] Undoubtedly, World War II and the struggle for control of North Africa between the Allied and Axis Powers made their lives more complicated, perhaps even dangerous.

Relatively little is known about the Belachhebs. Some accounts suggest that Mohamed and his family lived a hard, subsistence, agrarian life, an existence common to the people of the area. The accounts are almost certainly inaccurate, and Abdelkrim Belachheb likely did not grow up that way. In 1985, the ABC News program *20/20* confirmed that Mohamed was a respected businessman. As a trader, the father was rarely at home.[5]

The Belachhebs, like most of the people of the region, were Berbers—the people who, throughout history, had formed confederations of tribes that frustrated invaders and who "regularly imposed their desires on the Moroccan state by cutting off communications" between Fes and larger urban areas to the west.

The Berbers of northwest Africa are mostly light-skinned. They are not Arab. Thomas K. Park described them as a "group of people who epitomize the inutility of racial classifications." Many Europeans and Americans know little or nothing about the Berbers of North Africa.

References to Berber habitation of the Mediterranean coast of Africa, from Egypt to the Atlantic Ocean, date back to 3000 B.C. They are the indigenous people of the area. Mohamed Belachheb's Berber ancestors dominated the Mediterranean coast until the Arab invasions of North Africa that began in the Seventh Century. The Arabs were the only invaders to stay and permanently establish themselves in the area. As a result, many Berbers were pushed, or chose to withdraw, from the Mediterranean coast into remote interior regions where for centuries they were relatively, though not completely, isolated from the Arabs. Gradually, Berber culture did assimilate with Arab culture, so that by the Twentieth Century all Moroccan children, including Abdelkrim Belachheb, were attending Arabic–speaking schools.

During the Eight Century, the Berbers largely abandoned Christianity, Judaism, and "paganism" for Islam.[6]

On November 24, 1944, toward the end of World War II, after the Nazis had been driven from North Africa and things had qui-

eted down in Morocco, Tahra Abdeslam and Mohamed Ben
Mohamed Belachheb welcomed their fourth child, a handsome
and healthy son they named Abdelkrim.

On some occasions, Abdelkrim was to characterize his upbringing as severely disadvantaged. "Behind civilization by 500 years,
in total ignorance, we didn't play the games of sophisticated
American children," he claimed. (Behind which civilization? He
never said.) The family was large (Abdelkrim had eleven siblings)
and one account has them living in Beni Ammar in a small, square,
stone house on a plot of land with a few sheep. In 1978, thirty-
four years after Abdelkrim's birth, his first wife, a Belgian woman
named Jenny*, visited Beni Ammar and was utterly shocked by
what she saw. "Life is cruel there. Beni Ammar is like the time of
Jesus Christ." She was under the impression that the Belachhebs
were very poor. But then, Jenny may have seen only what
Abdelkrim intended to show her, which was whatever he wanted
her to believe.

On another occasion, Belachheb claimed to have lived in the
home of his grandfather, a man he admired and respected more
than his father. Reportedly, this grandfather was also an Imam who
owned a "castle" large enough to house over 100 family members.
At best, Belachheb might have been referring to a common practice of an Imam "being responsible" for or "caring" for a village,
because "castles," as such, are non-existent in villages like Beni
Ammar. During his *20/20* report from Beni Ammar in 1985, corre-
spondent Bob Brown interviewed Belachheb's father. In one scene,
Mohamed entered his house—it was not a castle.[7]

If Abdelkrim was merely indifferent to his father, he was outright scornful of his mother. He described her as "an ignorant peas-
ant who married into a family of some wealth." (Which, on other
occasions, he said was poor.) As an adult, Abdelkrim was to tell his
doctors that because of space limitations, he often slept with his
mother. Indeed, it was not uncommon for children and parents to
sleep in the same room, or even in the same bed; that is largely

true of any culture. But Belachheb claimed victimhood; he claimed to have suffered from recurring nightmares in which he had sex with her.[8]

According to an anthropologist who came to know Abdelkrim as a case study, Belachheb was raised in a strict Islamic Shiite tradition. The "psychological effect of that is that it produces a certain amount of mental rigidness, inflexibility, which contributes to his inability to adapt" Belachheb's strict upbringing allegedly included a "particularly heavy dose of indoctrination—especially since he was raised by an Imam—a religious figure—a mullah. They are the guardians and safe-keepers of religious detail."[9]

In truth, the Islamic Shiite tradition is virtually non-existent in Morocco. Muslims there are Sunni, living in one of the most liberal of all Islamic countries.[10]

The alleged mullah was his revered grandfather, and Belachheb later claimed to be a favored grandson. Indeed, he continued, his family called him "the pretty one" or the "special one." Soon after his grandfather died in 1960, the story went, a jealous paternal uncle vented his rage on the young Belachheb. According to Belachheb, his uncle inflicted severe beatings with a weapon resembling a shillelagh or a club. Belachheb also added that his teacher beat him daily for four years.[11]

His stories of a traumatic childhood were the earliest examples of a long list of instances of jealous tormentors who "picked" on him. And again, in truth, corporal punishment in grammar school was common and condoned, not only in Morocco.

By his own account, Belachheb's upbringing also included violent religious rituals. In 1984, while preparing for trial in the United States, he spoke to a psychologist about an initiation rite he witnessed at the age of ten. In 1985, ABC News identified the ceremony, which reputedly involved music and trances, practiced by the Brotherhood of the Hamadsha. The ritual reportedly included hitting oneself on the head with an axe in order to exorcise "she-demons." The shedding of blood was supposed to eliminate all traces of femininity from a masculine body. The self-inflicted torture allegedly included pouring boiling water over their heads, burning their tongues by licking heated knives, and then traveling over one hundred miles to a "sage" who healed them.

Belachheb claims to have gone home after the spectacle and bragged to his friends that he, too, could withstand the pain they had all witnessed. With friends who "didn't have anything else" to do, and while "playing the hero," Belachheb supposedly fashioned an axe from a sharp rock and a stick, and imitated the rites of that religious festival by burying the homemade axe into his own head. The other children, Belachheb continued, ran to get their parents who secured what medical attention they could. He claims to have been comatose for over eight months, remembering only the prayers to Allah for miracles recited by his father and grandfather.[12]

As an adult, when charged with serious crimes, Abdelkrim Belachheb attributed his violence to his upbringing and culture. Undoubtedly, some of his countrymen would have considered some of his characterizations a slander against Morocco and Berbers. His claims of repeated violence to his head later became the basis for a legal argument that he be sent to a hospital rather than a prison.

Indeed, Belachheb sought to portray the Meknes/Fes regions, where Beni Ammar lies, as frozen in time. He hoped that others would see the area as Martin Scorsese portrayed it in his film *The Last Temptation of Christ*. In his review of the movie, *Washington Post* writer Hal Hinson said of the locations that "Middle Eastern compositions (most of which were shot in Morocco) are rocky and desert-dry and bleached of color, and they seem almost to vibrate from the intensity of the sun. In the scenes set in the marketplaces and villages, the colors are jarringly sensuous; they burn into you and help Scorsese to evoke the barbarism of the age."[13] *Last Temptation* aside, Americans believing such stereotyped visions were more likely to accept Belachheb's tales of his native land.

Abdelkrim Belachheb grew up in an area surrounded by sacred Islamic sites. After Mecca and Medina, Fes is one of the holiest cities of Islam, founded during the great theological war that tore the Muslim world into the Shia and Sunni sects. The largest mosque in North Africa, the Qarawiyyin Mosque, is located there. Around 787 AD, during the time of the great war, Moulay Idriss El Akhbar (The Elder), a great-grandson of the Prophet Mohammed, and the founder of the Idrisid Dynasty (789-985), came to the area. He introduced Islam to Morocco. This was the nativity of the Moroccan state and it transformed the area.[14]

The Moulay Idriss, however, did not choose to be buried in Fes. Instead, his tomb is located even closer to the Belachheb homestead, on the slopes of the Jabal Zarhun between Beni Ammar and Meknes in the holy city named for him.[15] In 1985, ABC News reported that the Hamadsha ritual Belachheb claimed to have witnessed, and later imitated as a ten-year-old, took place on the other side of "Mount Zarhun" from Beni Ammar.[16]

South of Beni Ammar and only a few miles beyond the revered Moulay Idriss' grave is Meknes. Meknes is slightly closer to Beni Ammar than Fes, although contemporaneous maps suggest it is somewhat harder to get to. During Belachheb's time, it was accessible only by routes that were little more than paths through a wilderness.[17]

Indeed, Abdelkrim Belachheb was raised near revered, even sacred, Islamic sites. Years later in an American court, he attempted to use that fact to reinforce a defense centered on "culture shock."

II

The culture Abdelkrim Belachheb knew had been fashioned during the Nineteeth and early Twentieth Centuries when France and Spain, harboring visions of global empires, through military victories and treaties, brought Morocco and Algeria into their spheres of influence. In Morocco, the Spanish controlled a long, narrow strip of the Mediterranean coast and another narrow strip in the south. The French had a much larger area—including the regions around Fes and Meknes.

After World War I, the Berber and Arab populations began to seek greater autonomy. They were led by Muhammad Ibn Abd al-Karim al-Khattabi, more popularly known as Abd-el-Krim. He was to become a Berber hero and the symbol of Moroccan nationalism. Abdelkrim Belachheb was named after this Berber warrior, and years later Belachheb was to claim that as a result his father was imprisoned for twenty days for giving his son "delusions of grandeur." (He never identified who imprisoned his father.)

Belachheb's tales of the significance of his name suggested it had near-mystical power. Other Moroccans pointed out that the name "Abdelkrim" is as common in that area as "Charlie" is in America.[18]

That the Arabs and Berbers of Morocco are mysterious to geography-challenged Europeans and Americans is vividly illustrated by the march of the American Army through the area in 1942, only two years before Abdelkrim's birth. The Commander, the flamboyant American General George S. Patton, Jr., depended on intelligence that author Ladislas Farago called a "rather spectacular display of ignorance on the part of the State Department." Ever the equestrian, all Patton knew of Morocco was that "Barb," the ancestor of thoroughbred horses, came from the historic royal stables at Meknes. Patton had been told at a briefing conducted by his own intelligence officers that the Berbers hated the rather small population of Moroccan Jews and therefore were favorably disposed to Nazi Jew-baiting propaganda. Incredibly, the Jews, the briefing went on to illustrate, could be expected to attack the Islamic Berbers once the Americans arrived. (It would have been a suicidal act on the part of the Jews, who according to the same American intelligence, accounted for less than three percent of the Moroccan population.)[19]

In reality, Moroccan nationalist leaders easily saw that Nazism, however anti-Semitic, was not the path to an independent Morocco.

Sultan Mohammed V had pledged allegiance to France at the outbreak of the war and he never wavered. The Moroccans saw, as Moshe Gershovich has written, that two factors were to guarantee their independence: the decline of France as a military and political power (which the Nazis had assured) and, more importantly, the rise of "indigenous nationalist activism" that swept through Morocco.[20]

Desperate to hold on to its North African possessions, the French exiled the Sultan to Madagascar in 1953. The effect of this action was to further unite all Moroccans—the Berbers and Arabs in rural and urban areas. The sense of nationalism was particularly acute in the countryside, in villages like Beni Ammar, where young men swelled the ranks of the *Armee de Liberation.* But the *Armee* was not a well-equipped, fine-tuned military force winning glorious battlefield victories. They conducted stealthy guerilla attacks that constantly reminded the French that, in fact, no occupation forces could ever really control the countryside.[21]

If Belachheb had any political allegiance, it was to this nationalist movement, which was to flourish, as he became a young man. But unfortunately, Abdelkrim Belachheb would grow to learn that he could say almost whatever he wanted about Arabs, Berbers, and Morocco and many Americans would listen attentively and believe him.

Abdelkrim Belachheb claimed to be involved in guerilla activities as a young boy. On separate occasions, he told both of his wives that at the age of twelve he was involved in the bombing of a constable's office in his home village of Beni Ammar. In some versions, his alleged bombing was characterized as political resistance. Even if partially true, Belachheb would have celebrated his twelfth birthday in late 1956, about a year *after* France allowed for the return of the Sultan and several months after independence day had been celebrated in Morocco. Other versions of the story allege that the act was directed at the Arab-dominated government's oppression of the Berbers. If so, it would have been atypical of Arab-Berber relations at the time. As Gershovich wrote, "The manifestation of nationalist unity among Berbers and Arabs, rural and urban, nomadic and settled, spared Morocco the spectacle of civil strife characteristic of some newly established post-colonial societies."[22]

If the bombing occurred at all, it would not likely have served a political purpose; it is far more probable to have been a lawless act of juvenile delinquency, and most probably the result of a perceived insult by an official towards "the pretty one." The story's origin could also have been Belachheb's egotistical revisionist attempt to attach a larger meaning to his simple, youthful criminal behavior.

A far more reliable source of information on his childhood behavior than Abdelkrim Belachheb was his father Mohamed, who later admitted to ABC News that Abdelkrim was always a problem child. Through a spokesman the elder Belachheb admitted, "Since childhood he showed signs of disturbances and got himself in fights with other children his age. We received endless complaints about him from school, from his classmates, his teachers and the principal."[23] Undoubtedly, such a pupil was punished—often. Such corporal punishment was not only a Berber trait. Many cultures of the era, including American, disciplined problem-students harshly.

Clearly, from an early age he could not get along with anyone. Probably long before he hit himself on the head with an axe or bombed a police station, his behavior brought shame on the Belachheb family. In 1984, Abdelkrim was to tell the *Dallas Times Herald* that village officials presented the Belachheb family with an ultimatum: They could all leave the village, or they could send Abdelkrim into exile from Beni Ammar. The newspaper reported that, "[the Belachhebs] chose to forsake their son and he was banished."[24]

Afterwards, the newspaper account continues, Belachheb was moved frequently from one set of relatives to another, and at a very young age, about thirteen, he ended up in the gutters of Casablanca, selling his body and hustling food. He claimed to be bitter and determined to leave Morocco, so much so that he worked his way

north to the Strait of Gibraltar and earned passage to Spain. In
Spain he claims to have worked small jobs on farms from one town
to the next to get by, and there, too, moved northward past the
Pyrenees Mountains into France. There, he survived through the
force of his own personality, experiencing success, at first in me-
nial jobs as a waiter, driver, and handyman. As others recognized
his talent, he handled substantial deals for them, including Paris
car dealers, who trusted him to deliver luxurious cars to important
clients in the Middle East. Soon, Abdelkrim asserted, his activities
included making "runs" as a moneyman to Iran, Lebanon, and
Turkey, for liberation forces in Morocco and other North African
countries. He never indicated, and apparently was not asked, exactly who he was trying to liberate.[25]

Again, it is the elder Belachheb who sheds light on the truth.
Mohamed Belachheb claims that because of his son's continuous
troublemaking, the family moved to the larger city of Fes. (Why
moving to Fes was a solution of some sort was never reported.) It
was there, in 1963, at the age of nineteen, that Abdelkrim said
farewell to his father and decided to leave Morocco to go to Europe to study welding and mechanics.

It is difficult to believe that his motivation to leave was driven by
a desire to learn, especially since Interpol records from Rabat confirm that on June 21, 1963, during a time he claimed to be selling
his body and using his wits to survive the gutters of Casablanca,
Spain, and France, Belachheb criminally assaulted a Moroccan.
During the fight, Abdelkrim pulled out a pocketknife and wounded
the man. The case was referred to the King's Prosecutor attached
to the regional court at Taza. The record indicates only that he was
not convicted; it does not indicate that he showed up for the trial.[26]

Whether he appeared for trial or not, it would have been a very
good time for him to leave the country and he was probably a fugitive when he did so. His father, if so inclined, may have had the
connections and means to get him out of Morocco and send him
to Europe.

III

At the end of a turbulent childhood, Abdelkrim Belachheb left Morocco to begin an even more turbulent adult life. He left Africa, probably as a fugitive and certainly with a criminal record, for Europe. It was the beginning of the second phase—a period one of his doctors later called an "intermediate cultural stop."[27]

Throughout his life, Abdelkrim Belachheb's lies would have two common, but contradicting themes: grandiosity and victimization. He was the *pretty* one; he was the *special* one; he was the *favorite* of the revered grandfather, the Imam; he was a *fearless* religious zealot at ten and a *revolutionary* at twelve; his uncle was *jealous* of him; when he hit himself on the head with a homemade axe, he did such a good job he was in a coma for eight months and only a miracle from Allah saved him; he was so poor his family of fourteen lived in a small square stone house and had little more than a patch of land and a few sheep; but then, when he wanted to be rich, he lived in a castle that could house over 100 people; his uncle and teachers were *so jealous* of him that they beat him on the head with a club—every day for four years; he wasn't just a juvenile delinquent as a child, or a wandering, indigent as an adult—he was a *revolutionary* engaged in the romantic work of liberation! More of this odd combination of lament and romance was to come from Abdelkrim Belachheb.

Using primary sources currently available to researchers as public records, all that can be firmly established is that between his eighteenth and nineteenth birthdays, in June of 1963, Abdelkrim Belachheb was a knife-fighter in Morocco.

In many ways, Abdelkrim Belachheb's life as a young Berber growing up in Beni Ammar, Morocco, is mysterious, but only because he has muddled the record with lies he fed to the press on some occasions and his own defense team on others. Little about this period of his life can be documented much less verified, and stories about religious indoctrination, related beatings, head injuries, political activism, and other childhood traumas ultimately come from Belachheb himself. As a source, he is exceedingly un-reliable. His stories propagate stereotypes and contradict them-selves, sometimes grandiose and sometimes the laments of a victim, and thus, it is inescapable that at least half of everything he has ever said about his early years is false. Which half is true is the mystery.

But like information from others who became mass murderers, sometimes lies are as valuable to a researcher as the truth. They form a blueprint of what he wants us to believe, and maybe what he wants to believe about himself. Lies are windows into the mind of a killer. Belachheb's lies are like the others from multiple mur-derers—selfish and self-centered.

No doubt exists, however, about the time frame, conditions, and culture of the area in which he grew up. The region was shaped by thousands of years of poverty, exploitation (both internal and ex-ternal), invasions, and struggle. Years later, during a trial that would determine what was to be the rest of his life, Belachheb tried hard to convince others that in the more remote locations of his experi-ence, little has changed over the centuries. In truth, the Fes and Meknes areas made significant contributions to religion, architec-ture, and science. The people of the region endured aggression from outsiders for centuries, but they endured—especially during their post-World War II struggle for independence, which were Belachheb's formative years.

Without doubt, someone taken from that area and placed in Dallas, Texas, would experience culture shock. But then, so would other Moroccans, and virtually anyone else visiting from abroad. Would all of these visitors become killers? Would *all* of the Belachheb brothers, for example, have become killers had they moved to Dallas?

In 1984, as Belachheb faced trial for having committed six mur-ders, he made much about his Berber/Islamic upbringing, and how it was so dramatically different from his subsequent Euro-cen-tric and American experiences. It is amusing to ponder the reaction a scholar would receive today if he or she released a study that concluded that those raised in a North African Arabic or Berber culture were doomed to commit violent felonies if they were to move to America. But much of Abdelkrim Belachheb's defense was exactly that. Murder resulted, he said, as a result of confusion and culture shock.

His stories are a slander against his own people.

But it is pretty clear that Abdelkrim Belachheb did not function well in his native Berber culture either. Otherwise, his father would speak well of him, and he could still be in Beni Ammar, Meknes Province, Morocco.

---

[1] Thomas K. Park, *Historical Dictionary of Morocco* (London: Scarecrow Press, 1996), 1.

[2] Good Internet sources about the different areas of Morocco include www.cia.gov and www.arab.net/morocco. My use of those sites is current as of July 4, 2002.

[3] The Perry-Casteñada Library of the University of Texas at Austin has a large collection of maps developed shortly after World War II that are ideal for describing the Meknes/Fes area. Much of my description of the landscape and roadways is taken from this valuable source, which is hereafter cited as "PCL Maps"; Park, pgs. 42-47.

[4] United States Department of Justice: Interpol Rabat to Interpol Washington, July 31, 1984.

[5] The account of the Belachhebs living a harsh subsistence life is from an interview with Abdelkrim Belachheb's first wife, a Belgian woman named Jenny, *Dallas Morning News,* August 5, 1984; Ibid.

[6] www.cia.gov; www.arab.net/morocco; Park, 2, 42-47.

[7] Abdelkrim Belachheb quoted in *Dallas Morning News,* June 25, 1985 and Jenny quoted on October 28, 1984; *Dallas Times Herald,* October 28, 1985; ABC News: *20/20,* August 22, 1985.

[8] The *Dallas Times Herald,* quoted on October 28, 1984. The paper also reported that three experts were convinced that Belachheb's dreams were so vivid that the Oedipal experience might have actually occurred. But as we shall see throughout this book, very little of what Abdelkrim Belachheb says about sex can be believed.

[9] Dr. Harrell Gill-King quoted from testimony in *Texas* v *Belachheb,* 291st Judicial District, Cause no. F84-75078-SU, et. al., V, 1284-1390.

[10] I am indebted to Dr. Deborah Kapchan, Associate Professor of Anthropology, The University of Texas at Austin, for her valuable guidance in the area of Moroccan culture—an area I eagerly admit is not my specialty. In addition to her impressive credentials, Dr. Kapchan once lived in Morocco.

[11] Ibid.; *Dallas Times Herald,* October 28, 1984; *Dallas Morning News,* June 23, 1985.

[12] The authority on the Brotherhood of the Hamadsha is Vincent Crapanzano's *The Hamadsha: A Study in Moroccan Ethnopsychiatry* (Berkeley: University of California Press, 1973); Ibid.; *Texas* v *Belachheb,* 291st Judicial District, Cause no. F84-75078-SU, et. al., V, 1391-1567; ABC News: *20/20,* August 22, 1985.

[13] Hal Hinson quoted in *Washington Post,* August 12, 1988; Mark Ellingham, Don Grisbrook, and Sharen McVeigh, *Morocco* (New York: Rough Guide, 2001), 192.

[14] Park, 112-14; Ellingham, et.al., 196.

[15] Park, 151-52; www.arab.net/morocco.

[16] ABC News: *20/20*, August 22, 1985.

[17] PCL Maps.

[18] *Dallas Morning News,* November 13, 1984; *Dallas Times Herald,* October 28, 1984.

[19] Ladislas Farago, *Patton: Ordeal and Triumph* (New York: Astor-Honor, 1964), 192-95.

[20] Moshe Gershovich, *French Military Rule in Morocco: Colonialism and Its Consequences,* (London: Frank Cass, 2000), 206-10.

[21] Park, xxi-xxvii; Gershovich, 210-20.

[22] *Texas* v *Belachheb,* 291st Judicial District, Cause no. F84-75078-SU, et. al., V, 1284-1390; *Dallas Morning News,* August 5, 1984; *Dallas Times Herald,* October 28, 1984; Gershovich, 214-220.

[23] Spokesman for Mohamed Belachheb quoted on ABC News: *20/20,* August 22, 1985.

[24] *Dallas Times Herald,* October 28, 1984.

[25] Ibid.

[26] ABC News: *20/20,* August 22, 1985; United States Department of Justice: Interpol Rabat to Interpol Washington, July 31, 1984.

[27] *Texas* v *Belachheb,* 291st Judicial District, Cause no. F84-75078-SU, et. al., V, 1284-1390.

chapter three

"Pick on me"

> *"I can drive any woman in Belgium crazy."*
>
> —Abdelkrim Belachheb
> quoted from notes cited
> in trial testimony

I

According to Interpol Rabat documents, Abdelkrim Belachheb was in Morocco as late as June 21, 1963, when he assaulted and wounded a man in a knife fight. Months later, Interpol Washington has him in Europe at age nineteen. Where he went first and his movements for the next year and a half cannot be established with certainty. Various documents and conflicting testimony have him arriving in either France or Switzerland. There is no indication that his family had helped him to get to Europe or that they even knew where he was. The troubled son could merely have been a fugitive from justice who cared little for the concerns of his family.

While being processed in a Texas prison in 1984, Belachheb indicated that he went first to "Pepignons" in France. In this instance, he may have been telling the truth. During that same interview he admitted that he had lived in Fes from 1958 through 1962, which was consistent with what his father told ABC News in 1985. Anyway, this story was much more credible than the nonsense he told the *Dallas Times Herald* about using his wits to survive the gutters of Casablanca. On yet another occasion, he told the *Dallas Morning News* that his ambition was to go to Europe to "study lawyer or engineering or doctor to help the people of Morocco."[1]

Belachheb probably went to France first because he could speak French. But he seems to have wandered around Europe a great deal. In 1984, he indicated to his doctors that he had spent some time in Spain. ABC News reported that between late 1963 and August 1965 he was refused the necessary work documents to stay in Switzerland and The Netherlands.

Although his location changed, his slant on his experience in Europe varies little from his take on life in northern Africa. No one, he thought, wanted to give him a chance—not even other expatriated Moroccans. For example, while in Switzerland he claims to have been befriended by a woman who took him to the Moroccan embassy to get papers allowing him to attend school. Instead, he alleged, they beat him so severely that he was hospitalized for over a month. He recalled being in a coma, his second in less than ten years, for seventeen days. Yet, he claims not to remember who treated him or where he had been hospitalized.[2]

His wanderings in Europe were clearly the result of a series of unsuccessful attempts to get work papers. "I got to Europe and I have no chance," he was to say bitterly. While languishing in Spain, he continued, the penniless Belachheb had no money for food. He had only enough for cheap wine and as a result became an alcoholic.[3] But to another doctor, and on resumes he later fabricated to apply for jobs in the United States, he claimed to have attended French-speaking colleges.[4]

His circuitous European travels certainly indicate that he did not want to return to Morocco under any circumstances. Starving in Spain was better than going home to Morocco, the country from which he was probably a fugitive. He did eventually settle in Brussels, Belgium, and he brought along his violent and criminal behavior.

On August 20, 1965, he assaulted two people in Brussels. On November 5, he assaulted and struck a woman. On December 11, he attacked two men with a knife and threatened another one at a café. He was incarcerated from December 12, 1966 to January 11, 1967. Shortly afterwards, he broke out four windows in homes in his neighborhood and attacked another man in yet another knife fight. On February 6, 1967, and again on July 1, 1967, he assaulted men in fights. In less than two years, he had injured at least eleven people.[5]

Belachheb was jailed again on December 8, 1967, and by December 16, Belgian justice finally caught up to him. In addition to his many assault charges, he was also charged with carrying a prohibited firearm. In the correctional court of Brussels, the judges wrote: "These infractions constitute collective damages of such proportions that they cannot be sanctioned by anything other than the strongest punishment applicable."[6]

The "strongest punishment applicable" turned out to be a five year suspended sentence. It amounted to time served and two fines of 2,000 francs each.[7]

II

If a single city had to be designated the capital of Europe it would be Brussels. It boasts that non-Belgians are an integral part of its economy. A large number of its residents speak French, as did Abdelkrim Belachheb. This linguistic match and the welcoming cosmopolitan nature of the city made it perfect for him.

Soon after arriving in Belgium, probably during the summer of 1965, he became part of the Belgium nightclub scene. For the next two years, his life was little more than a series of fights and trips to jail.

From 1965 to 1967, he probably earned a somewhat meager living in a service position. Some reports have him working as a construction worker from 1965-75. From 1975 to the time he left Europe in 1981 (during which he spent at least one-third of his time in jail), he allegedly owned his own heating and air conditioning business called the *Establissements Belach'heb*.[8] Belachheb must have received some apprenticeship or training in refrigeration. Later, as a visitor to the United States, one of his employers would comment about how he fixed a refrigeration system that had been considered beyond repair.[9]

Into all of his autobiographical stories, even as a simple Brussels air conditioning and heating repairman, Belachheb managed to insert grandiosity and sexual bravado. He even claimed to his second wife that on a trip to repair a heating system in a parochial school in the nearby historic town of Waterloo, he made love to a nun.[10]

He made his "rounds" in more traditional locations as well. He became part of the Brussels entertainment scene and frequented cafés, bars, and nightclubs. In one of those spots, he met a very attractive Belgian woman named Jenny. She was a delicate-looking woman with long blonde hair. At age twenty-eight she was six years older than Belachheb. She recalled the moment she first noticed the Moroccan: "He is the only man I have ever met who really turned my head."[11]

Their relationship was intense and sexual, and she was very much in love with him even though she knew him to be occasionally brutal. "He was violent before I married him, but I was expecting a baby and I was crazy about him," she related later. She overcame her father's disapproval (at first sight he detested the man they both called "Karim") and on October 7, 1967, she and Belachheb were married by the Belgian equivalent of a Justice of the Peace.[12]

In late February of 1968, Jenny gave birth to their first child, a daughter they named Sabine.

"Karim" had standards: If a woman wanted to become his wife she had to be respectable, she had to be a good cook, and she had to be good in bed. He never indicated whether or not Jenny met that criteria, but time was to prove she certainly had one overriding quality he never came to appreciate—patience. "He always tries to be the center of attention. He always tried to run after the beautiful people," she said about her husband.[13]

The unusually perceptive Jenny spent the next thirteen years of her life married to a man who showed no evidence of reciprocal love or fidelity. Quite the opposite, he openly flaunted his adulterous hyper-sexuality to the extent that Jenny would later tell journalist Melinda Henneberger that "when he wasn't in jail he was out of the country looking for work or off with other women. Old, young, fat, thin, ugly, beautiful—he likes them all. Even a dog with a hat is good enough for him. You should see some of the pictures I found in his hip pockets."[14]

Of course, Belachheb saw things differently. "I marry this girl with love," he told the *Dallas Morning News*, "She was alone, lonely . . . I'm lonely. We find love together."[15] But he certainly did not love her enough to remain faithful to her. Stories of the *frequency* of his infidelity can be believed because Jenny confirmed them on numerous occasions. But with Belachheb, the tales became bigger lies as they got more grandiose.

Every woman he ever had sex with, it seems, flirted with him, demanded sexual favors from him, and gave him money as a result of her gratitude. Furthermore, his women were not the "dogs with a hat" Jenny described, but divas, and even stars like Romy Schneider, a hugely popular Austrian movie star and sex symbol of the 1950s and 1960s. He also claimed a ballerina from the Bejart Company of Brussels as one of his conquests. He reported that she spent a fortune on him.[16]

Even his description of Jenny, his wife, who surely endured great emotional pain during their marriage, descends into exaggeration: she was a very attractive woman, yet he described her as Swedish (probably believing Americans stereotyped Swedish women as the most beautiful in the world), but she was, of course, Belgian. It was important to Belachheb to project as manly an image as possible. Curiously, his psychiatrists later asserted that his aggressive pursuit of women, especially "northern" (i.e., north of the Mediterranean) and American women, and his obsessive desire to associate with the wealthy and beautiful were not displays of an exaggerated sense of self-importance, arrogance and grandiosity, but instead were manifestations of a poor self-concept and deep insecurity.[17]

This alleged poor self-concept and insecurity was apparently expressed by quotes like, "Moroccan people, accept [it] or not, have a superiority of sexuality in Belgium. . . . European women like men from the South."[18]

During her fourteen-year relationship with Abdelkrim Belachheb, Jenny probably came to know him better than anyone. "Nobody knows him like I do," she once said. Indeed. She was to add later, "He cannot love. He loves only himself."[19]

III

Abdelkrim Belachheb's marriage to Jenny did nothing to slow his troublemaking—or its resulting arrests and incarcerations. "We were scarcely married when he was sent to Foret Prison for a fight he got in to . . . [it was] a knife fight with a Spanish café owner and some other people," she remembered. Almost as soon as he got out, on February 24, 1968 he got into another fight with some patrons of the *Café des Ours* (The Bear's Café) in Brussels. According to Jenny, it was only two days after his first daughter, Sabine, was born. "Supposedly, he was out celebrating and he got mad and got up from the bar and drove a car he'd borrowed through the window [of the café]." He was immediately arrested and spent five days in jail, but his trial date for the incident was not until September 30, 1968. At that time he was sentenced to two months and served the time at a halfway house in Antwerp.[20]

Afterwards, Belachheb seemed to calm down for about a year. In 1971, he saw an ad in the newspaper calling for auditions for a bit part in a Belgian daytime drama called *Men of the Tiger*. He sent a picture of himself, auditioned, and landed a part playing a journalist. As a young man he had the attractive features of a Mediterranean playboy. But he never became a celebrity nor did it bring in a significant amount of money for his household. The series was rather short-lived and after its cancellation he returned to obscurity.

His short foray into the world of entertainment does indicate a probability that he had no real steady employment. During her visit to Jenny in 1984, journalist Melinda Henneberger got the definite impression that Belachheb did little or nothing to support his family—ever; Jenny was the breadwinner.[21]

In 1971, Belachheb also resumed his propensity for fighting. That year he attacked his Algerian employer in Brussels. In 1973, the Court of Charleroi sentenced him to two months in prison. He served two days at Foret Prison and was then transferred to St. Giles Prison outside of Brussels where he served the remainder of his term.[22]

During the early 1970s, he was hospitalized on a number of occasions for alcohol abuse at the *Centre hospitalier Jean Titeca* located on the Rue de la Luzerne in Brussels. In that institution a doctor named Yves Crochelet treated him. Dr. Crochelet also diagnosed a personality disorder and made some attempt to help him. Belachheb is said to have spent over three months at the Brierbeek psychiatric center near Brussels. There he received more treatment and was prescribed medication called Antabuse.

Antabuse was accidentally discovered as a medication for alcohol abuse in the 1930s when rubber industry workers were exposed to its active ingredient, tetraethylthiuram disulfide. The laborers became ill after having drinks after work. Antabuse, as a treatment for alcoholism, is an act of desperation. It is a horrifying drug. While it is considered nontoxic, it alters the body's metabolism of alcohol. While taking the medication it is impossible to drink without severe discomfort. Like a self-inflicted, massive hangover—the patient becomes hot, sweaty, and flushed. The neck and head throb with pain, and there is nausea and vomiting. The powerful drug even reacts to minute amounts of alcohol, like what would be ingested using over-the-counter cough medicines or mouthwashes, or inhaled fumes while using colognes and wood stains.[23]

How Antabuse made Belachheb's already unpleasant disposition worse can only be imagined, and even though the medication made him horribly ill, and may even have been an occasion for psychotic behavior, he managed to both abuse the substance and continue to drink. "One day he took a whole bottle [of Antabuse] with a whole bottle of wine and cut his veins open with a kitchen knife. He started vomiting and went screaming through the house like a wild animal," Jenny later related. The Brussels Police were called to the scene where they detained him and took him again to Brierbeek. He escaped by crawling through a window but was recaptured fairly quickly and returned to the hospital.[24]

But Belachheb never blamed Antabuse for his violence or the trouble he often got himself into. Instead, in the same way he had been victimized as a child for being "the pretty one" by a jealous and wicked uncle, resulting in severe beatings, Belgian men, he claimed, resented his "dark good looks" and picked on him. During his first televised interview, an August 1985 episode of *20/20*, Belachheb "explained" the series of violent incidents. As he spoke, perceptive viewers caught a glimpse of his dangerous temper; his eyes glazed and narrowed as his forehead wrinkled, his eyebrows angled upward, and the anger, though controlled (which is significant), showed.

The problem, he asserted, was that he looked like a number of different Eurasian nationalities: "If a Belgian man have trouble with an Italian, pick on me. If a Belgian man have trouble with a Turk, pick on me. If a Belgian have trouble with a French, pick on me. If they touch me, I do not permit that. I will never permit that." He continued, "For that I have a lot of accidents."

But during the same interview, he claimed not to remember the fights at all: "[I couldn't] believe I do this. It was an accident, or I don't know." In yet another attempt to explain his behavior, he said his problems were made worse by birthmarks on his hands and forearms.[25]

Real, swift, serious justice finally caught up to him in 1976, after he was arrested for robbery while on a construction job in Kuwait. There, he was sentenced and was to serve two years in prison. The nature of the theft is not known. Belachheb, infusing grandiosity yet again, claimed that it was a daring million-dollar robbery attempt sponsored by a mob leader in Casablanca. This shadowy figure had hired him and several Palestinians to pull off the job. His two years imprisonment, he claimed, was really the result of his refusal to identify his mob backer. And again, Belachheb re-introduced the fiction that he was an activist providing aid to Berber and other revolutionary causes.[26]

Belachheb's Kuwaiti stories are just as implausible as his explanations of other mishaps. Would a revolutionary with mob connections in Casablanca return to Brussels as a penniless ex-con from Kuwait? When he switched from his grandiose revolutionary mode to a humble victim mode, he said, "After two harsh years in Kuwait, I tell myself now I want be a good man. I want to be example man, live like every man—a normal life," he told the *Dallas Morning News* in 1985. Eight months earlier, back in a grandiose mode, he told the *Dallas Times Herald* that he had escaped from the prison.[27]

By 1978, after two years in a Kuwaiti prison, Belachheb returned to Jenny in Brussels. According to Jenny, he was interested in fathering a son and not long afterwards she was pregnant with her second child. Interestingly, in 1984, while being processed as an inmate in an American prison, Belachheb revealed that he had fathered an out-of-wedlock son named Smire, who had been born in 1972, and that the mother was a Belgian woman named Maggie.[28] American officials never checked the veracity of the story because there was no reason to. If he did have a son, the boy would have been six years old when Belachheb returned to Jenny. If the story of his out-of-wedlock son was not another of Belachheb's fantasies, he apparently ignored that son while longing for another.

Jenny's pregnancy did not spare her from Belachheb's abuse. She gave birth to their second child, another daughter they named Heidi.[29] Shortly after Heidi's birth, Belachheb's abuse of Jenny finally reached the breaking point. On his thirty-fifth birthday, November 24, 1979, he arrived home to announce he wanted to invite one of his former mistresses and her new boyfriend to dinner. He went to the refrigerator and opened it to find that there was not enough food to prepare the dinner he wanted. He calmly left the house, "and then he came home and nearly killed me," Jenny recalled.

He beat her mercilessly with one of her shoes and a wooden statuette of a bird. Sabine, who was twelve years old at the time, entered the room to see her mother being beaten. "I didn't hear my father come in. When my mama started screaming, I ran into her bedroom and saw him in the corner . . . I yelled for him to stop and he slapped me." The horror continued to the point where Belachheb's shirt had so much of Jenny's blood on it he stopped beating her long enough to take it off and place it in a laundry basket. That is when Jenny got away.

Then he turned to Sabine. "He handed me his tie and put on a raincoat and climbed out the window." It was the last time Jenny or Sabine would ever see Abdelkrim Belachheb.[30]

Battered and bloodied, Jenny was taken to the hospital where she was treated for injuries including four fractured ribs, a broken hand, and a punctured lung. Finally, from a hospital bed, she filed charges against him, and shortly afterwards, instituted divorce proceedings. "Not because I didn't love him, but because it was hell," she later admitted.[31]

The next day, November 25, 1979, Brussels police interrogated Belachheb, whose only response was, "I don't remember anything that happened last night between my wife and myself."[32]

In 1984, in Texas and under far more tragic circumstances, he would try that explanation again.

IV

After his release from jail for the beating of his wife, Abdelkrim Belachheb knew he was facing a certain prison sentence. On October 29, 1980, he was convicted, *in abstentia*, of beating Jenny and Sabine. There was a warrant out for him and he knew he could never return to Belgium without spending a considerable amount of time in prison. He almost certainly returned to Morocco—the only place he could have gone legally, i.e., as a resident. According to his father, Belachheb arrived and his father welcomed him by giving him land, undoubtedly in an attempt to get his son to settle down. Instead, Belachheb is reported to have wandered about aimlessly, probably getting into more arguments and fights.[33]

Without hesitation or apparent guilt, he departed Brussels leaving a pathetic wife and two daughters he cared nothing for. Six years after he nearly killed her, Jenny publicly admitted the truth about the man she loved. "I often asked myself, 'Did he love me?' But he didn't love me. He used me to have his papers to stay in Belgium. It could have been another woman. He would have done the same thing to her." Just as candidly, when asked if she thought "Karim" was crazy she replied, "As far as I know, he was O.K. mentally, except for a terrible inferiority complex. That's why he had to prove himself to every woman. And he lies more than he tells the truth—if that's a sickness."[34]

When informed of Jenny's quote about how he lies, Belachheb responded cynically, "I'm a liar like any other married man, because ninety-five percent of married men have girlfriends."[35]

After returning to Morocco, he surely realized that nothing in the Meknes or Fes Regions of Morocco could ever match the sensuality, excitement, and nightclub atmosphere of Brussels. Belachheb was hardly a farmer, herder, or trader frequenting *souks*. In a rejection of his native culture, Abdelkrim Belachheb sought to move away as soon as possible. He searched for a way to get out and a place to go. He claims to have been rejected by Canada, Switzerland, The Netherlands, and Italy.

Grandiosity reappears. He turned, he said, to the mob boss in Casablanca who hired him as a money runner for the Palestinians, only to find out that the man was in the United States.[36] Americans, it turns out, would not refuse Abdelkrim Belachheb entry, nor would they make any serious effort to find out who he really was as he applied for his visa.

Had a serious effort been made to discover who Belachheb was, American officials would have discovered that he was a hot-tempered knife fighter and wife-beater who had been given many opportunities to straighten himself out by a sluggish and tolerant Belgian criminal justice system and by his father in Morocco. He had an ex-wife who had supported herself and their children during their marriage while he chased other women or did time in jail. Indeed, Jenny's patience reached a level of co-dependency. He had wandered from country to country with no real attempt to adapt to any society in which he had lived. He was extraordinarily selfish.

As one of his friends was to say, "The guy didn't give a damn about anybody but himself."[37]

---

[1] *Texas* v *Belachheb,* 291st Judicial District, Cause no. F84-75078-SU, et. al., V, 1284-1390 and VII, 2290-2317; Dallas Police Department Files: Grant Lappin to Interpol Washington, July 18, 1984; Confidential Sources; *Dallas Times Herald,* October 28, 1984; Abdelkrim Belachheb quoted in *Dallas Morning News,* June 23, 1985.

[2] *Texas* v *Belachheb,* 291st Judicial District, Cause no. F84-75078-SU, et. al., V, 1284-1390, 1391-1567 and VII, 2290-2317; ABC News: *20/20,* August 22, 1985.

[3] *Dallas Morning News,* June 23, 1985.

[4] Dallas County District Attorney Files: E. Clay Griffith to Judge Gerry Meier, July 3, 1984; Abdelkrim Belachheb's resumes are in the Dallas County District Attorney Files.

[5] United States Department of Justice: Interpol Report, Translated from French, July 31, 1984; *Texas* v *Belachheb,* 291st Judicial District, Cause no. F84-75078-SU, et. al., V, 1284-1390; Ibid., August 4, 1984.

[6] Ibid.; The judges' sentence is quoted in *Dallas Morning News,* August 4, 1984.

[7] United States Department of Justice: Interpol Report, Translated from French, July 31, 1984.

[8] *Fort Worth Star-Telegram,* June 30, 1984; *Dallas Times Herald,* October 28, 1984; *Texas* v *Belachheb,* 291st Judicial District, Cause no. F84-75078-SU, et. al., VII, 2198-2236.

[9] Dallas Police Department Files: [Lisa], Restaurant Manager, Variety Arts Center, To whom it may concern, undated.

[10] *Dallas Morning News,* August 5, 1984.

[11] ABC News: *20/20,* August 22, 1985; Jenny quoted in *Dallas Morning News,* August 5, 1984.

[12] *Texas* v *Belachheb,* 291st Judicial District, Cause no. F84-75078-SU, et. al., V, 1284-1390; Jenny quoted in *Dallas Morning News,* August 5, 1984; United States Department of Justice: Interpol Report, Translated from French, July 31, 1984; Confidential Sources.

[13] *Dallas Times Herald,* October 28, 1984; Jenny quoted in *Dallas Morning News,* November 13, 1984.

[14] Jenny quoted in *Dallas Morning News,* August 5, 1984; *Texas* v *Belachheb,* 291st Judicial District, Cause no. F84-75078-SU, et. al., V, 1284-1390.

[15] Abdelkrim Belachheb quoted in *Dallas Morning News,* June 23, 1985.

[16] Ibid., August 5, 1984; *Dallas Times Herald,* October 28, 1984.

[17] Ibid.

[18] Abdelkrim Belachheb quoted in *Dallas Morning News,* June 23, 1985.

[19] *Texas* v *Belachheb,* 291st Judicial District, Cause no. F84-75078-SU, et. al., V, 1284-1390; Jenny quote from ABC News: *20/20,* August 22, 1985.

[20] United States Department of Justice: Interpol Report, Translated from French, July 31, 1984; *Texas* v *Belachheb,* 291st Judicial District, Cause no. F84-75078-SU, et. al., V, 1284-1390; Jenny quoted in *Dallas Morning News,* August 5, 1984.

[21] Melinda Henneberger, interviewed by the author on July 7, 2002; *Texas* v *Belachheb,* 291st Judicial District, Cause no. F84-75078-SU, et. al., V, 1284-1390; *Dallas Morning News,* August 5, 1984, and November 13, 2002.

[22] *Texas* v *Belachheb,* 291st Judicial District, Cause no. F84-75078-SU, et. al., V, 1284-1390; *Dallas Morning News,* August 5, 1984, and November 13, 1984.

[23] For more information on Antabuse see http://www.bartleby.com/65/an/Antabuse.html. Information current as of July 4, 2002; *Dallas Morning News,* August 5, 1984.

[24] Jenny quoted in *Dallas Morning News,* August 5, 1984.

[25] Abdelkrim Belachheb quoted on ABC News: *20/20,* August 22, 1985 and *Dallas Morning News,* June 23, 1985.

[26] Confidential Sources; *Texas* v *Belachheb,* 291st Judicial District, Cause no. F84-75078-SU, et. al., V, 1284-1390 and VII, 2290-2317; *Dallas Morning News,* June 23, 1985, and August 5, 1984; *Dallas Times Herald,* October 28, 1984.

[27] *Dallas Times Herald,* October 28, 1984; Abdelkrim Belachheb quoted in *Dallas Morning News,* June 23, 1985.

[28] Confidential Sources.

[29] Ibid.

[30] *Texas* v *Belachheb,* 291st Judicial District, Cause no. F84-75078-SU, et. al., V, 1284-1390 and VII, 2290-2317; Sabine Belachheb quoted in *Dallas Morning News,* August 5, 1984; ABC News: *20/20,* August 22, 1985.

[31] Ibid.; Jenny quoted in *Dallas Morning News,* August 5, 1984.

[32] United States Department of Justice: Interpol Report, Translated from French, July 31, 1984; *Texas* v *Belachheb,* 291st Judicial District, Cause no. F84-75078-SU, et. al., VII, 2290-2317; Abdelkrim Belachheb quoted in *Dallas Morning News,* August 5, 1984.

[33] Ibid.; ABC News: *20/20,* August 22, 1985.

[34] Jenny quoted in ABC News: *20/20,* August 22, 1985, and *Dallas Morning News,* August 5, 1984.

[35] Abdelkrim Belachheb quoted in *Dallas Morning News,* June 23, 1985.

[36] *Dallas Times Herald,* October 28, 1984.

[37] Unidentified friend quoted in *Dallas Times Herald,* October 28, 1984.

chapter four

America

> *"He believes that there is something extremely special about him."*
> —Dr. Sheldon Zigelbaum
> Psychiatrist for the Defense

I

The tragedy of September 11, 2001, the terrorist attacks upon New York City and Washington, D.C., focused attention on how visitors of other nations come to the United States. Some of the resulting debate included observations that it was too easy for dangerous people to penetrate American borders. Since that tragedy, pundits and many citizens voiced concern over the failings of intelligence services like the Central Intelligence Agency (CIA) and the Federal Bureau of Investigation (FBI) to preemptively identify visitors, legal and illegal, capable of such a monstrous crime. Included in the discussion were hard, pointed questions about the inability of the Immigration and Naturalization Service (INS) to keep track of those already within our borders.

Yet the United States clings to its heritage of openness. To close our borders is to close off ourselves to international ideas and influences. To close our borders is to reject our heritage. To close our borders is itself anti-American.

On a much smaller scale, a similar debate has been argued within America's borders for decades before September 11, 2001. One example grew up around Abdelkrim Belachheb in 1984. Even today, for Moroccans wishing to enter the United States, the web site of the American Embassy in Rabat and the Consulate in Casablanca answers the question "Why is there a visa requirement?" this way: "The United States is an open society. Unlike many other countries, the United States does not impose internal controls on most visitors, such as registration with local authorities. In order to enjoy the privilege of unencumbered travel in the United States, aliens have a responsibility to prove they are going to return abroad before a visitor or student visa is issued."[1]

If one version of his many grandiose stories is to be believed, Abdelkrim Belachheb could be considered a terrorist. He claimed to have worked for a mob boss in Casablanca and to have aided nationalist causes in northern Africa. But other than his word, there is no evidence that he ever had such connections. Abdelkrim Belachheb was not a terrorist; he was never that important. Nor was he ever selfless enough to dedicate himself to a cause of any type. However, he was a dangerous individual and a fugitive from justice. He was a criminal exploiting the largesse of America's open society.

During the summer of 1980, Belachheb made his way to the American Consulate in Casablanca and applied for the easiest visa he could get. Today, it is referred to as a nonimmigrant Type B visitor visa. It is granted almost routinely to two groups: a B-1 visa is given to persons wishing to enter the United States to conduct business; a B-2 visa is a tourist visa issued to persons wishing to travel "for pleasure." Both normally require documentation of some sort demonstrating an intent to leave the United States after a time specified by a travel authorization, usually not to exceed six months. The documentation usually takes the form of letters from friends in America who will be visited, confirmation of reservations for a planned or organized tour, or some other confirmation of subsistence such as hotel reservations and car rentals. Since the visa is based on visiting "for pleasure" the traveler is prohibited from gain-

ing employment while in the U.S. Thus, additional documentation is required to establish that the holder can support himself or
will be supported by someone already legally in the U.S.[2]

During the late 1970s and early 1980s, an average of more than
six million tourist visa applications were processed each year by
the embassies and consulates of the U.S. State Department.[3]
Belachheb's was but one.

The era also needs to be placed in context. In the early 1980s,
embassies and consulates were still reeling from the seizure of the
American Embassy in Teheran, Iran, by Islamic fundamentalist fol-
lowers of the Ayatollah Khomeini. Besides holding American hos-
tages, the fundamentalists also captured a trove of highly sensitive
U.S. intelligence documents. Shortly afterwards, the State Department instituted a policy whereby visa applications, and their ac-
companying documentation, were to be destroyed after a one-year
period. The intent was to protect native employees of the embassies.[4] So, if Belachheb was ever required to establish his intent to
return to Morocco, and his ability to support himself or be supported by someone else while in the U.S., those documents were
destroyed sometime around April 1982.

But the fact that Belachheb got a tourist visa at all means he
lied on at least two of the major questions that established his eligi-
bility. First, he would not have been granted the visa unless he had
stated that he lived in Morocco for the previous five-year period.
Second, when asked if he had a criminal record or a history of
mental problems, he had to have said, "no."[5]

The greatest enduring mystery of the relative ease of Belachheb's
success in getting the visa is whether he had any assistance in hiding his criminal background, and whether, if he was asked to document subsistence, someone in the U.S. assisted him in convincing
consular officials that they would support him. There is no surviving evidence ever made public implicating anyone in such collu-
sion. Again, the definitive answer, if one ever existed, was shredded
by the American Consulate in 1982.

Exploiting a system that depended on criminals and the mentally ill to identify themselves, Abdelkrim Belachheb received a nonimmigrant visa on July 17, 1980, and was later authorized to travel to visit the United States "for pleasure" for a period of six months beginning on April 22, 1981.[6]

II

As soon as he received his visa, Belachheb boarded a KLM flight to the United States. He later related to a friend that he felt "like a wounded animal" who had nowhere else to turn. It was a Moroccan friend, he said, who suggested that he go to California. He described his initial reaction after arriving as "the first time I love a country in my whole life." Shortly thereafter, reality set in: "In L.A., too many kinds of people. I can't handle that."[7]

But when in a victim mode, Belachheb vividly described how, upon his arrival in Los Angeles, he knew only enough English to get to a hotel from the airport. His English was so bad that he ate pancakes three times a day for a week because that was all he knew how to order. He did not want to expose his lack of language skills for fear of being "spotted" and sent back to Morocco.[8]

Eunice* was the first person in America to show Belachheb kindness. She provided a home for him for two months. Exactly how he connected with her is not a matter of record.

"He wanted to be an American," Eunice said. He went so far as to assume American names like Bill, Bob, or what seemed to be his favorite—Charlie.

Eunice remembers his having a problem securing a "green card." He searched for a job, in violation of the conditions of his visa, and found work illegally at restaurants as a waiter. His lifestyle would have been even more depressed had it not been for the money women insisted on giving him "for services"—or so he alleged. [9]

The first job he admitted to having in the United States was as a waiter in a restaurant owned by the Society for the Preservation of

Variety Arts, a non-profit corporation located in Los Angeles and chartered by the state of California. His immediate supervisor, a woman named Lisa*, found him to be an ideal worker. She wrote a glowing undated letter of recommendation for him addressed "To whom it may concern"—clearly for his use for numerous job applications over an extended period. She described herself as "highly satisfied with his work." Belachheb was "willing and cooperative" and "cordial." She continued: "Everyday, I receive compliments about Charly's Belachheb [sic] efficient service . . . I would recommend Charly's Belachheb [sic] for any work in which he is qualified, and that includes a wide range of activities."

Those activities included his repairing a refrigerator that had not functioned properly for some time. She seemed completely satisfied with both his work and his ability and motivation to please customers.[10]

Lisa made no comment whatsoever of any problems he may have had controlling his temper. In all likelihood, Belachheb controlled himself because he *had* to. He knew better than to cause trouble or draw attention to himself because his work was illegal in the United States, and soon his period of authorized stay would expire. Knife fighting and driving a car through a restaurant would undoubtedly have resulted in his deportation. And he did not want that.

It is important to remember that throughout his life Belachheb's movements were largely the result of being a fugitive from justice. He left Morocco at nineteen shortly after a knife fight and the resulting trial, which he skipped; he left Belgium immediately after he had severely beaten Jenny and shortly before he was sentenced to two years in prison for that offense. Now, he decided to leave Los Angeles, probably because on October 22, 1981, he officially became an illegal alien in the United States.

Shortly afterwards he moved to Dallas, Texas. Surely, he probably reasoned it would be harder for the INS to find him there.

III

Dallas was a boomtown in the late 1970s and even more so in the early 1980s. Everyone, it seems, was making big money. The atmosphere almost defied Economic Darwinism because everyone survived—and prospered. Construction typified Dallas' growth. In 1983, "Big D" was second only to the much larger city of Los Angeles in the issuance of construction permits, with a thirty percent increase in spending from the previous year to $1.3 billion according to a report by Dunn and Bradstreet. In 1984, Dallas moved to the top spot among growing American cities with $744 million in permits in just the first quarter. This was more than twenty percent above its closest rival, Los Angeles, twice as much as New York City, and over eight times as much as Chicago—all significantly larger metropolitan areas.[11]

Money was everywhere, jobs were plentiful, and it seemed as though businesses could not fail, no matter how ill conceived or poorly run.

Much of the new wealth and construction took place in north Dallas along an interstate highway loop numbered IH-635 and called the "LBJ Freeway." The thoroughfare, more or less, separated north Dallas from smaller suburbs to the north. Projected growth bordered on the unbelievable: in north Dallas alone office space was expected to increase ten fold, and multi-family and single family dwellings were expected to more than double.[12] New office buildings, and the infrastructure they required, combined with the sprawl created by malls and service establishments, with vast tracts of apartments, condominiums, and upper middle class neighborhoods, blended Dallas, Fort Worth, and their smaller neighbors into a megalopolis called the "Metroplex."

Such an influx of *nouveau riche* attracted an entertainment industry and the need for a number of "restaurant and club" establishments, which catered to people willing to pay membership fees in order to drink in the city's "dry" areas.

The opportunity created by so much growth and money attracted thousands from all parts of the country in search of jobs and fortunes.

If he was not running from the INS because of his illegal status, then Abdelkrim Belachheb, who had once held construction jobs in Europe, might well have taken his California friends' advice that Dallas was the place to be.[13] Undoubtedly, he and his friends reasoned, it would also be easier to get a green card in a place that had such a large demand for skilled construction workers.

In early 1982, some of Belachheb's friends in California called relatives of theirs named Abdul* and Debbie*, a married couple living in a northeastern section of Dallas. On Belachheb's behalf, "[They] asked us if we could take him in." Abdul and Debbie lived in a home on Listi Street with a thirty-two-year-old man named Mohamed*.

The Listi Street home was a modest dwelling in a middle class neighborhood. The houses were built on tiny lots along winding, very narrow streets, not always perpendicular to one another. The area was heavily shaded with mature trees and bordered on the west by a creek and a large undeveloped greenbelt, giving residents and visitors the illusion of isolation. Even though the area was only a few blocks from the LBJ Freeway, it was, and remains today, surprisingly hard to get to.

Abdelkrim Belachheb moved into the Listi Street house in early 1982. Soon, his hosts realized their guest was much more than they had bargained for. He stayed for four months before Mohamed finally asked him to leave. Debbie was to recall that on one occasion Belachheb had a severe toothache. "My husband took him to the dentist and he gave him a bottle of Tylenol 3 for pain. He ate the whole bottle." The Listi residents called an ambulance but the attendants would not take him to the hospital because he had not lost consciousness. Abdul brought him to the hospital, but there are no reports of his being admitted for treatment.[14]

One of the first activities Belachheb engaged in was to enroll at the Center for the English Language in Dallas. Exactly how he paid the tuition is a matter of speculation, but he probably managed to get low-paying, service jobs similar to those he held in Los Angeles. He attended with a friend named Yanouri*, who was also an acquaintance of Mohamed.

His teacher remembered that Belachheb was a very poor student who behaved in "a generally offensive manner." He often arrived for class at 8:30 A.M., after a night of partying, smelling like a barroom, with the heavy stench of alcohol on his breath. He could not take criticism and often responded with no sense of social grace.[15]

But, within a few months he was to place the following statement on his resume: "I speak French, Arabic, Italian, Dutch and English."[16]

On the other hand, there is little doubt that Belachheb could be charming when he wanted to be. He used whatever money he could make to cultivate a Mediterranean playboy image. He used his French accent to his advantage when trying to pick up women. He preferred, of course, rich women who could afford to spend money on him. And some of them did. "The kid's got sex appeal," said the woman who was to become his second wife.[17] And because of booming times, the north Dallas nightclub scene was fertile ground for him to plow.

If his first wife, Jenny, was correct when she said Belachheb would settle for "a dog with a hat" when it came to sex with women, then he must have felt like an enormously successful playboy. Along the LBJ Freeway, especially near the Dallas/Addison border, many nightclubs catered to virtually all age groups and tastes. The younger, louder throngs tended to go north into Addison where a strip of clubs had sprung up that were more like discotheques. Further south, quieter joints catered to a more subdued, middle-aged crowd. If a lonely, divorced, middle-aged woman with a good job making good money wanted to go out for a drink, she could do so in relative safety in north Dallas. Abdelkrim Belachheb preyed on such women. He often boasted that he successfully cultivated relationships with rich white women who gave him money and memberships in exclusive Dallas nightclubs.

While Belachheb's fondness for grandiosity always creates suspicion, in this case there is some evidence to support at least some of what he claimed. In 1984, the *Fort Worth Star-Telegram* interviewed a neighbor in an apartment complex where he lived and quoted her as saying that many women paraded in and out of his residence. "He has a good personality. If you meet him face-to-face he could sell you anything. But over the phone he couldn't even make an appointment," said an unidentified friend to the *Dallas Morning News*.[18]

He preferred rich women and chased them. But they had to be American, because he needed his "papers" to become a legal resident of the United States; he was searching for an "American Jenny" to marry.

During that time, he continued to exhibit signs of his narcissistic personality. American women, he observed, were interested in him because they could learn so much. And they always wanted sex, "even before they give me a cup of coffee," he said. He thought every occupation he held was beneath him and so he changed jobs frequently. He complained, for example, about how restaurants in Los Angeles would not make him a manager without first evaluating him as a waiter. He also complained that they would not take the time to teach him English. (That a working knowledge of English was a preferred qualification for a managerial position in a restaurant in America seems not to have occurred to him.)[19]

But even as a waiter, he was reportedly an anal retentive perfectionist, which could have been a reflection, not of the importance of the position he held, but of how grandiose he considered himself to be.

"He felt he had to be a millionaire," a coworker said, "everything was too low class for him." The solution to his immigration and occupational dilemma was to marry a rich American woman.[20]

IV

Back in Belgium, Jenny's petition for a divorce from Abdelkrim Belachheb was granted on February 25, 1982. Shortly afterwards, she changed her name.[21]

Four months later, Belachheb attended a small party at an apartment complex located near the Trinity River at 111 Continental Street in Dallas. He appears to have been living in the same apartment complex at the time. The hostess was a friend named Beth* who was a secretary in a Dallas law firm. At the party she introduced Belachheb to a friend named Joanie*.

By her own account, Joanie was living in a "ghetto" at the time. But then, any Dallas real estate was considered gold. She had purchased a house as an investment even though it was a "shack." She had no furniture and her car was ten years old. She was certainly not Belachheb's ideal for a wife. She was a personnel consultant for the Girl Scouts of America and not rich.[22] Additionally, although quite attractive, at age fifty-three, she was fifteen years older than Belachheb and she had been married twice before.

But she was also an American citizen. The *Dallas Times Herald* reported that Belachheb proposed marriage to her two weeks after he first met her.[23]

Joanie was immediately attracted both to Belachheb's arrogance and innocence, and the "little boy eyes" that always looked "scared and suspicious." She thought he had an affectionate nature and that their chance meeting was almost mystic. "I knew the minute he walked into the room. It was him. I had even seen him before, in a dream, and I had been praying for God to send him to me." That evening they talked well into the morning hours; Belachheb telling her fanciful stories of his world travels.[24]

But she also had reservations: "My first thought was, 'O.K., he just wants to legitimize his position here, right?' So, I told him he needed to see some other women first and then we'd see. He laughed really hard and said, 'More women?'"[25]

Joanie and Belachheb dated for several months. She called him "Charlie," another of Belachheb's adopted American names. Their relationship grew closer when, in October of 1982, Joanie's house was damaged by fire. His experience in construction put him in a position to be of great help, and according to Joanie, he supervised the reconstruction of the dwelling. By November 27 she moved back into the house—and he moved in with her. At that time he proposed marriage again, and again Joanie put him off. She was reported to have asked him to wait six months. Six months later, on May 28, 1983, the Justice of the Peace of precinct one in Sherman, Grayson County, Texas, married them.[26]

Abdelkrim Belachheb had been in the United States illegally from October 22, 1981, to the day of his marriage—583 days later. His marriage guaranteed that he could remain in the United States. All he had to do was repeat the lies he told successfully that allowed him to enter the United States in the first place. He petitioned the INS for permanent residency in July 1983. Joanie took on the burden of handling the paperwork and bureaucratic red tape. In sworn testimony, she related that "[W]e didn't have the money to hire an attorney to get his immigration papers, and I did all that myself and every time you have to ask one question you have to stand in that long line which is three or four hours, and I was doing all that and he was dissatisfied with things and he was depressed and I was just exhausted."[27]

On his petition for legal alien status (i.e., permanent resident alien) Belachheb repeated the lies he used to get his visitor visa fraudulently: he stated that he had been a resident of Morocco before coming to the United States, and he indicated that he had no criminal record. These falsifications should have excluded him from attaining his legal resident alien status, but as an INS official from Los Angeles readily admitted at the time, "We don't track them after they enter the country unless we get information that would prompt us to question the legality of their entry. In this case nothing was even brought to our attention about the guy." He was officially declared a permanent resident alien of the United States on January 16, 1984.[28]

When Debbie, the friend who lived with Belachheb in Mohamed's house on Listi Street, found out Belachheb had gotten married, she was relieved because, she thought, "the lady had money."[29]

Joanie described her marriage to Belachheb as warm and loving, even as she described his continuous abuse of her. "We had a very loving relationship," she said, "but there were times when Charlie's mind would snap. His eyes would glaze; it was almost like something wasn't making a connection . . . he was in terror like he was defending himself from me . . . Then he seemed to snap back and he was confused when he saw the state I was in. I knew he had no remembrance of what had happened."[30]

On another occasion, he threw a drink in her face as he accused her of embarrassing him in front of his Arabic-speaking friends. "We were entertaining some Egyptian friends, a man and a woman, and they were talking Arabic and sort of ignoring my presence. And when they left I mentioned to Charlie that they were rude to me in my own home." The innocuous comment sent Belachheb into a rage. After throwing the drink in her face, he grabbed her head and fractured her skull on the back of a sofa. A couple of days later she had to be admitted to the hospital for swelling. Later, in sworn testimony, she claimed that he had no memory of the incident: "He was confused."[31]

On yet another occasion, he came in late on a Monday night and she swore at him. He reacted by pinning her to the floor with his knees and threatening to beat her. Still another fight had her running from him into their bedroom and placing a chest of drawers against the door to keep him out. He forced the door open anyway and the chest fell on her.[32]

His behavior toward Joanie was fashioned by his attitude toward women, in general. His eyes were not glazed nor was he under any trance or hallucination when he told Dr. Kevin Karlson, a psychologist, that "If you be nice with women, all women be bored. I'm not nice; women like that." At the time of his comment, if Belachheb had been anything other than lucid the doctor would surely have noted it and testified to that fact. Belachheb's cultural background might explain his thinking of women as subservient, but his violence toward them, especially his two wives, is more attributable only to his towering ego. In 1984, Joanie admitted to Dallas police that he simply could not stand to be rejected by a woman. If true, it certainly explains the problems he perceived he had with American women, especially the kind he pursued—rich and independent-minded. He saw them as aggressive and insolent.[33]

Neither is it surprising that during his second marriage he repeated his infidelity and shamelessly exploited another wife who loved him. Allegedly, when Joanie changed the listing for their phone from her own last name to "Belachheb" the phone rang constantly because of calls from women he had picked up. He fancied himself as a ladies' man and spent a considerable amount of money on himself. He wore fashionable, designer clothes, and reportedly used money Joanie gave him to buy memberships in private nightclubs. He also purchased a wig to hide his balding scalp. It was of such quality that some of his friends did not know he was bald. (He was so meticulous and demanding about it, however, the salon that sold it to him gave him back his money and let him keep the wig so he would go away and leave them alone.)[34]

By July 1983, only two months after her marriage, Joanie decided to leave. His paranoia was too much for her to handle, she said. She left for Las Vegas and got a job working for a friend at a mining company. During her nine-month stay in Nevada, Belachheb visited her several times and they reportedly kept in close touch by phone.[35]

Joanie's departure meant nothing to Belachheb, except possibly the end of a revenue stream. He continued to go as he pleased, attempting to live the life of a playboy and pursuing rich women foolish enough to spend money on him. He did have jobs, mostly low-paying positions as a waiter or a chauffeur, and there were many because he did not hold any for longer than a few weeks. What money he did make he spent on his self-centered addictions. He drank to the point of alcoholism. Since his days in Brussels, his favorite drink was Johnny Walker Red and Coke—sometimes he had "JW Red with 7Up."

Of all of his jobs, the one least suited to his training or temperament was as a business broker for G&G International in north Dallas. "Actually, I don't know why he was working with me," the owner later admitted. "He tried to do the business, but he never did. He came and disappeared." Belachheb had no business experience remotely related to the job. He could barely speak English. He could never have comprehended the complicated contracts he was expected to consummate. After only two months, observing Belachheb's hopeless incompetence and chronic absenteeism, the owner asked him to leave. He took it well, but fellow workers do remember how enraged he got when a colleague got a date with a woman who had originally called for Belachheb.[36]

By the spring of 1984, Joanie was ready to return to Texas, and when she did she found her husband penniless, unemployed, and living with another woman. At the time, he was driving a white Chevrolet station wagon he had financed with his girlfriend's co-signature. Eventually, he moved back in with Joanie, only to abuse her again and throw her out of her own house—twice. On those evenings she drove around aimlessly or just slept in the car.[37]

Like Jenny in Belgium, Joanie's patience with the unpleasant Abdelkrim Belachheb bordered on co-dependency. Meanwhile, Belachheb had nothing good to say about her. "She is a white American, unfortunately. She puts me down . . . She made me a slave, forced me to do things that I should never have done," he later told a psychiatrist.[38] And to Beth, the woman who introduced them, he called Joanie a "filthy, dirty person that never took a bath, smelled bad, stupid, old, ugly—you name it," she recalled. And when Beth asked him if it was true that he beat Joanie badly enough to put her into a hospital, he replied, "Yeah, I sure did. Bitch deserved it."

When Beth asked him why he had married her in the first place, he said that he needed a green card.[39]

[1] See http://www.usembassy.ma/Services/Consular/visa.htm. Site visited on July 28, 2002.

[2] Ibid.

[3] ABC News: *20/20*, August 22, 1985.

[4] *Dallas Morning News,* August 7, 1984.

[5] Ibid., August 5, 1984; *Dallas Times Herald,* August 7, 1984; ABC News: *20/20*, August 22, 1985.

[6] A copy of Abdelkrim Belachheb's visa is in the file of the Dallas County District Attorney's Office; U.S. Department of Justice: Immigration and Naturalization Service: *Memorandum of Creation of Record of Lawful Permanent Residency, Abdelkrim Belachheb,* stamp dated January 16, 1984, and *Application for Status as Permanent Resident,* July 12, 1983; Dallas County District Attorney Files: Unidentified and undated note; Ibid.

[7] Dallas County District Attorney Files: Norman Kinne to Eugene Gee, July 6, 1984; Abdelkrim Belachheb quoted in *Dallas Morning News,* June 23, 1984.

[8] *Dallas Times Herald,* June 23, 1985.

[9] Eunice quoted in *Dallas Times Herald,* August 5, 1984; Ibid., October 28, 1984.

[10] Dallas Police Department Files: Lisa to whom it may concern, undated; *Fort Worth Star-Telegram,* June 30, 1984.

[11] Details of the Dunn and Bradstreet report are covered in *Dallas Morning News,* August 10, 1984.

[12] Ibid., June 29, 1984.

[13] *Dallas Morning News,* June 23, 1985.

[14] *Texas* v *Belachheb,* 291st Judicial District, Cause no. F84-75078-SU, et. al., VI, 1934-65; Dallas Police Department Files: Handwritten notes from an interview with Mohamed, June 29, 1984; Debbie quoted in *Dallas Times Herald,* June 30, 1984.

[15] Dallas County District Attorney Files: *Affidavit,* by Yanouri, June 29, 1984; The teacher is quoted the file and in the *Fort Worth Star-Telegram,* June 30, 1984.

[16] Dallas Police Department Files: Application for Employment, Charley [sic] Abdelkrim Belachheb, October 29, 1983; *Texas* v *Belachheb,* 291st Judicial District, Cause no. F84-75078-SU, et. al., VII, 2384-2413.

[17] Second wife quoted in *Dallas Morning News,* August 5, 1984.

[18] *Fort Worth Star-Telegram,* June 30, 1984; Belachheb friend quoted in article.

[19] A court-appointed psychiatrist contributed the Belachheb quote in *Texas* v *Belachheb,* 291st Judicial District, Cause no. F84-75078-SU, et. al., VII, 2198-2236.

[20] *Texas* v *Belachheb,* 291st Judicial District, Cause no. F84-75078-SU, et. al., VI, 1653-77; Belachheb coworker quoted in *Dallas Morning News,* June 30, 1984.

[21] Melinda Henneberger; Kingdom Of Belgium: Province of Brabant: Territory of Brussels-Capital: District of Schaerbeek: Extract from Registry of Divorce Certificates, 1982, # 164 RS; *Dallas Morning News,* August 5, 1984.

[22] *Texas* v *Belachheb,* 291st Judicial District, Cause no. F84-75078-SU, et. al., V, 1237-84 and VI, 1653-77.

[23] *Dallas Times Herald,* October 28, 1984.

[24] Dallas County District Attorney Files: Unidentified and undated newspaper clipping; Melinda Henneberger; *Texas* v *Belachheb,* 291st Judicial District, Cause no. F84-75078-SU, et. al., V, 1237-84; Joanie quoted in *Dallas Morning News,* August 5, 1984; *Dallas Times Herald,* October 28, 1984.

[25] Joanie quoted in *Dallas Morning News,* August 5, 1984.

[26] State of Texas: County of Grayson: *Marriage Certificate:* Abdelkrim Belachheb and [Joanie], May 28, 1983; *Texas* v *Belachheb,* 291st Judicial District, Cause no. F84-75078-SU, et. al., V, 1237-84; Ibid.; *Dallas Times Herald,* October 28, 1984.

[27] Joanie quoted in *Texas* v *Belachheb,* 291st Judicial District, Cause no. F84-75078-SU, et. al., V, 1237-84; *Fort Worth Star-Telegram,* June 30, 1984.

[28] U.S. Department of Justice: Immigration and Naturalization Service: *Petition to Classify Status of Alien Relative for Issuance of Immigrant Visa,* July 12, 1983 [Redacted].

[29] INS official quoted in *Dallas Times Herald,* August 7, 1984; Debbie quoted in *Dallas Morning News,* August 5, 1984.

[30] Joanie quoted in *Texas* v *Belachheb,* 291st Judicial District, Cause no. F84-75078-SU, et. al., V, 1237-84.

[31] Ibid.

[32] Ibid.

[33] Ibid., 1391-1567; Dallas Police Department Files: Handwritten notes from an interview with Joanie, undated; Dallas County District Attorney Files: E. Clay Griffith, MD to Judge Gerry Meier, July 3, 1984.

[34] *Texas* v *Belachheb,* 291st Judicial District, Cause no. F84-75078-SU, et. al., VI, 1653-77 and 2198-2236; *Dallas Times Herald,* October 28, 1984; Jeff Shaw, interviewed by the author on June 14, 2002.

[35] *Texas* v *Belachheb,* 291st Judicial District, Cause no. F84-75078-SU, et. al., V, 1237-84; *Dallas Morning News,* August 5, 1984.

[36] *Dallas Morning News,* June 30, 1984; G&G owner quoted in *Dallas Times Herald,* June 30, 1984.

[37] *Texas* v *Belachheb,* 291st Judicial District, Cause no. F84-75078-SU, et. al., V, 1237-84; *Dallas Times Herald,* October 28, 1984.

[38] Belachheb quoted by Dr. Clay Griffith in *Texas* v *Belachheb,* 291st Judicial District, Cause no. F84-75078-SU, et. al., VII, 2198-2236.

[39] Beth quoted and Beth's quote of Abdelkrim Belachheb in *Texas* v *Belachheb,* 291st Judicial District, Cause no. F84-75078-SU, et. al., VI, 1653-77.

chapter five

The North Dallas Nightclub Scene

"He is violent even when he is not drink-ing. But when he does, it's all over. I used to say, 'It's a good thing you can't get a gun here [in Brussels].' How did he get one in Texas?"

—Jenny, Belachheb's first wife
quoted in the *Dallas Morning News*

I

To one of the waitresses he encountered, Abdelkrim Belachheb was merely a five-foot six-inch man with a wig and crooked teeth.[1] To some others, he apparently represented romance from the Mediterranean and mystery from Africa. The frequency of his sexual conquests is as much attributable to his tenacity as to his charm.

His compulsion for sexual conquests, especially of rich women, took him to the nightclubs that sprang up along the LBJ Freeway; the center of the Dallas construction boom. The wilder action was further north in Addison, where the clubs were louder and more raucous. But those establishments attracted a younger crowd—people emerging from high school and college, with good jobs and plenty of money to spend.

On the edge of the area, for the middle aged, especially the single and divorced who would rather not spend nights alone at home, there were more formal and quieter places to go. Each of these had a regular clientele, some of whom frequented two or three of these "clubs." For the most part the customers all knew one another, and they came to know the owners, bartenders, and waiters.[2]

This nightclub crowd was far from the wealthiest in Dallas, but most of the people who frequented the clubs were comfortable with themselves. Others were "wanna-be big shots." Either way, they worked for their money. Generally, they had high-paying jobs they depended on to support their lifestyles. Many were living better than they ever thought possible. Ken Kercheval, one of the stars of the television megahit show, *Dallas,* observed that, "Back then, people [in Dallas] sweat money."[3]

Abdelkrim Belachheb had never seen such widespread free spending among so many common people. An anthropologist was to testify later that to Belachheb the women of these clubs represented a great deal of wealth. The accoutrements included nice cars, coiffed and colored hair, bejeweled necks, ears, wrists and ankles, shoes that matched purses, credit cards, "boob jobs," and buying whatever you want when you want it just because you want it. The men wore shiny dress shoes, had nice three-piece suits, smelled good, and bought drinks for the women. Some of these men had coiffed and colored hair and bejeweled necks, too.

For some, the freedom went beyond spending. They were too old to go to the Addison clubs. Yet they were healthy, single or divorced, easily bored watching television, had no parents to answer to—and had normal sex drives. Some of them did what they taught their children, now grown, not to do. They drank and drove, and sometimes made decisions based on urges. The north Dallas nightclub scene had relatively nice places to get picked up by someone from a somewhat "safe" group of people.[4]

The liquor laws of Dallas County complicated business for these clubs. They were infuriatingly complex because they were codified and enforced on the precinct level. A career prosecutor for the Dallas District Attorney's Office once said, "I never did understand all of it." Some precincts were completely "dry." The adjacent precinct might allow for the purchase of liquor, but only in licensed liquor stores. The next precinct might allow for the purchase of beer and wine in a grocery store but hard liquor in a liquor store only. The next precinct could be completely "wet." Some Dallasites had to cross the Trinity River to buy a six-pack of beer. Restaurants and bars had to contend with this local autonomy by getting around the law, which allowed for individuals to buy drinks if they held membership in a private "club." Some places presented the illusion of a separation of the restaurant, which anyone could enter, and the bar (or the club), which required a membership.

Generally, the "membership" fee was not exclusionary; it amounted to a small payment for a card that allowed the holder to buy a drink. "You could afford that on a wino's salary," a Dallas policeman was to say.[5] The exclusivity came from price and loca-

After two generations of hard work, the Ianni family moved their restaurant to a booming section of north Dallas on the corner of Midway and LBJ Freeway. (Dallas County District Attorney Files)

tion; in that area of Dallas, prices, for almost everything, were steep—but the times were good and the money was there.

Ianni's Restaurant and Club was just such a place.

II

Joe Ianni was born in Italy in 1920 and immigrated to the United States at an early age. By 1928 he had come to Dallas from New York City. He was married to a woman named Marie, better known as "Totsy." (Marie Ianni's nickname has been spelled a number of different ways. "Totsy" is my phonetic version.) Joe and Totsy first served their Italian dishes in a small restaurant on Ross Avenue in the early 1950s. They eventually moved their restaurant to an area called "lower" Greenville Avenue. Here the restaurant gained a reputation as one of the finest and most authentic Italian eateries in Dallas. Connoisseurs from all parts of the Metroplex went to Joe Ianni's restaurant for his homemade pastas and sauces. The restaurant had a quiet, Old World atmosphere with candles and a "heavenly smell of garlic."

Ianni's was the kind of restaurant where people actually went to eat as much as socialize. Dallas legends, like baseball great Mickey Mantle and jockey Willie Shoemaker, were often seen there eating their favorite Italian dishes. Joe was particularly good at preparing veal. One of the dishes was a veal cutlet pounded paper-thin, stuffed with crabmeat, and rolled.[6]

Joe Ianni died in 1973, and Totsy and their daughter, Mary*, took over the management of the restaurant. Ten years later, in early 1983, the Iannis decided to move the restaurant to the center of the Dallas business construction boom during its height. The new address was 12801 Midway Road, on the southwest corner near the LBJ Freeway. The new restaurant shared a building with a few other, smaller, specialty shops and was sort of an island in the parking lot of a strip mall called the Harvest Hill Village Shopping Center. It was near destinations of the *nouveau riche*, such as the Galleria and Valley View Shopping Center.[7]

Ianni's Restaurant and Club from entrance to back. After entering the front door, customers walked through a hallway to the back where the barroom was located. (Dallas County District Attorney Files)

The new Ianni's was a larger establishment with three dining rooms. Toward the back was a barroom crowded with small, round tables, each surrounded by four royal blue-padded chairs with casters. The Formica tabletops matched the wallpaper, a red background with small white patterns that from a distance looked like polka dots. To the left was a well-stocked, U-shaped bar with padding that matched the royal blue upholstery on the chairs. The high-back stools, though, were covered with beige vinyl and swiveled so that the customers could easily face the bar or turn around to see the dance floor located in the back right corner. In this corner, a pianist used a black, baby grand piano to play soft music from 5 to 8:30 P.M. each evening. From 9 P.M. to 2 A.M., a band, usually a trio or quartet, played. The rich, dark blue carpet was spliced up against a small hardwood parquet floor where people danced. The club stayed as busy as the restaurant.[8]

It was built to be one of the nicer places in Dallas. It specifically targeted upwardly mobile north Dallas businesspeople, either singles or couples, who wanted to enjoy a night out. The soft music didn't attract teens and wasn't loud enough to drown out conversation. Stretch limousines parked out front were a common sight. Reportedly, coats and ties were required, but some entered with fashionable open-collar leisure suits. Because it was in a "dry" precinct, patrons usually went through the routine of "applying" for a membership in order to buy liquor.[9]

Ianni's was also a popular spot for women who wanted to go out and not be bothered by lecherous men. "It was a nice place to be. It's a happy place to be," said a regular named Anna, who went there almost every night. "The food is good [and] the service is good," said another regular named Kelly. Occasionally, call girls and drug dealers came in as well, but as long as they made no attempt to do "business" there, they were not asked to leave. Mary and her employees were careful to protect Ianni's good name and reputation.[10]

Ianni's reputation for being a nice, quiet place for mature people to have fun without being bothered, and having good food and service, followed the restaurant and club from lower Greenville Avenue to its location on Midway in north Dallas. Anything less would have meant going out of business; across the parking lot was another restaurant and club called Cappuccino's, and just down the LBJ Freeway was Farfallo's.

III

Abdelkrim Belachheb continued to spend whatever money he had on expensive designer clothes and other accessories for blending into the north Dallas nightclub scene. He probably lived largely on what others gave him. His ego and temperament were such that he could not hold a job for more than a few weeks. "He was nervous, high-strung, not very stable. He couldn't hold a job, but he was never violent," said his former housemate Debbie. Another resident in the house on Listi Street, Mohamed, wondered aloud whether Belachheb had any money. Another friend knew him to be talented. Reportedly, Belachheb was offered a teaching job in a welding school, but "he didn't have the patience. He was too high strung to teach." As a waiter he was anal-retentive and a perfectionist who demanded respect. This was complicated by his paranoia: "He thought people were talking about him," a coworker once said.[11]

While Belachheb's friend, Debbie, never saw him get violent, his wife, Joanie, told a different story to the Dallas Police. She indicated that every time he lost a job, he got more abusive towards her.

If so, the abuse must have been frequent. His resume was a maze of job and educational experiences that even a novice human resources person could easily see was fantasy. According to Belachheb's resumes:

- He attended primary school in Moulay Idriss in Morocco from 1951-1957. (Which was confirmed by his father in 1985.)
- From 1958-1962, he attended *College Chaumane*, in Paris. (In truth, that was when his family had to leave Beni Ammar and move to Fes because of his juvenile delinquency.)
- From 1958-1965, during a time the same resume said he was in school in Paris, he listed experience as a waiter in the Brumel Hotel in Luzanne, Switzerland. He noted a promotion to maitre' d at this location (which is highly unlikely since he was fourteen in 1958).
- From 1963-1965, he attended the *École Technique De Lausanne* in Switzerland where he earned a technical diploma.
- From 1966-1968, he attended the *École des Beaux Art de Brussels* in Belgium where he specialized in Mechanics and Business Management. He apparently worked his way through that school by being a waiter/captain at the Westbury Hotel in Brussels at the same time.
- But from 1965-1975, he also worked for Fabricum General Construction on the *Ave de Ville Vorte*, in Brussels as a "techni-

cian and executive for all natural gas instruments." He was instrumental in the company's acquisition of natural gas contracts. He also received certification by *Ecole des Art et Metier* in heating and plumbing. He was also a supervisor in welding for all of Belgium, Holland, and the Middle East.

- From 1969-1980, he added food service to his construction jobs. He was a "passive" partner who participated (which is oxymoronic) in catering services like weddings. He had experience in "continental food preparation while working with gourmet chefs in Italian, French, Moroccan, and Spanish foods." (Of course, he failed to mention that he was in a Kuwaiti prison from 1976 through 1978.)

- From 1975-1981, he ran another business called *Establissement Belach'heb* where he employed twenty-seven people in his heating, air conditioning, and plumbing business. (Again, he does not explain how he could have operated this business while in prison for two years in Kuwait. He sold this business, he claims, in 1981, the year after he fled to Morocco to escape a two-year prison sentence for nearly killing his wife.)[12]

On a separate resume he submitted for a car salesman position he indicated that he was in car sales in Belgium from 1976 through 1981. His grandiosity displayed itself most prominently when he wrote narrative statements: "I worked for Citrogen *[sic]* in Belgium for six years selling cars. I spent five years independently buying Mercedes, BMW, Peugeot, and Volvo and selling them in Turkey and Teheran." He added, "During the years that I owned my own business, *Establishment Belachheb,* I made many contacts with investors and businessmen in Europe, Iran, Turkey, Lebanon, Tunisia, and Morocco in the sale of automobiles, real estate, land, and commodities." But when asked why he was interested in working for that particular dealership, he wrote, "I believe in Chevrolet."[13]

His resume for his employment in America was only slightly more truthful. He overstated his position and tenure in almost all of his jobs. For example, he indicated that he worked at the Hyatt Regency Hotel's Universal Restaurant for a year. In truth, he was a part-time waiter for only thirteen days. He had himself working at G&G International Business Brokers for six months when he was there for barely two and had been asked to leave because of chronic absenteeism. He also listed his friend Mohamed as a reference, saying he knew him for five years, which would have been for three years before he even entered the United States.

A final fraudulent statement came when he was asked if he had ever been arrested; he checked "no."[14]

Indeed, he could not hold a job because he could be a very unpleasant individual. Most accounts by those who knew him cite his paranoia and his compulsiveness. Or perhaps he simply did not want to work for a living.

According to her own sworn testimony, Joanie tried to help him get started in his own business. She tried extraordinarily hard to satisfy his fleeting interests. "Nothing is ever good enough for his grandiose ideas. I helped him or tried to help him get started in construction, when he rebuilt my house, and he wanted to go into construction. Then it was welding. Then it was bar tendering. Then it was—and I was always trying to help him, and when we almost get it ready, it was just not good enough."[15]

Joanie was so accommodating that she agreed to sell two of her properties, valued at about $125,000, to finance his business aspirations. They met a real estate agent in an apartment Belachheb had on Forest Lane in Dallas and signed a contract for the sale of the properties. (This was the same domicile Belachheb had once shared with another woman while still married to Joanie.) The agent remembered that Belachheb was calm at the time, except when Joanie signed the contract. He insisted that Joanie add "Belachheb" to her signature.[16]

Abdelkrim Belachheb's treatment of his wife Joanie is a story of heartbreaking exploitation and abuse. "[Charlie] has a severe personality problem that turns him into a monster with little or no provocation," she was to say later in a written statement. "He is violent, suspicious, accusing, and verbally and physically abusive. At those times he has no control over his behavior."[17]

Joanie testified that on the occasion where he beat her badly enough to put her in the hospital, he came to pick her up to take her home, but because of a one hour delay in her out-processing, he left her stranded; he was unwilling to wait. She had to call his friend, Mohamed, to take her home. When she did leave him to live in Las Vegas for about nine months, he visited her there, and in April 1984 she returned to him in Dallas. Shortly afterwards, he attacked Joanie violently at least twice in a three week period. Accounts differ, but the first incident appears to have been brought about by Belachheb's belief that Joanie called his workplace and caused him problems. "Don't you ever call my work again. If you ever make trouble for me again I'll kill you," she quoted him as saying. Then he threw her out of the residence. She fled to a gas station where she called Mohamed for help. In a courtroom, she later reconstructed her conversation:

"Mohamed, Charlie is crazy. He is going to kill someone. I have got to get help for him."

According to the *Dallas Times Herald* Mohamed replied, "Maybe someone will kill him."

Joanie left him, again, only to return to celebrate their first wedding anniversary (May 23, 1984).[18]

She stayed a little more than a week. In her own words, Joanie related that on June 2, "[Charlie] came home and the phone had been turned off, and I realized it was Friday night. Early in the day [I] had gone to get another phone, but it wouldn't be reconnected until the following Wednesday, and he was demanding the receipt and he was just, you know, in a frenzy, and I was so frightened I didn't know where it was. I couldn't find it, and he opened the door and he took my clothes and just started throwing them out and all my creams all over my clothes. He was just wild." She continued, "I finally did find my car key. I drove, it's just a half a block to [a grocery store] parking lot, and I was going to call the police, but there was a policeman in a squad car there, and I ran up to him and I told him that my husband had a gun, that he was crazy and I needed help."

The officer told her to get a divorce.[19]

Belachheb had purchased that gun exactly one year earlier on June 2, 1983, less than a week after he had married Joanie. While his marriage assured his being able to stay in the United States, he would not be granted his permanent legal resident status for another six months. It was illegal for him to purchase a firearm. But he entered the Hines Boulevard Pawn Shop and presented a Texas driver's license as identification. It still had Mohamed's Listi Street address on it and Belachheb used that on the ATF Form 4473 he completed for the purchase. (The pawnshop worker completed the seller's portion of the form six days later on June 8.)

Belachheb had purchased a Smith and Wesson model 459, 9mm semi-automatic pistol. It was a double action, which means that it can be fired with or without cocking back the hammer. It holds more rounds than most pistols. The magazine, or "clip," can hold fourteen rounds, and it is possible to load a full clip while a live round is in the chamber. Thus, it is possible to fire off fifteen rounds without reloading. It is a semi-automatic—the force of each blast automatically ejects an empty shell and reloads a live round.

And history repeated itself. ATF Form 4473 asked the following questions:

- Are you under indictment
- Have you ever been convicted in any court of a crime punishable by imprisonment for a term exceeding one year
- Are you a fugitive from justice
- Are you an unlawful user of, or addicted to, marijuana or a depressant, stimulant, or narcotic drug
- Have you ever been adjudicated mentally defective or committed to a mental institution

- Have you ever been discharged from the armed forces under dishonorable conditions
- Are you an alien illegally in the US
- Are you a person who, having been a citizen of the U.S., renounced his citizenship

Belachheb answered "no" to all of the above.[20] Yet again, the United States Government depended on a criminal and/or a mental patient to identify himself.

IV

Linda Thomas Lowe was a pianist and a lover of music. She was considered one of the best. For twenty years, she played background music in some of the finest hotels and clubs, not only in Dallas at places like the Dallas Hilton and the Registry, but also in locations like the MGM Grand Hotel in Las Vegas. She loved her work and was able to support herself comfortably, especially since she was divorced and her only child was grown and had a family of her own. Indeed, Linda had two granddaughters, but she did not look like a grandmother. She took care of herself and her looks, including breast augmentation. She was not just attractive; she was quite beautiful. She stood at a little less than five-feet two-inches tall, but she walked and danced gracefully on high-heel shoes, and her slim, 114 pound figure undoubtedly made her look taller. She had clear, green eyes, expertly accentuated by her makeup. She was style-conscious, into fashion, and always wore nice clothes.[21]

It was not always like that for Linda Lowe. She was born in a central Texas hamlet called Bremond (pronounced *Bree*Mon). She was close to her brother, Wade, in part because they grew up together in a poor and strict environment. Their parents were very dogmatic members of a fundamentalist Assemblies of God Church. Their faith prohibited short pants, lipstick, movies (even at school), dancing, and many other amusements routinely enjoyed by their peers. Her younger brother Wade remembers seeing Linda in a schoolyard standing in a white skirt that went all the way to her

Linda Lowe was a musician who loved to listen to bands play in Dallas's trendy night spots. Her boyfriend introduced her to Abdelkrim Belachheb. Several weeks later she said, "I don't like him. He stares at me." (Texas Court of Criminal Appeals, Second District)

ankles, while all of the other children played in shorts in the Texas heat. Wade had to wear long white pants. He and his sister bonded because they often found themselves alone together because they could not participate in some school activities.[22]

Soon after Linda graduated from high school in Fort Worth, she put her rigid religious upbringing behind her and lived the way she wanted. Although she continued to attend church services in different denominations, and played and sang in their choirs, her music now focused on entertainment. She basically told her mother that she was grown and would do as she pleased, but she did not do it in a bitter or rebellious way.[23]

Linda's first marriage was to a man named Bobby, who did gigs with Willie Nelson during his early days. The marriage lasted only a year. Her next husband, a Mr. Lowe, was in the construction business. That marriage was ill fated as well.

Her career in music was her real love, and while she did demo tapes, she never recorded professionally. She was a good friend of popular country singer Lee Greenwood and had ambitions to record with him, but she supported herself by playing background music. She changed jobs often, as musicians do, playing at Dallas' more exclusive nightspots. On July 11, 1984, she opened at Farfallo's, a competitor of Ianni's. Since she usually played during the late afternoon and early evening hours, it was easy for her to stay and listen to the band that followed, or even check out the competition in places like Ianni's. Both places were also close to her home; she had just moved herself and two cats into a condominium only a few blocks away on Preston Oaks Boulevard.[24]

In January 1984, Linda had become seriously involved with a Dallas businessman named Nick*. He owned a car dealership that sold both a domestic line and upper-end exports like Mercedes, Rolls Royce, Ferraris, Porche, and Lamborghini. Nick first met Abdelkrim Belachheb while Belachheb worked as a chauffeur for the Walker Limousine Service. Belachheb was the driver who responded when Nick called for a limousine to pick him up at the Registry Hotel. Belachheb drove Nick and his stepson to the airport to pick up his ex-wife, but when they arrived they learned that the plane's arrival would be delayed for one to two hours. Nick asked Belachheb if he wanted to leave and return, but Belachheb said "no," got into the back seat and fixed drinks for everyone.

In trial testimony, Nick described what happened next: "I asked him if he was the owner of the limousine service and he said no, he was just the driver. I asked him if he had anticipated any plans of owning his own limousine service at a later date. He indicated yes, he would be very interested in that. I stated to him that we were anticipating an opening at approximately the first of May in [a suburb of Dallas], and if he was interested in purchasing a limousine to come over and see me. He took a card out [and] he wrote his name out, 'Pierre' and he gave me his home phone number and he said that he wanted one of my cards. However, we didn't have any at that point because we hadn't opened up for business yet. So, he thanked me and he said he would be in contact with me." The plane arrived and Nick surprised his ex-wife with a limo ride to a grand hotel.[25]

Two weeks later, Belachheb called Nick and indicated that he had quit his job at Walker's Limousine because he was not making enough money. Nick, a man of considerable business connections, told Belachheb that he had a partner who was getting ready to purchase a couple of limos for use by top-level executives of a company called First American Investments and Finance Corporation housed in the Alpha Towers in Dallas. Nick knew they would need a couple of drivers. "What kind of money do they pay?" asked Belachheb.

"I don't know. You have to negotiate with my partner over there or whoever you are going to drive the car for," Nick replied.

Belachheb ended up driving for the firm. During his short-lived tenure as a driver, he met and charmed another prominent businessman named Jim*. Jim and Nick were business partners in the auto sales business. They both thought that since Belachheb was fairly good looking and had a foreign accent he had the potential for selling the expensive and exotic foreign cars that were soon to fill their lots. They picked out an office for him and even introduced him to the sales manager. The sales manager interviewed Belachheb for nearly three hours and concluded that Belachheb's international aura made him a "natural" to push the top line inventory. The job, however, was not available for another month; the dealership was still under construction. For the time being, Belachheb had to be satisfied with his role as a limo driver. The wait did not suit his impatient temperament.

Jim went so far as to say that Belachheb "was more a friend than an employee. I had done him a couple of favors and he was always willing to do me favors. . . . I had loaned him personal money from time to time and I liked the guy as a matter of fact."[26]

Belachheb might have ingratiated himself with the "big shots," but he quickly got into arguments with his immediate supervisor, the man he was supposed to drive around in one of the three company limos. The trouble started when Belachheb was given a company credit card to buy one new suit to wear as a driver; he spent $3,000 on clothes. Then he complained about his pay. He was making over $2,000 a month, which was quite good (in 1984) for a driver, but he demanded a $500 a month raise. So, he ended up quitting, only to find out that the company withheld his last paycheck because of the money he spent on the credit card. This sent him into a rage. He directed his fury at his supervisor, whose name was Dan*. Belachheb showed Nick's son the Smith and Wesson semi-automatic he had purchased a year earlier and indicated that "[Dan] was going to get this," if he did not get his last paycheck.[27]

Shortly afterwards, Belachheb visited Nick. He was still upset over not getting his last paycheck. "He said he would do whatever he had to to get his pay," Nick recalled. Belachheb indicated that he had tried to reach Jim, but the secretaries stopped him. "He said he would go over there and grab [his former supervisor] and kill him if he had to."

Nick got Jim on the phone, and Jim told Belachheb to come on over. Nick was worried about what Belachheb would do once he got there. They walked outside and Nick tried to calm Belachheb down:

"Don't go over there because there is bankers over there at the office at First American and there is business people there. If you go in there to cause a scene I am going to hear it from [Jim], and I made the introduction for you. [Jim] is going to lash back at me and I'd appreciate it if you stay away. I will make sure you get your last week's pay check." Then Nick asked, "Do you have any money on you?"

"Why, what difference does that make?" replied Belachheb.

"Because it seems like you are upset over this past week's pay check. Turn the key on your ignition. Let me see your gas gauge."

"For what?"

"I want to make sure of something. Pierre, you don't have any money?" asked Nick. (At the time, Belachheb was using the name "Pierre.")

When testifying about the incident, Nick concluded the story by saying, "So, I reached into my pocket and gave him $150-200."[28]

V

During the evening of June 19, 1984, Abdelkrim Belachheb and his wife, Joanie, sat together for what was to be their last meal together. According to her statements to Dallas Police, and sworn testimony, they discussed his mental problems after he confessed to her that he had been depressed. During this conversation, she testified that she first found out about his many trips to psychiatric hospitals in Belgium. He was rational, at first, and had prepared a nice meal. They talked more about his problems, but eventually he got angry and started accusing her of "all kinds of things." She continued, "I told him I was afraid of him because the monster was appearing too often now. I told him about a psychiatrist who had a new method for determining the cause of depression. . . . He became defensive about my references to his mental condition and started to become verbally abusive."

During the evening Belachheb watered some plants he had in the apartment. "I take better care of my plants than my wife," he said.

Joanie finally had enough. She got up and started for the door.

"You have my number at work," he said. "Will you call me?"

"I never intend to see you or call you again," Joanie replied. Then she left.[29]

---

[1] Dallas Police Department Files: *Investigative Supplement Report,* by Catherine Arnott, June 29, 1984.

[2] Terry Rippa, interviewed by the author on July 12, 2002; John McNeill, interviewed by the author on July 12, 2002; Richard Paul Jones, interviewed by the author on July 14, 2002; Norman Kinne, interviewed by the author on June 14, 2002; Jeff Shaw; Melinda Henneberger.

[3] Ken Kercheval's quote was from a Travel Channel special on famous movie and television location sites. The *Dallas* locations were included in the special.

[4] Ibid.; *Texas* v *Belachheb,* 291st Judicial District, Cause no. F84-75078-SU, et. al., V, 1237-84.

[5] Bill Parker and Norman Kinne are both quoted during interviews.

[6] *Dallas Morning News,* June 30, 2002; Richard Paul Jones.

[7] Ibid.; *Dallas Times Herald,* June 29, 1984; *Fort Worth Star-Telegram,* June 30, 1984.

[8] Much of my description is from the Dallas District Attorney Files: Crime scene photos.

[9] Wade Thomas, interviewed by the author on July 13, 2002; Richard Paul Jones; *Fort Worth Star-Telegram,* June 30, 1984.

[10] Patrons quoted in *Dallas Times Herald,* June 29 and 30, 1984; Dallas County District Attorney Files: Unidentified and undated newspaper clipping; Richard Paul Jones.

[11] Quotes are from *Dallas Times Herald,* June 30, 1984 and *Dallas Morning News,* June 30, 1984.

[12] Dallas Police Department Files: Handwritten notes of an interview with Joanie, and *Resume of A. Charles Belachheb,* circa October 1983.

[13] Ibid.

[14] Ibid., *Dallas Times Herald,* June 30, 1984.

[15] Joanie quoted in *Texas* v *Belachheb,* 291st Judicial District, Cause no. F84-75078-SU, et. al., V, 1237-84 and 1391-1567.

[16] Dallas Police Department Files: Handwritten notes of interview with real estate agent, undated; *Dallas Morning News,* June 30, 1984; *Fort Worth Star-Telegram,* June 30, 1984.

[17] Dallas Police Department Files: Handwritten notes of an interview with Joanie, undated; Joanie quoted in unidentified and undated newspaper clipping in the Dallas County District Files.

[18] Joanie quoted in *Texas* v *Belachheb,* 291st Judicial District, Cause no. F84-75078-SU, et. al., V, 1237-84; Mohamed quoted in *Dallas Times Herald,* October 28, 1984.

[19] Joanie quoted in *Texas* v *Belachheb,* 291st Judicial District, Cause no. F84-75078-SU, et. al., V, 1237-84.

[20] *Texas* v *Belachheb,* 291st Judicial District, Cause no. F84-75078-SU, et. al., IV, 952-968, 1196-1224, and State's Exhibit 8 (ATF Form 4473).

[21] Wade Thomas; Dallas County District Attorney Files: Unidentified and undated newspaper clipping.

[22] Wade Thomas.

[23] Ibid.; *Texas* v *Belachheb,* 291st Judicial District, Cause no. F84-75078-SU, et. al., IV, 861-864; Dallas County District Attorney Files: Unidentified and undated newspaper clipping.

[24] Wade Thomas; Dallas Police Department Files: Unidentified and undated notes; Dallas County District Attorney Files: Unidentified and undated newspaper clipping; *Dallas Morning News,* June 30, 1984

[25] Nick quoted in *Texas* v *Belachheb,* 291st Judicial District, Cause no. F84-75078-SU, et. al., VI, 1792-1840.

[26] Jim quoted in Ibid., 1792-1840 and 1987-2015.

[27] *Texas* v *Belachheb,* 291st Judicial District, Cause no. F84-75078-SU, et. al., V, 1391-1567, VI, 1792-1840, 1841-45, and 1987-2015.

[28] The conversation is reconstructed from Nick's testimony in Ibid., VI, 1792-1840.

[29] Joanie quoted in Ibid., V, 1237-84; Dallas Police Department Files: Handwritten notes from interview with Joanie, undated; Belachheb quoted in *Dallas Morning News,* August 5, 1984.

chapter six

A Position for Tragedy

> *"I don't like him. He stares at me."*
> —Linda Lowe

I

Linda Lowe was not one to sit home alone with her two cats. She very much enjoyed patrolling the Dallas nightclub scene to listen to musicians. On different occasions she had been a member of several "all-girl" musical groups. On Tuesday, June 26, 1984, she called her brother Wade and told him that later in the week she was going to a place called Ianni's to listen to a band. Wade later related that she was looking for talented musicians to form a new group.[1] She was an outgoing person who clearly liked being around others, so she may have grown tired of playing the piano by herself.

Linda was planning to surprise Wade for his upcoming birthday by picking him up in a limo and taking him out for a nice dinner. Those who knew Linda would not have been surprised by her "very generous" and considerate nature, her mother later said. Linda even sent her brother a Father's Day card. The bartenders at the nightclubs, who came to know her as a person and a performer, all gushed about how "sweet and nice" she was.[2] No one, it seems, had anything negative to say about her—except Abdelkrim Belachheb.

Nick, the businessman and car dealer who had befriended Belachheb by helping him get a limo driver job, started dating Linda in January 1984. Wade thought that Nick was in love with Linda and that the feeling was mutual.

There was also talk of Linda opening her own nightclub. She wanted to call it "Fluffy's" (after one of her cats). Presumably, with Nick's business connections, financing for the business could have been arranged.

One of Nick's favorite restaurants was a place called Augustus' Gourmet Restaurant in Addison. In May, Belachheb had landed a job there as the maitre d'. Nick was to become fond of the owner, a man named Pete*. Apparently, Nick still considered Belachheb a friend and potential employee. He made it a point to have business events there. He also recommended Augustus' to other businesses looking to have luncheons and dinners. It was there that Belachheb first met Linda Lowe. Nick introduced them.

Nick remembered, "He greeted us with open arms; he introduced us to the owner, [Pete], and he had kissed Linda's hand and I remember he would go out of his way—if she went to light her cigarette he would run over there with his cigarette lighter; he would light it. He was very gracious, very polite, well-mannered."[3]

Given his attraction to rich women, and Linda's beauty, Belachheb must have been enamored with her. And at first, she was taken in by his charms.

But soon, Linda became unsettled by the way Belachheb and Pete constantly stared at her. Although Nick asked her to relax, that they were only out to be as helpful as they could be, Linda reached a point where she refused to go there.

Linda and Belachheb's association reached a low-point when Nick visited the restaurant and complained to Belachheb about a stomach condition he suffered from called sigmoid ulcer colitis. Belachheb said he knew of a remedy from France that would help. He guaranteed a cure in two to three months. He told Nick to swallow a raw egg and then a tablespoon of olive oil first thing in the morning.

According to his testimony, Nick tried it and it made him violently ill, giving him cramps and causing him to vomit. "Why did you listen to him?" Linda asked incredulously. She wanted nothing to do with Belachheb and did not want to be around him. On June 17, 1984, while on a date, Nick said he needed to go to Augustus' to pay a bill for a dinner he had thrown for his parts manager.

"Well, I don't want to go in there. I don't want to have anything to do with that restaurant, and especially with Pierre [Belachheb]," Linda insisted. But Nick persisted and talked her into going inside—a decision he was soon to regret.

"Why would you have prescribed something like olive oil and a raw egg for a colitis condition?" she said pointedly to Belachheb.

"It works wonders in Europe," Belachheb replied.

In his testimony, Nick continued, "Then they got into a name-calling situation. She called him an idiot, that type of thing, and I kind of settled both of them, backed them off."

"What's the matter? Isn't this restaurant good enough for you?" Belachheb shot back. Linda apparently replied with a direct and definitive "no!"

Linda never went back to Augustus' Restaurant.[4]

II

Abdelkrim Belachheb continued to drift from one job to another. His brief career as a waiter was an utter failure. The month before he worked at Augustus', he waited tables at the Dallas Palace Restaurant; that tenure lasted only three weeks. His maitre d' position at Augustus' lasted only slightly longer.

The staff at Augustus' must have thought he was crazy. On Wednesday, June 27, 1984, he threatened to fire a number of employees after he had discovered that a knife on one of the tables had not been polished. Then he had a serious argument with the chef and walked out. Pete arrived to find Belachheb outside the restaurant sitting on a curb. "I'm leaving. I quit," he is quoted as saying.

Pete tried to calm him down by saying, "Go home, calm down. We will talk about it tomorrow."

The next day, Thursday, June 28, 1984, Pete talked to Belachheb on the phone and, more or less, fired him. "Why don't you come today and I'll just give you your pay check, pay you what I owe you," Pete is quoted as saying. Belachheb arrived at 7 P.M. and picked up his check.[5]

June 28 was a bad day for Belachheb. In addition to losing his job, he had received a call from his first wife, Jenny. She informed him that their oldest daughter, Sabine, had failed her past year in a Belgian high school. Jenny claims that Belachheb got upset over the news, although, given his treatment of Jenny and their daughters, it is hard to believe he had genuine concern for them. According to Jenny, they were all to meet in a few weeks in Spain. Undoubtedly, he told her a number of grandiose lies, and when he hung up he surely knew that he could never go to Spain, or anywhere else, in his penniless condition.

That same evening he called Nick at home and said he needed to see him right away. Nick told him to come by the dealership early the next morning or later that evening. Belachheb's latest ambition involved the purchase of a restaurant called Agnew's, located in the Adelstein Plaza very near the Registry Hotel, one of Dallas' finest locations. He had previously discussed the idea with Nick's business partner, Jim. Jim reportedly had opened a file for providing financing, but Belachheb needed collateral.

His distress also manifested itself in a new urgency to get his hands on some of Joanie's assets. He called the real estate agent that had the contract to sell Joanie's properties and asked for the agreement to be extended. The agent reminded him that Joanie had the title to the properties and that she, not he, would have to sign the new contract. Belachheb replied that he had papers to show that he had the authority to sell the property, but he never actually produced them. Finally resigned to not being able to consummate the deal by himself, he ended the conversation by saying he would find Joanie and bring her to sign the document, even though she had told him only a few days earlier that she would never talk to him or see him again.[6]

So, on Thursday, June 28, 1984, Abdelkrim Belachheb had in hand only his final paycheck from Augustus' Restaurant and no immediate prospects for gainful employment. Whatever chance he had for selling cars, or opening his own business, at the very least required his patiently waiting for a period longer than he had ever been able to hold a job in Dallas. The clothes he wore, he had purchased with the misuse of his employer's credit card. The car he drove, an ugly white station wagon, he was able to buy only because the woman he lived with while Joanie was away in Las Vegas had cosigned the loan. He had nothing but the hope of getting his hands on Joanie's money and welshing on his friends, as he had done to his friend Mohamed, who had welcomed him into his home when he first arrived in Dallas, and as he had done to Jenny in Belgium. Ten days earlier, Mohamed had asked Belachheb to repay a personal loan only to hear Belachheb reply, "I am starving and you are calling me about your money. I will never talk to you again. You will never hear from me." Then Belachheb hung up the phone. It would have been extraordinarily fortunate for Mohamed if Belachheb had kept that promise.

In his mind, of course, Belachheb was not responsible for any of his problems. Later, in an interview with the *Dallas Times Herald,* Joanie related that, "He said to me one time, 'Why God abandoned me?'" That was while he was in a victim mode. While grandiose, he told his friends that he knew someone in France who would soon be sending him $500,000.[7]

III

It was a slow night, even for a Thursday, but the customers in Ianni's Restaurant and Club still received the special treatment they had come to expect. Mary, a second generation Ianni, now running the establishment, had never seen Belachheb before that fateful evening, but he had been there two nights earlier when one of her bartenders sold him a membership. Another of her bartenders, the one on duty that Thursday night, was Richard Jones, who had been with the Ianni family since he was seventeen. He vividly remembers his first night on the job; he saw Mickey Mantle in one of the dining rooms. The Iannis had more or less adopted Richard as one of their own.[8]

Ata*, an Iranian who had been in the United States for eight years, was a waiter at Iannis. He had finished his shift at 11:30 P.M., but Mary allowed employees to have a drink and stick around; it was always better to have more employees on hand to help handle the few customers who got more and more inebriated as the evening turned into the early morning hours.

A poster near the club's entrance told customers that the Mike Harris Quartet would be playing that night. They featured a young and attractive singer billed as Sherlyn*. They had taken over for Billy Cole, who played during happy hour. Only a few blocks away, Linda Lowe played the happy hour for the competition, Farfallo's, located on the corner of Preston Road and LBJ Freeway in the North Dallas Bank Building. But, as soon as Linda finished her last set of songs, she intended to go to Ianni's to check out the Mike Harris Quartet.[9]

Abdelkrim Belachheb was to tell a court-appointed psychiatrist that, on June 28, he went out at about 4:30 P.M. and started drinking. He went to Farfallo's first, where he listened to Linda's soft music.

According to her brother Wade, she had agreed to meet her friend Janice Smith at Ianni's later that evening. They could check out the Mike Harris Quartet together. Linda left Farfallo's at 10:15 P.M. and arrived at Ianni's in the time it took her to drive two miles down the LBJ Freeway. Belachheb claims to have arrived at Ianni's at almost exactly the same time.[10]

Janice Smith was already there. The one-time legal secretary who was now a real estate agent was born and raised in Fort Worth, where she worked for different real estate companies. She had been living in Dallas for about five years. As a real estate agent for the Preston Royal Henry S. Miller Company she did extraordinarily well for herself. As a certified residential specialist, and a graduate of the Real Estate Institute, she won the "Dozen Award" in 1983, which was given only to multi-million dollar sellers who ranked in the top five percent of sales people nationwide.

Janice's first marriage ended with the death of her first husband, Gene. They had two sons who, by 1984, were grown and on their own. Her second marriage was to a bank executive in Dallas; it ended in divorce in 1983. At age forty-six she was single, comfortable, extraordinarily vibrant and energetic, and like her friend, Linda, she lived alone in an area not far from Ianni's.[11]

On Thursday, June 28, 1984, Janice and a colleague named Jo* headed for Ianni's at about 7:30 P.M. after a business meeting at the Marriott with a client. As soon as they entered the bar, Janice and Jo conversed with several people Janice knew from her days as a Fort Worth resident. Jo and Janice then had dinner. Jo had a dish of manicotti, and Janice had veal, or possibly chicken, and vegetables. They talked about a recent mini-vacation they had taken together to Padre Island. Janice loved the beach and had a dark, rich tan her co-workers admired. She took particularly good care of herself. She was five-foot six-inches tall and weighed only 114 pounds.

That evening she wore a purple sweater with a white skirt. She also wore a pair of gold earrings, and around her neck were both a pearl necklace and a gold chain with a diamond stud. She had four gold bracelets on her right wrist, and a gold ring with a blue stone on the fifth finger of her right hand; on her left hand she wore diamond rings on her fourth and fifth fingers. Her hairdresser had done her short blonde hair that morning.

Janice was dressed for business and her extraordinary success spoke for itself. But she also "looked like a million dollars," had a

Janice Smith, a successful real estate agent, had arrived at Ianni's earlier in the evening and had dinner with a colleague. Janice was in the barroom when her friend, Linda Lowe, arrived to listen to music. (Texas Court of Criminal Appeals, Second District)

"wonderful sense of humor," and knew how to have a good time. By the end of the evening her blood alcohol level was .17, nearly twice the level prohibited by law for her to drive herself home. (In 1984, the legal limit was .10).

Ianni's was her favorite restaurant, in part, because women could go there without being harassed. She and Jo paid their dinner tab at about 9:15 P.M. Jo left and Janice stayed to rejoin her friends at the bar, and probably wait for Linda to show up as planned.[12]

Janice was at the bar with friends for about an hour before Linda arrived at about 10:30. Her friends left and she and Linda joined another Ianni's regular named Marcell Ford. They sat in the first booth on the right.

Marcell Ford did not suffer fools lightly—and that was a nice way to put it. She worked as a secretary/bookkeeper for a demolition company called Dallas Demolition Excavating, Inc. At one time,

Although he spoke to many women on the night of June 28/29, 1984, Abdelkrim Belachheb kept returning to Marcell Ford, who forcefully pushed him away when he attempted to put his arm around her. Belachheb reacted by backing off, blowing her a kiss, and going to his car to load a semi-automatic pistol. (Texas Court of Criminal Appeals, Second District)

she had been a heart specialist nurse in the United States Air Force where she did a tour of duty in Germany. In 1984, the company she worked for housed its offices across the LBJ Freeway from Ianni's, and so it was easy for Marcell to stop by after work whenever she wanted. At thirty-four, she was one of the younger customers in the bar that night; she was single and free to do as she pleased.

Marcell liked to hang "around some high class people and some high class places," one of her nieces told the *Dallas Morning News*. She lived, however, in her own house a good distance away from north Dallas in another, more blue-collar suburb called Grand Prairie. She lived in that neighborhood for several years, but was not well known there. The Ianni's staff and regulars recognized her as one of their own, although her brusque and confrontational nature turned some of them off. "You can spot people to stay away from," an Ianni's customer once said about her. On the other hand she had gentle hobbies like reading, drawing, and bird watching.

She collected glass and clay figures and lived alone with a terrier named Gamby.[13]

Marcell and the Ford family had been toughened by tragedy. Six years earlier, in 1978, her father, George Haskell Ford, had been shot to death during the robbery of his Star Liquor Store in downtown Dallas. According to newspaper reports, her mother, Ozella, was severely beaten as well. But the incident did not drive the Fords out of the business district. Ozella ran the Busy Bee Grill in what the *Dallas Times Herald* called a "rough strip of bars and liquor stores" on San Jacinto Street next door to the liquor store where her husband had been killed. Indeed, the newspaper reported that she once dealt with a beer-drinking troublemaker by putting a gun to his face and backing him right out of the door.[14]

Marcell also felt like she knew how to deal with troublemakers, especially men who drank too much and came on too strong.

On that Thursday night, she wore a black and white patterned long-sleeved dress and white, low-heeled sling-back shoes. At five-feet nine-inches, she had a stocky build and weighed 170 pounds, but her dark brown eyes and curled brown hair made her attractive. She had not eaten much, probably a baked potato earlier in the day, but she had plenty to drink; by the end of the evening her blood alcohol level reached .16.[15]

When Abdelkrim Belachheb approached Marcell that night, the bartender on duty got the definite impression that the two knew one another. Another of Ianni's bartenders believed he witnessed Marcell leaving with Belachheb earlier that same week.[16] According to Belachheb, on that first evening he and Marcell kissed at the bar and as they left she handed him her car keys. He alleges that she performed a sex act on him while he drove them to a house in north Dallas. Once at the house, they joined a "Jacuzzi party" in progress where as many as thirty people were frolicking nude. Belachheb continues by saying that he, Marcell, and another, unidentified woman, had a *ménage à trois* in a hot tub until he felt he was "being used." At that point, he alleges further, he asked Marcell to take him home.[17]

There are good reasons to be extraordinarily skeptical of Belachheb's Jacuzzi party story. First, the story itself neatly fits the profile of a Belachheb lie. It chronicles his sexual prowess, and as it develops it gets more grandiose—*thirty* naked people. Belachheb is also at the center of the story—thirty naked people and they were *all watching him*. And finally, he switches to a victim mode— he was being used and he asked to go home. Second, no one involved in the investigation from the District Attorney's Office or the Dallas Police Department, or the investigative reporting of Melinda Henneberger of the *Dallas Morning News*, has ever uncovered hard evidence that such an event took place. The *sole* source of the story is Belachheb.

More believable is the observation by the Ianni's bartender that earlier in the week Marcell left the bar with Belachheb. No one, except possibly Belachheb, knows what happened after that.

Of course, Marcell was not the only woman in the bar that Belachheb had hit on. Earlier that week he had bought a drink for one of Mary's waitresses.[18]

After Belachheb arrived on that Thursday night, he immediately prowled for sex. He first set his sights on a woman named Sara* who had arrived about an hour before he did. He sat next to her and introduced himself as "Pierre."

"You have a French accent," Sara observed.

"Yes," replied Belachheb.

Then they exchanged a few phrases in French. She danced with him twice. Even though they were seated in a restaurant, he asked her if they could go out and get a bite to eat. When relating the story in a packed courtroom, Sara remembered that he did not seem depressed. Quite the contrary, he made a pass at her. "No, I'm separated from my husband. I'm here to meet a girlfriend. You seem like a nice guy; there is a lot of cute girls here. Go for it," she said. He smiled, seemed to understand and left her alone.[19]

His next attempt was with the singer of the Mike Harris Quartet, who went by her first name only—Sherlyn. She remembered seeing Belachheb in Ianni's before. In a handwritten statement on her personal stationery in the Dallas County District Attorney files, Sherlyn described his "come-on."

"Hello. How are you?" she quoted him as saying.

Her narrative continues with "I didn't have a good feeling standing there so I tried to excuse myself but he still held on to my hand as I tried to move on, he still held my hand and then kissed it," she wrote to the District Attorney.

"You'll forgive me. I must go sing," she said to him as an excuse to get away.

Sherlyn believed that really good musicians are sensitive to their audience, and on that Thursday night, she felt "disharmony everywhere."

Belachheb then turned to the bartender, and said, "It's nice to work around so many beautiful girls," as he motioned toward Sara and Sherlyn.[20]

One of the first women Belachheb approached was Marcell Ford. At some point, she, Linda Lowe, and Janice Smith moved from their booth to the bar, probably for Linda to get a better look at the band. Belachheb walked up to Marcell and began talking to her. Belachheb ordered his favorite, Johnny Walker with 7Up. When the bartender asked him if he had a membership, Belachheb looked at him as if bewildered. Marcell then said to put the first drink on her membership. Shortly afterwards, Marcell left Ianni's and went to Cappuccino's.[21]

As Thursday night crept closer to Friday morning, the crowd thinned out. But there were still twenty to thirty people in the bar. One of the late arrivals was a newcomer to Dallas, a forty-five-year-old unemployed bartender named Ligia Koslowski. She had moved to Dallas from Chicago only six months earlier and was not yet a regular in the north Dallas nightclub scene. She lived in an apartment complex called the Stone Terrace in nearby Irving. Her neighbors recall that she had lived with a male roommate who had left her about two months earlier. They described her as very quiet and even shy, and as a result, no one knew much about her. She may not have been certain that she wanted to make Texas her home; she still had an Illinois driver's license. She had no known friends in the area, and it was not until several days later that police would find out that she had a daughter in Illinois. To this day no one knows how she got from Irving to the corner of Midway and the LBJ Freeway. All that is known about her movements that night is that when she arrived in the parking lot between Ianni's and Cappuccino's, she asked a woman named Barbara Watkins if either place served good food.[22]

Ligia first went to Cappuccino's. There she met the owner of a Rolls Royce dealership and limousine service named Dick*. He and his driver, a young man named Glen* walked with her across the parking lot to Ianni's. Most likely, she was looking for a bartending job. She was dressed to impress, wearing a tan blouse with a matching skirt and belt with fashionable white shoes. She

Ligia Koslowski was an unemployed bartender who had recently moved to Dallas from Chicago. She was probably in the area looking for a job at one of Dallas's nicer clubs—like Ianni's. (Texas Court of Criminal Appeals, Second District)

also wore a necklace with a medallion engraved with her name, "Ligia." Her fingernails and toenails were carefully polished with dark pink enamel. Her long-term effort to look her best had also included breast augmentation.[23]

John McNeill liked socializing in private north Dallas clubs because he "always avoided the crazies." He was a lifelong Dallasite who had been to Ianni's before. He had a degree in marketing and business administration from East Texas State University in Commerce (Texas A&M-Commerce today). He was a partner in a new company called New Age Refrigeration of Dallas, Inc. It was a design group engaged in research and development. Their major project at the time was the development of a system for food production and distribution for the U.S. Department of Agriculture. John, only thirty-eight years old at the time, splendidly represented the generation of upwardly mobile Dallas business people. One of his partners in business, and his companion on that Thursday night, was Terry Rippa. Terry was a graduate of the University of North Texas in nearby Denton. His parents knew Joe and Totsy Ianni well, which meant that Terry was an acquaintance of Mary. They had gone to high school together.[24]

Earlier during the evening, John went to Farfallo's for a drink. While there, he heard Linda Lowe playing and singing. As he drank at the bar, he noticed the odd dress of the man sitting next to him. The man wore an open, wide-collar leisure-type vested suit. He looked foreign, had what John thought were Arab features, and when he ordered a drink, John heard an unmistakable French accent. Other than that, there was nothing remarkable about the guy, who drank and danced with women without incident. That was John's first brush with Abdelkrim Belachheb.

At about that time, Terry Rippa was driving north on Dallas' Central Expressway, heading for the LBJ Freeway to meet his friend. He had an ominous feeling—and he did not know why.[25] He met John at Farfallo's a short time later. While they were there, a woman John was dating at the time, an insurance company employee named Barbara Watkins, (the same woman who recommended Ianni's to Ligia Koslowski) called and asked them to meet her at Cappuccino's. They went there but couldn't find her. They immediately crossed the parking lot and entered Ianni's at about 10:30 P.M.

They found Barbara talking to friends. John and Terry sat at one of the small red-topped tables very near the bar, no more that a few feet away from the barstools. Barbara joined them a few minutes later.

Terry remembers seeing Linda Lowe, Janice Smith, and Marcell Ford sitting in the first booth, all apparently having a good time. He loved to dance, and as he was coming off the dance floor, he met Linda Lowe, who told him, "You sure are a real good push dancer for as young as you are."

"I'm older than you think," Terry replied.

Mightily impressed by Linda's beauty, Terry wanted to dance with her, but he decided to wait for the band to play the right song. To his disappointment, they were not playing good dance music that night.

Well-known to Dallas Police Officers, Frank Parker had a long criminal history. He was also a regular at Ianni's and was allowed in the kitchen to prepare his own sandwich. (Texas Court of Criminal Appeals, Second District)

The women had moved to the bar by the time Belachheb arrived. John saw him talking to Marcell and Linda.

Terry nursed a white wine, continued to wait for a good dance song, and kept his eye on Linda, now seated at the bar between Janice (on the left) and Marcell (on the right). John had a beer and Barbara had his attention.[26]

Frank Rance Parker, however, was not at Ianni's to dance. If he had his eye out for girls, it was probably to check out the "competition" or hire them as one of his own. He was a former United States Marine—and a pimp with a long criminal record. He lived in Arlington, and at only five-feet eight-inches tall, weighing 218 pounds, he looked older than his real age of forty-nine. He was somewhat like Belachheb in that his dress was exaggerated, i.e., a little too "mod," especially for a man his age and size, and it made him stand out. He wore a tan leisure suit with a tan open-collar short-sleeved shirt. He also wore a gold necklace with two prominent medallions and a gold bracelet around his left wrist.

Frank's arrests dated back to early 1957 and included vagrancy, assault, burglary, and narcotics possessions. In 1960, he had been sentenced to two years in prison for burglary. He apparently got out early, only to be convicted and sentenced to eleven years for controlled substances violations. In 1969 and 1970, he was convicted of two separate instances of aggravated assault. Indeed, Dallas police knew Frank Parker by name and sight and had the attitude that, "If Frank Rance Parker was there it was not completely innocent."[27]

But Frank was a regular at Ianni's; he never caused any trouble, was a good tipper, and was liked by the other regulars and the staff. Indeed, he was one of the few customers who could arrive after the restaurant closed and walk into the kitchen and make himself a snack.[28]

The midnight hour turned Thursday night into Friday morning. It was June 29, 1984, by only a few minutes when Joe Minasi entered the bar for a drink. He had called his wife earlier that evening and told her not to prepare a meal for him. His business

During the evening of June 28/29, 1984, master mechanic, Joe Minasi called his wife to tell her not to prepare supper because he would go out to eat. (Texas Court of Criminal Appeals, Second District)

partner said, "He was Italian and he liked Italian food." But because he was a regular, Joe knew that the restaurant at Ianni's was closed at that hour. He wanted a drink, and had probably been drinking before he arrived. By 12:15 A.M., he was legally drunk with a blood alcohol level of .12. Joe sat on one of the beige stools near the entrance.

He was still dressed in mechanic's garb: a light blue work shirt and darker blue pants held up by a wide, shiny, black leather belt with a wad of keys hanging on his right hip. Only a workaholic could be dressed that way in a nightclub after midnight, and that was what Joe was. He routinely put in eighteen to twenty-hour days.

He had come to Dallas by way of Phoenix from his native hometown of White Plains, New York, to take a job with an oil leasing company. But he loved mechanics and had become a master mechanic for Rolls Royce, Jaguar, and Mercedes. He was good at what he did, often taking out a stethoscope to listen to pistons and valves inside churning engines to diagnose problems. He and his partner, a man named Eddy*, co-owned European Connections, a garage on Denton Drive. Ianni's was on his way home.[29]

IV

Shortly after the stroke of midnight, everyone was in position for tragedy. Ianni's barroom included a U-shaped bar at the room's entrance. On the left, stood two Ianni's employees named Ata and Ahmed*, now off-duty, having a drink, and keeping an eye on the place. At the bottom of the "U" nearest the door, from left to right, Joe Minasi, the mechanic, sat next to the limo driver named Glen, both were talking and having a drink. To their right, Ligia Koslowski sat near the right corner. Just around that corner from her, on the right side of the "U," sat Janice Smith, Linda Lowe, and Marcell Ford. Abdelkrim Belachheb stood between Linda and Marcell. At the bar's top right, stood Mary, Ianni's proprietor, and Dick, Glen's boss and the owner of a limo parked outside. As soon as the band took a break, Sherlyn joined them. The bartender was inside the "U" tending bar. Almost directly behind Linda, John McNeill, his date Barbara Watkins, and Terry Rippa continued drinking at one of the small tables. Frank Parker was in the kitchen making himself a sandwich.

Nearly all of them saw Marcell push Belachheb.

---

[1] Dallas County District Attorney Files: Unidentified and undated newspaper clipping in Linda Lowe folder; Wade Thomas.

[2] Ibid.; Richard Jones; *Dallas Morning News,* June 30, 1984.

[3] Nick quoted in *Texas v Belachheb,* 291st Judicial District, Cause no. F84-75078-SU, et. al., VI, 1628-1748 and 1792-1840.

[4] Ibid. The argument is reconstructed from Nick's sworn testimony, 1792-1840.

[5] Quotes are reconstructed from testimony of Dr. Sheldon Zigelbaum, a psychiatrist who examined Abdelkrim Belachheb in preparation for trial testimony. See *Texas v Belachheb,* 291st Judicial District, Cause no. F84-75078-SU, et. al., VI, 1628-1748; *Dallas Morning News,* June 30, 1984; *Fort Worth Star-Telegram,* June 30, 1984.

[6] Dallas Police Department Files: Undated handwritten notes of an interview with real estate agent; *Dallas Morning News,* August 5, 1984.

[7] Abdelkrim Belachheb quoted in Mohamed's trial testimony in *Texas v Belachheb,* 291st Judicial District, Cause no. F84-75078-SU, et. al., VI, 1934-1965; Joanie quoted in *Dallas Times Herald,* undated clipping in the Dallas District Attorney Files; *Dallas Morning News,* June 30, 1984,

[8] Dallas County District Attorney Files: *Prosecution Report, Dallas Police Department,* by

Robert B. Counts, June 29, 1984; Dallas Police Department Files: *Supplement Report,* by G. Reynolds, June 29, 1984; Richard Jones.

[9] *Texas* v *Belachheb,* 291st Judicial District, Cause no. F84-75078-SU, et. al., IV, 865-892 and 969-1012; Dallas Police Department Files: *Investigative Supplement Report,* by Catherine Arnott, June 29, 1984.

[10] Dallas Police Department Files: Unidentified notes dated July 2, 1984; *Texas* v *Belachheb,* 291st Judicial District, Cause no. F84-75078-SU, et. al., VI, 1792-1840; Wade Thomas.

[11] *Texas* v *Belachheb,* 291st Judicial District, Cause no. F84-75078-SU, et. al., IV, 857-60; Dallas County District Attorney Files: Unidentified and undated newspaper clipping in the Janice Smith folder; *Dallas Morning News,* June 30, 1984; *Fort Worth Star-Telegram,* June 30, 1984.

[12] Southwestern Institute of Forensic Sciences: *Autopsy Report of Janice A. Smith,* Case no. 1904-84-0851, June 29, 1984; Dallas County District Attorney Office Files: Unidentified and undated newspaper clipping in Janice Smith folder; *Dallas Morning News,* June 30, 1984.

[13] Ronnie Ford, interviewed by the author on August 4, 2002; Terry Rippa; Dallas County District Attorney Files: Unidentified and undated newspaper clipping in the Marcell Ford folder; Marcell Ford's niece quoted in *Dallas Morning News,* June 30, 1984.

[14] Ibid.; *Texas* v *Belachheb,* 291st Judicial District, Cause no. F84-75078-SU, et. al., IV, 849-52; *Dallas Times Herald,* October 20, 1991.

[15] Southwestern Institute of Forensic Sciences: *Autopsy Report of Marcell Mae Ford,* Case no. 1904-84-0855, June 29, 1984.

[16] Richard Jones.

[17] Abdelkrim Belachheb's version of the Jacuzzi party is covered in detail in *Dallas Times Herald,* October 28, 1984.

[18] Dallas Police Department Files: *Affidavit in Any Fact,* by [waitress], June 29, 1984, and *Investigative Supplement Report,* by Catherine Arnott, June 29, 1984.

[19] The conversation between Abdelkrim Belachheb and Sara is reconstructed from her sworn testimony in *Texas* v *Belachheb,* 291st Judicial District, Cause no. F84-75078-SU, et. al., VI, 1897-1907; Dallas County District Attorney Files: *Affidavit in Any Fact,* by Sara, June 29, 1984.

[20] The conversation is reconstructed from Dallas County District Attorney Files: Unidentified handwritten notes on stationery. The notes are unsigned, but the details are such that it could only have been written by the singer Sherlyn. The facts described in the notes also match Dallas Police Department Files: *Investigative Supplement Report,* by Catherine Arnott, June 29, 1984, which is a report of an interview with Sherlyn; Richard Jones confirmed the Belachheb quote during my interview with him.

[21] Dallas Police Department Files: *Investigative Supplement Report,* by Catherine Arnott, June 29, 1984; Richard Jones.

[22] Dallas County District Attorney Files: Unidentified and undated newspaper clippings in Ligia Koslowski folder; *Fort Worth Star-Telegram,* June 30, 1984; *Dallas Morning News,* June 30, 1984; Barbara Watkins, interviewed by the author on August 22, 2002.

[23] Southwestern Institute of Forensic Sciences: *Autopsy Report of Ligia Koslowski,* Case no. 1904-84-0854, June 29, 1984; *Texas* v *Belachheb,* 291st Judicial District, Cause no. F84-75078-SU, et. al., IV, 1012-62.

[24] John McNeill; Terry Rippa; Dallas County District Attorney Files: Unidentified and undated newspaper clipping in John McNeill folder; John McNeill quoted in *Dallas Morning News,* July 7, 1984; *Texas* v *Belachheb,* 291st Judicial District, Cause no. F84-75078-SU, et. al., IV, 865-92.

[25] John McNeill; Terry Rippa; *Texas* v *Belachheb,* 291st Judicial District, Cause no. F84-75078-SU, et. al., IV, 865-92; Dallas Police Department Files: Handwritten notes from an interview with John McNeill, July 5, 1984.

[26] Ibid.; Barbara Watkins; *Dallas Morning News,* July 7, 1984.

[27] Southwestern Institute of Forensic Sciences: *Autopsy Report of Frank Rance Parker,* Case no. 1904-84-0856, June 29, 1984; Dallas County District Attorney Files: Unidentified and

undated newspaper clipping in Frank Parker case folder; *Dallas Morning News,* June 30, 1984; Police quote is from Bill Parker interview.

[28] Richard Jones.

[29] *Texas* v *Belachheb,* 291ˢᵗ Judicial District, Cause no. F84-75078-SU, et. al., IV, 853-57; Southwestern Institute of Forensic Sciences: *Autopsy Report of Joseph John Minasi,* Case no. 1904-84-0852. June 29, 1984; Dallas County District Attorney Files: Unidentified and undated newspaper clippings in Joe Minasi folder; *Dallas Morning News,* June 30, 1984; Eddy quoted in *Fort Worth Star-Telegram,* June 30, 1984.

chapter seven
——————————

"Take that . . ."

> *"The movies don't even come close."*
> —Norman*
> piano player for the Mike Harris Quartet

I

The Mike Harris Quartet had been playing soft music since 9 P.M., and by the time midnight came along, they were getting no requests or tips. "Hey, it was a Thursday night," said Norman, the piano player. They played Duke Ellington's *C Jam Blues* before taking a break just after midnight. Sherlyn, the featured singer, turned on taped music and went to the end of the bar where Mary and Dick were talking and laughing.

From the time Belachheb arrived to just after midnight, he had three or four Johnny Walker and 7Up. He roamed around the entire barroom and spoke to nearly all of the women. He even danced with a few, but he always came back to Marcell.

"Marcell was the kind of person if she was annoyed with somebody you could tell quite immediately," Dick observed. He noticed, as did almost everyone else, that Marcell wanted less and less to do with Belachheb as the night wore on. Some of the other regulars, less than enchanted by her brusque ways, recall that she could, at times, be cruel. "I had seen her before come on to a man sitting next to her and then belittle him in front of people," remembered a Ianni's bartender.

That night with Belachheb, she was just "egging him on" for about two hours. At first, he laughed it off, even after she called him a "sand nigger." A couple of times, he just walked off and danced with someone else—only to return. She merely continued her unambiguous insults. Whether or not they had ever had a relationship, or had ever been to a "Jacuzzi party," on that evening it was clear that Marcell wanted Belachheb to go away. Right before midnight, the bartender, standing right in front of both of them, and other patrons nearby recalled that the argument began to get "nasty."[1]

Marcell spent most of two hours insulting Belachheb and rebuffing his advances. Equally clear is that he controlled himself through that period and chose to stay rather than leave. According to a psychologist Belachheb's attorney later retained, the critical moment came when Marcell is alleged to have said, "I can't believe I ever made love to a monkey like you." Belachheb claims to have turned to walk away. Linda Lowe, Belachheb's story continues, grabbed him by the hair and said, "Leave this lady alone or it's all off with Nick," an apparent reference to the job he was to get in about a month at Nick's car dealership.

The three most reliable witnesses to the final moments of the argument were Ata, the employee seated across the bar from Marcell, who had a direct view of what was going on; Richard, the bartender; and Terry Rippa, who had been watching Linda for an opportunity to dance with her. None saw Linda do anything but look straight ahead or lean forward to light a cigarette.[2] Other people were very near, and surely if she had grabbed Belachheb's hair, it would have caught someone's attention, but no one else saw such a thing. Linda was so close to the action that she had to have known what was going on, but it is highly unlikely that she inserted herself into an argument that did not involve her with a man she openly detested.

Marcell had enough when Belachheb tried to put his arm around her. She pushed him back violently and said something like, "If you ever do that again you will be taken care of. . . . " The bartender believes that at that moment it is possible that Linda and Janice, two friends enjoying each other's company, may have laughed at something unrelated to what was going on and that Belachheb might have thought they were laughing at him.

Now, Belachheb had enough. He backed off, blew Marcell a kiss, and turned left to head toward the front door. As he turned to walk away, Marcell blew him a kiss, looked at Ata and Ahmed seated across the bar, and rolled her eyes upward.[3]

Ata was accustomed to "following" troublemakers out the front door—just in case—and he watched Belachheb leave. He thought the trouble was over.[4]

Belachheb exited Ianni's and went straight to his white, 1983 Chevrolet station wagon. An anthropologist, who later testified at Belachheb's trial, stated that at that time Belachheb's expectations, however unrealistic, of good things to come came crashing down. The "precipitating stress" was the realization that all along he had lived an adult life in which he largely depended on women for his subsistence. It was a gender role reversal he could not handle.[5]

If, indeed, it was a time of honest reflection for Belachheb, he knew that the only time in his life he ever dominated women was when he beat them. That was not an option in Ianni's. The accoutrements of wealth inside the barroom, the gold bracelets, diamond earrings, three-piece suits, styled hair, and thick wallets were things he had never earned for himself. Later, his defense was to argue that at that moment he had a seizure and was out of control.

Far from being out of control, Abdelkrim Belachheb went to his car to equip himself to avenge his bruised ego, to be the center of attention, to be a dominant force in as unambiguous a way as possible. He began to prepare for the ultimate domination. As Jack Levin and James Alan Fox have written, mass murderers demonstrate that they are "very much in control in the most forceful way possible—they play God."[6]

Belachheb's white station wagon was parked closer to Cappuccino's than Ianni's. On the front passenger side floorboard sat a full bottle of Seagram's Whiskey. Belachheb pulled out a carton that once held fifty 9-mm rounds. They contained two kinds of bullets: full metal jackets and Remington Peters, a hollow point designed to slow and flatten upon impact. It tears into tissue and inflicts horrifying damage. He loaded two clips holding fourteen rounds each and placed one in his coat pocket. He put the other one in the gun.[7] He closed the car door and looked up at the red-lighted sign—"Ianni's," and headed back to settle with Marcell—and everyone else who had been laughing at him.

II

Terry Rippa knows that Belachheb left Ianni's for fifteen to thirty minutes because the band played four songs in that time and all of them were Latin-type rhythm selections, not the slow song he waited for to dance with Linda. Finally, he gave up and stood to pay his tab when the waitress told him he ought to have the "special."

"What's that?" asked Terry.

"Bailey's, coffee, and Kahlua," she replied.

"No, no thank you," Terry said, but she brought one anyway.

So, he sat and drank it and tried to leave again. "I think I'm getting ready to go on," he told John and Barbara. The band was not even playing at that time; they had taken a break. "And that's the time I started to get up from my chair. He [Belachheb] came back in and I was reaching in my pocket to get money."[8]

"He brushed by me when he came back in," remembered Terry, who was now determined to pay his bill and leave. Belachheb stopped three or four feet behind Marcell.

Sherlyn had just put her cigarette down when she saw him pull a gun from underneath his jacket with his right hand. Richard was reaching below the bar to get a bottle of Bailey's Irish Creme. He, Dick, Ata, and Glen remember vividly the sound the slide on Belachheb's semi-automatic pistol made when he ejected the live round already in the chamber to prepare to shoot.

"There are sounds you hear that you never mistake for anything else, [like] a switchblade knife, a pump shotgun, or the slide on an automatic. I heard that slide and in my mind that was an automatic pistol and I'm outta here!" Glen related to a Dallas County Prosecutor. Indeed, even before the first shot Glen was on the floor crawling for the safety of the kitchen. In an instant, he got on his feet and hit the door of the kitchen with such speed and force he knocked a waiter to the floor. Dick, a man who owned pistols, recognized the sound and instantly grabbed Mary and Sherlyn and pulled them to the floor.[9] He may well have saved their lives.

Terry and Richard remember that there was "no discussion" between Belachheb and Marcell, but others remember differently.

"I have enough bullshit from you," Belachheb shouted.

"Oh no, Pierre, don't do that!" pleaded Marcell.

To some the first shots sounded surreal. John McNeill thought it was a champagne cork. Ata, looking directly at what was happening, remembered, ". . . I thought, 'the bullets are not real.' I thought it was a play because I did not see any reaction of anger or madness or anything that, you know—that's why it was so shocking to me, I mean I could not believe it."[10]

"It didn't sound as loud as you would think," Richard remembered. "It sounded more like a cap gun." But he remembers the rush of hot air and particles of gunpowder hitting the right side of his face. His first thought was that Belachheb was out to get Marcell only; he ducked to get out of the way so as to not get "accidentally" shot. Once on the floor, Richard crawled toward Mary and Dick.

Carol*, a waitress, was walking toward the kitchen at the time and heard the noise, but she didn't think it was a gun. She was more alarmed by the flashes the exploding gunpowder made in the dimly lit barroom; it looked like an orange strobe light. Immediately, she hid in one of the kitchen's freezers.

Sherlyn heard a bullet go by as she ran into the office. Mike Harris, the leader of the band, saw the flashes as well. He made it out the back door and headed for his car.[11]

As in most cases in which things happen fast, witness testimony is conflicting, and each is certain of what he or she saw. But there is no doubt about the order in which Belachheb picked off his victims, and the autopsy reports of each gives a convincing picture of what happened and in what order. [12]

Marcell was first. Standing directly behind her, he shot her twice as she was seated with her arms resting on the bar. One bullet entered the back of her left arm, near her armpit, and traveled through the top of her left shoulder and exited there. Then it re-entered the left base of her skull, not penetrating but severely bruising it before it exited the back of her head. This wound clearly shows that she was leaning forward and looking over her left shoulder. A second shot entered her left back just below the scapula. Since she was bent over, the missile moved upward through her left shoulder area, fracturing three ribs before slicing through her lung and shattering her left clavicle. Then it exited the base of her neck and grazed her chin.

Marcell was shot twice from behind, never directly facing her assailant, and she immediately fell to the floor to the right of her barstool. Both wounds had "stippling," which means Belachheb was close enough for the force of the gunpowder to produce its own microscopic wounds—a reddish circle around each entry wound resembling a bruise. [13]

Terry Rippa dove under the table and pulled a chair over himself. John grabbed Barbara and pulled her so hard he jerked her out of her shoes. The narrow aisle between the barstools and the tables where they were was no wider than three or four feet. Belachheb could have turned around and killed John, Terry, and Barbara at point blank range. Instead, he methodically went down the bar shooting people sitting there like a line of plastic ducks at a carnival. [14]

Linda was next. She was so close to Marcell that Belachheb just turned slightly to shoot her. She might have had some time to react because Belachheb was to her right, but he shot her in the left, mid-back area. This may have indicated that she swiveled in her chair to the left in a hopeless effort to escape. But he was too close. Stippling around this entry wound indicated that he was about three feet from her. The bullet went through both of her lungs and exited her right side just under her armpit.[15] She fell straight down to the base of her barstool. The butane cigarette lighter she was using when the shooting started landed on the dark blue carpet right next to her.

Of all the victims seated at the U-shaped bar, Janice was the only one found in a place other than near where she was sitting. Most likely, she moved about ten feet to her left before he shot her in the left thigh, crippling her and sending her to the floor near the entrance to the barroom. Another possibility is that he shot her where she sat and she crawled to where she was found, but there was no stippling on the wound. Belachheb was more than four feet away from her. Ata indicated that Belachheb had to take a couple of steps before he shot her. The chances are that she was moving. The bullet exited her left hip after destroying her femur and fracturing her pelvis.[16] While it must have been extraordinarily painful, there is little doubt that she could have survived this leg wound—if that was all he had done to her.

Before turning around the lower right corner of the U-shaped bar, Belachheb looked across and saw Ata and Ahmed looking back at him. He pointed the gun in their direction and both men quickly hit the floor. Belachheb fired. The bullet shattered Ata's glass of red wine and lodged in the wall behind them. The two men quickly crawled into the kitchen.[17]

When Belachheb turned the corner, he literally came face to face with Ligia Koslowski. The probable first shot was fired at point blank range, or what pathologists call a "tight contact" wound. It entered her upper jaw just below her right ear, traveled through her oral cavity and exited her left cheek near her lips. From the back, Dick saw the shot and said that her "head just kind of puffed." Indeed, the force of the missile destroyed the inside of her mouth and blew out chunks of her false teeth. In a haunting scene, she landed on the floor next to the blood-streaked upper right portion of her dentures.[18]

Immediately, Belachheb moved to Joe Minasi, who stood up, but not fast enough. Belachheb put his gun against Joe's upper right jaw, just below the ear, and fired. It was another tight contact wound; the bullet exited the left side of Joe's face after it fractured his jaws and bruised his brain. Joe must have held on to the bar for a moment because he bled onto the counter, leaving a ghastly, congealed pool around his drink and two ashtrays.[19]

Terry Rippa and John McNeill could not figure out how a pistol could hold so many rounds. Terry counted thirteen shots and John stopped counting after nine.

"They were like rag dolls falling off those bar stools," remembered Terry. John thought of making a move for the gun, but Belachheb moved so fast that such an attempt would have been too late and certainly suicidal. In retrospect, Terry summarily dismisses the idea: "If the mass of people had thought as one, maybe five or six could have got up and rushed him. . . . But you don't think like that, because it happens so quickly."[20]

The lead detective of this case believes that after Belachheb dropped Joe Minasi, his Smith and Wesson 9mm semiautomatic jammed on him, causing him to retreat temporarily to the foyer near the front door. Indeed, an unspent round was found there after the shooting, convincingly suggesting that he got the weapon into working order and pulled back the slide, ejecting the live round to fall where it was found on the brick floor near a potted plant by the front door. As Belachheb fiddled with his gun, of course, "there was a lull there where nobody moved and we figured he's left," remembered John McNeill.

"Is he gone?" someone asked. No one answered.

Richard, the bartender, remembers that about thirty seconds later someone else said, "Let's go! He's gone to get another clip! He's reloading again!"

Someone else screamed, "He's back!"[21]

Now, standing at the entrance, Belachheb faced the entire bar-room and he could see everyone. The singer, Sherlyn, in a state-ment to the Dallas County District Attorney, wrote: "Mary kept say-ing 'I've got to call the police' over and over. Since I was closest to the office, I said 'stay here' I'll go. There was another shot. I ran in the office, closed the door, and got to the phone. I was standing by the desk [and] had the operator on the line... then I heard shots again." She grabbed the phone and crawled under the desk.

Sherlyn had called the Farmer's Branch Police Department. (Farmer's Branch is a suburb north of the LBJ Freeway.) The dis-patcher who answered was named Michael Blum. It was 12:16 A.M. The recorded telephone conversation went as follows:

Michael Blum: Farmers Branch police emergency, Blum.

Sherlyn: Officer, we've got trouble at Ianni's Restaurant at LBJ Freeway. There's a man firing a gun. I mean he is shooting every-body.

Blum: At the restaurant?

Sherlyn: Ianni's

Blum: Ianni's

Sherlyn: LBJ and Midway

Blum: O.K., can you stay on the phone with me. That's Dallas. I'm going to give you to them, but you stay on the phone with me so I can give you to them. Stay on the phone with me so I can give them a description, OK?

Sherlyn: Please hurry.

Blum: OK, you stay on the phone with me.

Sherlyn: OK.

At that moment Blum called the Dallas Police Department.

Blum: I got a hold of the Dallas Police Department; they are on their way. Now, can you answer me about how many there are?

Sherlyn: Just one.

Blum: What does he look like?

Sherlyn: A light gray suit. I'm the singer here. I had spoken to him earlier. He has a very heavy accent, extremely black hair.

Blum: OK, has he shot anybody?

Sherlyn: I don't know.

Blum: Do you know what he is shooting with? Is it a pistol or a rifle?

Sherlyn: No, it's some kind of a . . . you'll forgive me, I don't know much about weapons. It's an automatic. Oh, God . . .

Blum: Do you know this man? Do you know his name or anything?

Sherlyn: No, officer. Please come here. Please save me.

Blum: OK. Has someone been shot?

Sherlyn: Oh yes, sir. Evidently.

Blum: Is he still in the building?

Sherlyn: I don't know. I am in the office, sir. I've been under the desk.

Blum: OK. Stay on the line with me. I'm going back with Dallas.

Sherlyn: Don't leave me long.[22]

Because he had already gunned down five people, and their bodies were on the floor, Belachheb limited his own mobility. He could no longer walk around the bar on the right side because the small space between the barstools and the tables was now littered with bodies. Belachheb would have had to hop over Ligia, Linda, and Marcell to get near the dance floor. Seemingly determined to kill more people, he started shooting people who were already on the floor. Two witnesses, John McNeill and another patron named Stanley*, saw the overkill.[23]

Janice Smith was directly in front of Belachheb. She was almost certainly still alive, having only a wound in her leg and hip. As she lay face down on the dark blue carpet, he coolly walked up to her, placed the barrel of the gun against the back of her head, near the top, and shouted, "Take that, bitch!" He pulled the trigger. The explosion splattered his pants with her blood and brains.[24]

Only inches to the right, Ligia lay on her face as well. She was probably already dead. He placed the barrel of his 9mm against the back of her neck and fired. The bullet came out of her right cheek just below her eye.[25]

At the corner of the bar, Linda lay on her back—also probably already dead. Belachheb could not walk up to her directly and probably had to aim a bit to shoot her behind the left ear. "Take that, Linda!" he said just before pulling the trigger. The bullet went through her head and partially exited near her nose.[26]

During the "lull," and while Belachheb was firing at Janice, Ligia, and Linda again, there was a general stampede across the dance floor toward a back door. About twenty people made it out safely and ran toward the closed shops of the strip mall. There were large pillars that many of them hid behind. Still inside, John, Terry, and Barbara were in a particularly vulnerable spot. During the second round of shooting Belachheb was making his way closer and closer to the trio of friends. Barbara screamed and ran toward the dance floor. She slipped and skidded across the hardwood to the black, baby grand piano. She lay on the floor and hid her head behind the foot pedals.

John and Terry ran toward the back. Almost at that same moment, Frank Parker came running out of the kitchen. Belachheb fired a number of rounds at the three men.

John was trying to get to safety around the corner of the bar. After hopping over Marcell, he ran in a stooped position, and it saved his life. "It hit me in the lower back," John related at Belachheb's trial. But the bullet traveled up his torso and lodged in his chest between skin and his sternum. That he was not killed instantly was miraculous. The long path of the bullet did not sever any vital blood vessels. John thought, as he lay on the dark blue carpet, he would bleed to death within minutes—but he survived. His luck did not end there: he had been shot with a fully jacketed round, not a Remington Peter hollow point that would surely have torn through his internal organs and blood vessels and killed him instantly.[27]

Terry made it into the kitchen. "[Belachheb] was shooting at me and he got John and the other guy and I ran in between them," Terry recalled.

At approximately 12:15 A.M. on June 29, 1984, Abdelkrim Belachheb took a 9mm semi-automatic from his jacket and murdered five of the patrons seated at Ianni's bar. From left to right: Glen (who hit the floor as soon as he heard Belachheb pull the slide on his pistol), Joe Minasi, Ligia Koslowski, Janice Smith, Linda Lowe (lighting a cigarette), and Marcell Ford (the first victim). (Illustration by Karen T. Taylor, Facial Images)

After shooting Marcell Ford, Linda Lowe, and Janice Smith, Belachheb moved around the corner of the bar and took aim at Ligia Koslowski and Joe Minasi. (Illustration by Karen T. Taylor, Facial Images)

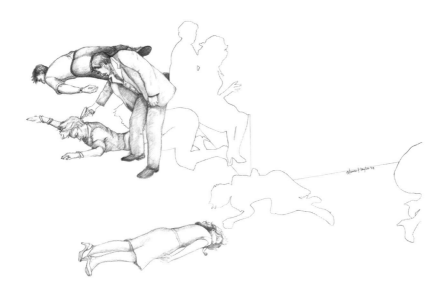

After shooting Joe Minasi, Belachheb's gun jammed. He moved to the foyer to fix his weapon and then returned to shoot all of his victims again, and two more people—Frank Parker and John McNeill, who survived his injury. (Illustration by Karen T. Taylor, Facial Images)

View of the right side of Ianni's bar. (1) Where Marcell Ford fell mortally wounded. (2) Linda Lowe. (3) Table where John McNeill, Barbara Watkins, and Terry Rippa were seated. (4) Location of Sherlyn, Mary and Richard. (5) Location of Richard, the bartender. (Dallas County District Attorney Files)

The other guy was Frank Parker. Frank was in the relative safety of the kitchen making himself a sandwich when the shooting started. Ata, who had escaped one of Belachheb's bullets, remembers that, "Parker was in the kitchen, too, and he was so nervous when we heard shooting again—he told me his girlfriend got shot and somebody had to stop him." Unarmed, and using extraordinarily poor judgment, Frank ran out the back kitchen door toward Belachheb. He did not get far.

Dick witnessed the death of Frank Rance Parker: "Parker was coming from the back of the restaurant to the front where I was. . . . Frank got hit and it kind of stood him up, and then he got [shot] twice more and it dropped him back in the drums." Dick saw Parker jerk in a *dance macabre* three times before Parker fell to the floor. Frank was a big target, and the three shots damaged nearly

Ianni's barroom, looking toward the back. This photo was taken from where Terry Rippa, Barbara Watkins, and John McNeill were sitting when Abdelkrim Belachheb started firing his semi-automatic pistol. (1) Marcell Ford fell here. (2) Where John McNeill fell critically injured. (3) Where Frank Parker was shot and killed. (4) The covered body of Linda Lowe. (Dallas County District Attorney Files)

all of his vital organs. He fell dead almost immediately near a pot-ted plant by the back entrance to the kitchen.[28]

Many of the twenty or more people who escaped out of the back door of the restaurant were still hiding behind the wide pil-lars holding up the breezeway along the front of the stores. Rich-ard was there with Mary and they saw Belachheb heading toward his car. Sara and Mike Harris got into his car, and they, too, saw Belachheb running through the parking lot. Dick was near the back corner of the building; he saw Belachheb near the front cor-ner. Ahmed, who minutes earlier had escaped Belachheb's bullets, was caught in between them and completely exposed. Belachheb shot at him but missed.

"Hey, mother fucker, I didn't do anything to you. Don't shoot me," Ahmed screamed.

Dick remembered, "[Belachheb] just kind of looked at him and put the gun in his belt and ran over and got in his car and left."[29]

---

[1] Dick quoted in *Texas* v *Belachheb,* 291st Judicial District, Cause no. F84-75078-SU, et. al., IV, 1012-62; Dallas Police Department Files: *Investigative Report,* by Catherine Arnott, June 29, 1984; *Dallas Morning News,* June 30, 1984; Richard Jones.

[2] *Texas* v *Belachheb,* 291st Judicial District, Cause no. F84-75078-SU, et. al., IV, 893-951 and 1391-1567; Terry Rippa; Richard Jones.

[3] Ibid., 893-951 and 956-1012; Marcell Ford quoted in Dallas Police Department Files: Unidentified handwritten notes from an interview with Richard Jones and *Investigative Supple-ment Report,* by Catherine Arnott, June 29, 1984.

[4] *Texas* v *Belachheb,* 291st Judicial District, Cause no. F84-75078-SU, et. al., IV, 1012-62.

[5] See testimony of Dr. Harrell Gill-King in *Texas* v *Belachheb,* 291st Judicial District, Cause no. F84-75078-SU, et. al., V, 1284-1390.

[6] Jack Levin and James Alan Fox, *Mass Murder: America's Growing Menace* (Plenum Press: New York, 1985), 82.

[7] *Texas* v *Belachheb,* 291st Judicial District, Cause no. F84-75078-SU, et. al., IV, 1081-86 and 1196-1224; Dallas Police Department Files: *Investigative Supplement Report,* by G. W. King, June 29, 1984.

[8] Quotes are from *Texas* v *Belachheb,* 291st Judicial District, Cause no. F84-75078-SU, et. al., IV, 893-951.

[9] Ibid. Dialogue with the Ianni's waitress is from 1012-62 and 969-1012 and other infor-mation is from 893-951 and VII, 2384-2413; Dallas Police Department Files: *Investigative Supplement Report,* by Catherine Arnott, June 29, 1984 and unidentified and undated hand-written note; Glen's quote is from an interview with Norman Kinne; Terry Rippa.

[10] Belachheb and Ata quotes are from *Texas* v *Belachheb,* 291st Judicial District, Cause no. F84-75078-SU, et. al., IV, 893-951 and 969-1012; Terry Rippa; John McNeill; Richard Jones; Dallas Police Department Files: *Investigative Supplement Report,* by Catherine Arnott, June 29, 1984, and handwritten notes from an interview with eyewitness, undated.

[11] Richard Jones; Dallas Police Department Files: Handwritten notes from an interview with Carol, undated; Dallas County District Attorney Files: Unidentified handwritten note dated June 30, 1984 and *Prosecution Report, Dallas Police Department,* by Robert B. Counts, June 29, 1984; *Dallas Morning News,* June 30 and July 1, 1984.

[12] Reconstructing Belachheb's monstrous crime with absolute certainty is not possible. What I have presented is my best interpretation of the sequence of the shooting. It is based on the autopsy reports, eyewitness testimony, and known positions of the victims at key points in time.

[13] Southwestern Institute of Forensic Sciences: *Autopsy Report of Marcell Mae Ford,* Case no. 1904-84-0855, June 29, 1984; *Texas v Belachheb,* 291st Judicial District, Cause no. F84-75078-SU, et. al., IV, 1147-96.

[14] *Texas v Belachheb,* 291st Judicial District, Cause no. F84-75078-SU, et. al., IV, 893-951; John McNeill; Terry Rippa; Barbara Watkins; Dallas Police Department Files: *Investigative Supplement Report,* by G. Reynolds, June 29, 1984.

[15] *Texas v Belachheb,* 291st Judicial District, Cause no. F84-75078-SU, et. al., IV, 1147-96; Southwestern Institute of Forensic Sciences: *Autopsy Report of Linda Thomas Lowe,* Case no. 1904-84-0850, June 29, 1984.

[16] *Texas v Belachheb,* 291st Judicial District, Cause no. F84-75078-SU, et. al., IV, 969-1012 and 1147-96; Southwestern Institute of Forensic Sciences: *Autopsy Report of Janice Smith,* Case no. 1904-84-0851, June 29, 1984.

[17] *Texas v Belachheb,* 291st Judicial District, Cause no. F84-75078-SU, et. al., IV, 969-1012.

[18] Southwestern Institute of Forensic Sciences: *Autopsy Report of Ligia Kozlowski,* Case no. 1904-84-0854, June 29, 1984; Dick quoted in *Texas v Belachheb,* 291st Judicial District, Cause no. F84-75078-SU, et. al., IV, 1012-62.

[19] Southwestern Institute of Forensic Sciences: *Autopsy Report of Joseph Minasi,* Case no. 1904-84-0852, June 29, 1984; *Texas v Belachheb,* 291st Judicial District, Cause no. F84-75078-SU, et. al., IV, 1012-62 and 1147-96.

[20] *Dallas Morning News,* July 7, 1984; Terry Rippa quoted in interview and *Dallas Times Herald,* October 20, 1991.

[21] John McNeill quoted in interview; *Texas v Belachheb,* 291st Judicial District, Cause no. F84-75078-SU, et. al., VII, 2384-2413; Dallas Police Department Files: *Affidavit in Any Fact,* by Kristi*, June 29, 1984, *Investigative Supplement Report,* by G. Reynolds, June 29, 1984, and separately by Catherine Arnott, June 29, 1984.

[22] The emergency phone call to the Farmer's Branch Police Department was reported in *Dallas Morning News,* July 1, 1984, and played on ABC News: *20/20,* August 22, 1985; Dallas County District Attorney Files: Unidentified handwritten notes dated June 30, 1984.

[23] Stanley's observations are in Dallas Police Department Files: *Investigative Supplement Report,* by G. Reynolds, June 29, 1984; John McNeill; Terry Rippa.

[24] *Texas v Belachheb,* 291st Judicial District, Cause no. F84-75078-SU, et. al., IV, 1147-96 and 1777-95, Abdelkrim Belachheb is quoted by Stanley on 2290-2317; Southwestern Institute of Forensic Sciences: *Autopsy Report of Janice Smith,* Case no. 1904-84-0851, June 29, 1984.

[25] Southwestern Institute of Forensic Sciences: *Autopsy Report of Ligia Koslowski,* Case no. 1904-84-0854, June 29, 1984; *Texas v Belachheb,* 291st Judicial District, Cause no. F84-75078-SU, et. al., IV, 1147-96.

[26] Southwestern Institute of Forensic Sciences: *Autopsy Report of Linda Thomas Lowe,* Case no. 1904-84-0850, June 29, 1984; *Texas v Belachheb,* 291st Judicial District, Cause no. F84-75078-SU, et. al., IV, 1147-96; Abdelkrim Belachheb is quoted by Stanley in Dallas Police Department Files: *Investigative Supplement Report,* by G. Reynolds, June 29, 1984.

[27] John McNeill quoted in *Texas v Belachheb,* 291st Judicial District, Cause no. F84-75078-SU, et. al., IV, 865-92; Dallas Police Department Files: *Investigative Supplement Reports,* by Catherine Arnott, G. Reynolds, and *Prosecution Report* by Robert B. Counts, June 29, 1984; John McNeill; Barbara Watkins.

[28] Ata and Dick quoted in *Texas* v *Belachheb,* 291st Judicial District, Cause no. F84-75078-SU, et. al., IV, 969-1062 and 1147-96; Terry Rippa quote from interview; *Dallas Morning News,* November 3, 1984; Southwestern Institute of Forensic Sciences: *Autopsy Report of Frank Rance Parker,* Case no. 1904-84-0856, June 29, 1984.

[29] Richard Jones; Dallas Police Department Files: *Investigative Supplement Report,* by Catherine Arnott and G. Reynolds, June 29, 1984, and *Affidavit in Fact,* by Sara, June 29, 1984; Ahmed quoted by Dick in *Texas* v *Belachheb,* 291st Judicial District, Cause no. F84-75078-SU, et. al., IV, 1012-62.

chapter eight
_____

"I came to kill you."

"I did what I did and now I have jobs to finish; I still have people I want to kill."
—Abdelkrim Belachheb
quoted by his friend Mohamed

I

As the red taillights of Belachheb's white station wagon faded and disappeared to the north, seven of his victims lay on Ianni's floor bleeding to death—or already dead. Terry Rippa was the first to return to the barroom. "And nobody was in the bar at all, and I went down and checked with John and he was conscious, and then I walked up to the front and I did not check pulses or anything. It was quite a mess—the tables, broken glass, and the victims—and I checked on all five the best I could by observing, and they all appeared to be dead except for a few minutes later Marcell was moving."[1]

With his military medical training on his mind, John McNeill thought he was going to bleed to death in a matter of minutes. But he was surprisingly alert. "That son-of-a-bitch was in Farfallo's an hour or two before," he told Terry.

"Just hold on," Terry replied.

Barbara Watkins, who hid under the piano during the second round of shootings, had already checked on John. But she was in a state of near-hysterics, and John told her that she couldn't help him. He said that he was probably bleeding to death and that she should call an ambulance. Barbara decided to make that call from Cappuccino's.

Barbara had to run through the aisle between the rows of tables and the bar to get out of Ianni's. In her way lay Marcell, Linda, and Ligia. "In order to get out the door, I had to step over the bodies. And the blood was all over the floor, you know, real thick. And I thought, I guess one of my main thoughts was, 'if I slide and fall, I'll never get up again.'"

But Barbara did make it out through the front door. A bartender named Pam* remembers Barbara entering Cappuccino's. "She came in hysterical, grabbing her head, and all she could blurt out was that people had been shot. Then she started to fall down."

"Where?" asked an astonished Pam.

"Ianni's," answered Barbara before she collapsed.[2]

Others had already called for help. Sherlyn, the singer, was on the phone with the Farmer's Branch Police Department as the second round of shots was being fired. As she remained hidden under the desk in the office, some of those outside returned after Belachheb drove away. Richard Jones, the bartender, thought to use the same phone Sherlyn was already on. When he reached for it under the desk he touched Sherlyn and "scared the living daylights out of her." Sara, who earlier during the evening had danced with Belachheb and refused his advances, called as well.

Two Dallas police officers, Thomas Hall and Catherine Arnott, were patrolling northwest Dallas at that time. They arrived at 12:21 A.M., five minutes after Sherlyn's frantic call. Several Ianni's customers were running around the parking lot searching for friends they had lost during the melee. Most were afraid to go inside. Arnott was the first to enter. Terry Rippa witnessed her entrance. "The first officer that came in was a female. She was up front with her gun pulled and everything. I yelled at her 'He's gone'. She stepped around the bodies and put her gun up and came around the back and walked up to me and hugged me."

Soon, other police officers, at least thirty more, including a tactical team, arrived. Medics checked out the bodies at 12:27 A.M. Terry pointed to John and told them, "Why don't you help this guy first? At least he is alive."[3]

They set up a triage, but only two victims had any chance of being saved.

Within seconds John McNeill was on his way to a hospital. He had not felt anything, at first. Then he was overwhelmed with excruciating pain. Ironically, the only other victim still alive was Belachheb's first target and the catalyst for the carnage—Marcell Ford.

Norman, one of the musicians, remembers Marcell saying, "Get some help. Get an ambulance. I'm dying."

Sherlyn recalled that "she kept crying [and] she couldn't breathe. I tried to talk, to make her be still but blood was pouring all over me, her, [and] the floor. I couldn't tell where she was shot— but I held napkins on her back shoulder and front. I tried—I tried. I prayed with her. Then she cried 'Mama, Mama.'" Those were Marcell's last words. She died en route to Parkland Memorial Hospital where she was pronounced dead on arrival.[4]

II

Officer Bill Parker grew up in the Oak Cliff section of Dallas. His dad was a postal worker and his mother was a stay-at-home mom. He joined the Army right after graduating from Sunset High School and was in the Airborne Infantry from 1961 to 1964. He applied for a job with the Dallas Police Department even before he was discharged; he was just looking for a job. He had not yet graduated from a police academy class, so he was first assigned to the auto pound until he could join a new set of recruits. Bored beyond belief, he could not wait to get out of that auto pound.

During his career, Bill worked in a variety of law enforcement positions. After leaving the academy, he was a patrol officer for three years. His first investigator's position was in auto theft, followed by burglary and theft and then vice. During the time he spent in vice, he came to know, and arrest, Frank Rance Parker (no relation to Bill). After vice, Bill was a sergeant in the tactical unit (SWAT). By 1973, he was transferred to the "Crimes Against Persons Unit," which included homicide.

Just after midnight on June 29, 1984, Bill Parker had barely gotten to sleep when the phone rang. He had been out to dinner that evening, had a few drinks, and after nineteen years as a Dallas policeman, eleven of them in homicide, he was used to getting up in the middle of the night to go to a murder scene. This one was different, of course, because of the number of bodies.

During his career, Bill has seen many gruesome crime scenes. He does not let the horror or sadness of it all affect his concentration, judgment, or get in the way of finding out who the murderers are. In Bill's mind, emotion obstructs justice, and he won't have it. Terry Rippa may have been thinking of Bill Parker when he observed, many years later, that the police at the scene seemed cold and indifferent. If so, what he saw in Bill Parker was a veneer hiding a quiet determination to catch the man who littered the Ianni's barroom with dead bodies.

His substantial investigative gifts more than make up for his small physical stature. By 1984, he had "earned a reputation for psychological craftiness and gamesmanship." He amazed his colleagues and prosecutors with his uncanny ability to get confessions and solve crimes.

"He's not brutal and he's not threatening. He's as good as any I've ever seen at worming his way into the confidence of the defendant," commented a defense attorney.

"There might be another interrogator in the country as good as he is, but I can't believe there's one any better," said a district judge.[5]

Indeed, at times Bill seemed to do the impossible. Dallas County Assistant District Attorney Norman Kinne still marvels at the case of a murdered woman found in a park who had been sexually assaulted with a tree limb. Again, intensely disciplined, Bill was not distracted by the senseless horror. Instead, he studied the victim carefully, stood up, turned to the crowd of onlookers, and picked out the murderer. A few minutes later he had a confession.

When asked to explain how he picked out the culprit from a crowd, he modestly replied, "I've seen that look in a man's eye before."[6]

Once on the Ianni's case, Bill took nothing for granted. He parked his car beyond Cappuccino's so as not to disturb anything in the parking lot. When he entered the club, he found the place being processed by forensics teams. The bodies were still there, but Bill was just as interested in the bits and pieces of debris on the floor. Paul Lachnitt, a fourteen-year veteran, and Robert Counts of the Crimes Against Persons Unit, joined him. J. P. Schreck of the Physical Evidence Section took photographs and collected evidence.

Lachnitt and Counts gathered up all the witnesses and interviewed them separately so as not to allow them to "contaminate" one another. They came up with a description of the murderer, his vehicle, and the name "Charlie."

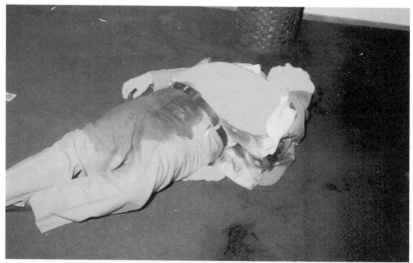

A witness at Abdelkrim Belachheb's trial testified that Frank Parker was in the kitchen when the shooting started in the barroom. He allegedly made an attempt to "rush" toward Belachheb in an effort to stop him. Parker was shot and killed almost immediately. (Dallas County District Attorney Files)

The witnesses also told of how the murderer ran out of ammunition and went to the foyer, only to reload and return and shoot two more people (John McNeill and Frank Parker), and overkill the others already on the floor. Others told him that they thought the murderer might have had a machine gun. From witness recollections of the sound of a "slide" and the discovery of a live round near where Marcell Ford fell mortally wounded, Bill quickly surmised that the murderer used a 9-mm semi-automatic pistol. The moving of the slide ejected a live round from the gun's chamber. Bill knew that the killer would not have left the room if he had run out of ammunition; if possible, he simply would have loaded a new clip rather than leave and return. Bill thought that the killer must have had trouble with the gun; it probably had jammed on him. If so, there should be a live round somewhere in the foyer.

View from the barroom to the front foyer. After his gun jammed, Abdelkrim Belachheb ran to the front foyer and fixed his gun for more murder. The "x" indicates where Bill Parker discovered a live 9-mm round that had been ejected from Belachheb's pistol. (Dallas County District Attorney Files)

On the foyer's brown brick floor, to the left of a wooden bench, below the leaves of a potted plant held in a wicker-covered vase, he found a live 9-mm bullet.[7]

III

Meanwhile, Abdelkrim Belachheb sought to put distance between himself and Ianni's Restaurant and Club. In his white, 1983 Chevrolet station wagon, he turned left onto Midway and then immediately turned right onto the entrance ramp of the LBJ Freeway. He headed east for approximately nine miles before exiting onto Church Road and then right onto Plano Road, a larger thoroughfare. He drove a little less than a half-mile before turning left onto Kinglsey Road. He then took an immediate right onto Bryson Drive. The route is complicated even with a map in hand, but Belachheb knew exactly where he was going. He had been there many times before.

The seventh block down Bryson was Listi Drive, where his friend Mohamed lived. It was the first home Belachheb had known in Dallas.[8]

From Kinglsey, Bryson Drive is straight and narrow for four blocks. A thickly wooded greenbelt and riverbed borders the street to the west, where there are no sidewalks or homes. The shoulder is about ten feet wide before the ground drops considerably into the riverbed. At the fifth block, near Giddings Street, Bryson makes slight curves to the left and then to the right. As Belachheb drove south on Bryson he hopped the curb and rammed the passenger side of his car into a telephone pole. The noise awakened several nearby residents. Some told police that they saw a man leaving the area, running further down Bryson in the direction the car was headed.

Belachheb rammed the front right fender of his car into the pole, and forward motion destroyed both passenger side doors. The metal tore from its frame. The car finally stopped when the back wheel struck the utility pole with such force that it deflated the tire and put a gash in the hubcap. The pole was only inches from the street's curb, so the car still obstructed the right lane of the 9200 block of Bryson. The force of the crash sent Belachheb's head into the rear-view mirror where several of his toupee hairs were recovered from the cracked glass.[9]

Listi Street was only two blocks away. Belachheb ran south on Bryson past McCree Road and turned left on to Listi. Mohamed's house was on the right.

At the time, Mohamed was a chef at Mario's Restaurant in Dallas' trendy Turtle Creek Village. He had finished work at eleven P.M. and had just returned home. It was just after midnight when his girlfriend, Anne*, arrived. Yanouri, Mohamed's cousin who lived with him at the time, was also in the home. (Debbie and Abdul, the married couple who had lived there at the same time as Belachheb had since moved.)

The residents of the house were watching Richard Attenborough's epic movie *Ghandi*. Yanouri lay on an Oriental rug in front of the brown sofa that faced the windows in the living room. Mohamed, Anne, and Yanouri were getting ready to eat a large meal after having fasted during Ramadan. Yanouri remembered what happened next. "It was after midnight and the three of us were watching a video taped movie when there was a knock on the front door. My cousin Mohamed got up and answered the door. He opened the door but I could not see who it was. He greeted the person in Arabic and then I heard a struggle. My cousin yelled out to me to help him. [Anne] and I ran over to the door and I saw my cousin struggling with a man that I know as Charlie. They were fighting and my cousin was trying to pull a handgun away from the man called Charlie. My cousin was able to get the gun and the bullets fell out of the gun and I grabbed them."[10]

Belachheb had taken a leather coat from his car and draped it over his right arm. (He still had on his leisure suit coat as well.) When he approached Mohamed's house and rang the doorbell, Mohamed had greeted him with, "Welcome, come in." Belachheb answered by dropping the coat and pointing the gun as if to shoot.

"I jumped for him and grabbed him by the arm. Charlie fell down and I got the gun away from him." As he wrestled Belachheb to the ground and took the gun away from him, Mohamed called for Yanouri for help.

"Kill me! Kill me! I came to kill you!" Belachheb screamed in the front yard as Mohamed held the gun on him and told him to calm down before he woke up the whole neighborhood. Anne came to the door, and Mohamed told her to get back. In her statement, Anne remembered that Yanouri got so upset that Mohamed had to slap him and tell him to get back into the house and be quiet.[11]

Mohamed took Belachheb into his house to a back hallway that connected three bedrooms. Anne and Yanouri stayed in the living room, while Mohamed and Belachheb went into the middle bedroom to talk.

"Why did you want to kill me? What did I do wrong to you?" asked Mohamed.

"I came to kill you in hope that you would kill me," replied Belachheb.

"Why?" asked a puzzled Mohamed.

"I killed some people in a bar on Midway," said Belachheb.[12]

They did not believe him at first. "[Charlie's] normal behavior is highly aggressive and his interest is to be the main attraction. He makes loud and angry outbursts, he drinks a lot and is prone to extreme exaggeration," Anne later told the *Dallas Morning News.*

Their initial disbelief is understandable. Even though he had pulled a loaded gun on Mohamed, Belachheb had no intention of killing him. "Hell, I think if he wanted to kill [Mohamed] he would have," thought a Dallas County prosecutor. Thinking this was another of Belachheb's cheap stunts for attention was not unreasonable. But, the first thing Mohamed and Yanouri did was to make certain that Belachheb could not get his hands on that gun again. Mohamed hid it between the mattress and box springs of his bed, and Yanouri hid a clip of live rounds in a utility closet in the kitchen.[13]

While their initial disbelief was reasonable, within a matter of minutes, Mohamed and Yanouri knew, or should have known, that Belachheb had done something very terrible.

Belachheb wanted the gun back and threatened to implicate Mohamed in the murders. "If you are going to call the police somebody else is going to come and kill you," threatened Belachheb.

"I will not give you the gun back," answered Mohamed.

Belachheb then told Mohamed to tell the police that he had taken the gun back by force. He needed the gun back, he said, because he had a list of people he wanted to kill—then he was going to kill himself. He had to finish what he had started. "They will kill me by injection or electric chair. If you don't give me the gun I'm going to buy another and come back and kill you," Mohamed remembers Belachheb saying.[14]

Mohamed still had trouble believing Belachheb had actually killed people in a bar on Midway. Belachheb told him to get a radio. In the bedroom while listening to the newscasts, Mohamed began to take him much more seriously. Mohamed told Yanouri to get Anne to call the police but to do it without Belachheb hearing. Yanouri then went into the bedroom and joined Mohamed and Belachheb.

As Mohamed and Yanouri sat on chairs on either side, Belachheb lay on a mattress with his head propped up in his hand and told of the murders he had just committed. The two men had to have seen the blood spatters and human tissue on his pants near his shoes.

"I really don't want to kill you, you know. I came to provoke you, then you turn around and you kill me," Belachheb said.

"Why would I do that? I mean, I have no reason for killing you," answered Mohamed.

Then Belachheb said he had enough of this life. No one, it seems, wanted to give him a chance. While in that victim mode, he took his final paycheck from Augustus' Restaurant and threw it at Mohamed. "I am starving and you ask me for money." (Mohamed had lent Belachheb about $100 and had asked him for his money back a couple of days earlier.)

Shortly afterwards he said. "I have just shot some people, killed some people—a bunch of people."

"Where?" asked Mohamed.

"Midway."

"Why?"

Belachheb explained that he had a conversation with a young lady and she told him, "They don't allow monkeys in the club."[15]

He said he was determined to kill when he woke up that morning. "I was trying to kill all of them," he said.

At 1:30 A.M., Anne opened the door to the bedroom and asked if she should prepare dinner for four. (The dinner hour was consistent with Ramadan fasting.)

"My life is finished. I did what I did and now I have jobs to finish. I still have people I want to kill," Belachheb told Mohamed.

Belachheb reasoned that he had time; the police would not catch him for several days.[16]

IV

DPD Officer Thomas Haney was patrolling northeast Dallas during the graveyard shift when he received a call to respond to an accident on Bryson, near the corner of Giddings Street. He arrived shortly after 12:30 A.M. to find a severely damaged white Chevrolet station wagon lodged against a utility pole. Haney shined his flashlight into the car, and in plain view, he noticed a bullet in one of the creases of the seat. He could also see a box of bullets on the floorboard on the driver's side and a large bottle of Seagram's Whiskey on the passenger side. The bullets looked like 9-mm rounds. By that time, radio traffic on police channels alerted everyone listening to the horror of what had happened at Ianni's. Haney knew he was on to something.

Within minutes, police swarmed the area. Helicopters did an aerial search, but they focused on the thickly wooded riverbed to

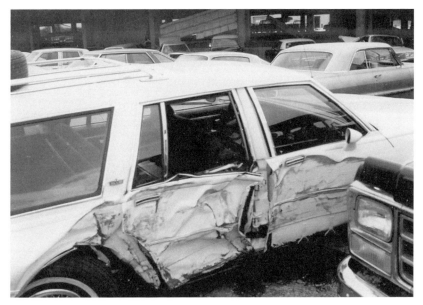

Abdelkrim Belachheb's car. After fleeing Ianni's Belachheb headed for a friend's home in far northeast Dallas. Apparently while trying to reload his gun, he jumped a curb on Bryson Street and plowed into a utility pole. From that location, he ran two blocks to his friend's home where he was arrested. (Dallas County District Attorney Files)

the west. Bloodhounds picked up a scent but lost it rather quickly.[17]

Back at Ianni's, Bill Parker had been on the scene for only about fifteen minutes when he heard that a uniformed officer reported discovering a white station wagon with a live 9-mm bullet. He and Paul Lachnitt immediately decided to take a look at the car. All they had when they left the restaurant was a description of the suspect and the name "Charlie."

"My heart was beating so fast my tie was jumping," Bill remembered later that year. He arrived there to find a disheveled car full of junk. The registration had a southeast Dallas address, "so this guy was not going home." There were many documents with many names and Bill called Ianni's in an attempt to match any of them to Ianni's membership list—with no luck. On a job application,

Bill saw "Charley" [*sic*] used as a nickname for Abdelkrim Belachheb. Another of the names, "Mohamed," a reference on a resume, lived on Listi Street. It was the same address as the one found on a checkbook for Abdelkrim Belachheb. A patrol officer familiar with the neighborhood pointed to the south, the direction the car was heading, and said that Listi was only about two blocks away.[18]

Parker and Lachnitt drove to the corner of Bryson and Listi. Then they walked slowly down the street, searching for the house. It was about 2:15 A.M., and they found it—the only home in the neighborhood with the lights still on. Lachnitt took a position directly across the narrow street behind a parked car while Parker went to the residence and began looking into each of the windows. While standing near the garage door, he saw the front door open and Anne walked out. Bill stayed quiet as she walked across the front porch and down the walkway toward the street. She was out for a cigarette. Parker quietly approached her. He proceeded from the assumption that his killer was there.

"Where's Charlie?" he asked quietly.

"He's in the house," Anne replied.

"Where's that weapon?"

"He's harmless now. We took it away from him." Bill knew he had the right place.

"Does he live here?" Bill asked.

"No," Anne replied.

"Do you live here?"

"Well, sort of." Bill knew he could go inside without worrying about search and seizure problems.

"What are they doing?" Bill asked.

"Talking," Anne replied.

"How many are there?"

"Three."

"How about you inviting me in. I'd like to get acquainted with Charlie."[19]

Anne appeared to be uncomfortable allowing the two men, both dressed in civilian clothes, into the house.

"It's alright. I'm the police. Where's the man?" Bill assured her.

"In the bedroom in the back of the house," she said.[20]

Bill then calmly told her "there is one of two ways we can do this. I can go in there quietly like the way I met you, or you can scream and carry on and someone will get hurt."

She pointed him to the hallway, then to the door. Parker and Lachnitt stood outside the bedroom door—guns drawn.

Bill thought about how some of the people at the restaurant had talked about machine guns—he knew better—or so he thought. In two weeks President Ronald Reagan and the Republican National Convention were going to be in town; there was no telling what was going on or who was planning to do whatever in Dallas at a time like that. But such thoughts were fleeting, and they did not stop Bill from kicking open the door.

Belachheb was smoking a cigarette and lying on a small mattress near the corner of the room. He had his head propped up in his hand.

"Get down or I will kill you all!" shouted Bill, who for a moment, did not immediately recognize which of the Middle Easterners was Belachheb. Belachheb and Mohamed hit the floor immediately, but Yanouri's English was not very good and he did not readily understand; Bill used his gun to speak a universal language. Very soon, Bill was able to pick out the Ianni's murderer. Belachheb still had on the same clothes, and on his pant legs near his ankles Bill saw blood and specks of bone and brains. He signaled Lachnitt to radio for help, which arrived in minutes.[21]

To this day, Bill is not completely convinced that the people in the Listi Street house did not believe Belachheb when he first spoke of the mass murder he committed. How could they not notice the blood on his pants? "I don't see how they could miss it."

Nor was he positive that they would have turned him in if he and Lachnitt had not gotten there. Mohamed, Yanouri, and Anne all assert that they intended to turn him in and claimed to have called the police as soon as they were able to get Belachheb into a bedroom where he could not hear the call being made. Yanouri even claimed that Belachheb wanted to leave, but he and Mohamed continued to talk to him until the police arrived. Bill is not sure when the call was made. His gut tells him that it was after he had arrived. It is always possible that they were "covering their ass."[22]

But it did not matter. The Ianni's murderer was on the floor at Bill's feet. Bill ordered him to get up. A search uncovered a fully loaded 9-mm magazine in Belachheb's inside left coat pocket. He told Belachheb to get face down on the floor. To all instructions, Belachheb responded quickly, clearly not in a trance or intoxicated.

Once the police arrived, Mohamed, Anne, and Yanouri became models of cooperation. Mohamed took Officer Billy Joe Hill to his bedroom and lifted the mattress to expose Belachheb's hidden gun. Yanouri led him to the utility closet where he had placed the clip. There was an extra round as well.[23]

From the moment he was in custody, Belachheb was thinking about his defense. Before he could be locked up he would try charm, grandiosity, and victimhood to impress those who arrested him. Lachnitt placed handcuffs on him and walked him to a waiting car. Bill got in the back seat with Belachheb and asked Lachnitt to turn on the dome light. Then he read Belachheb his Miranda rights.

"How did you catch me so fast?" Belachheb asked.

"It really wasn't that fast. It's been two hours," Bill replied.

The Listi Street house was located in extreme northeast Dallas, almost in the suburb of Garland. Neither Parker nor Lachnitt knew the neighborhood and they "were about half-lost." They wondered aloud how to get back to police headquarters in downtown Dallas. At some intersection, Lachnitt asked if they should turn left to get to the freeway. Parker answered that he thought so. Then Belachheb interjected, "If you want to go downtown the best way is to take Highway 75. Don't take a left. Take a right and I'll show you when we get up a little farther." Belachheb was trying to be charming.

Bill Parker thought to himself, "I'll have to remember to tell Norm [Dallas County Assistant District Attorney] about this."

"I had a vision that I killed some people tonight," Belachheb blurted out.

"Oh, you did," replied Bill. "Have you lost your memory since you left the house? Turn around and look behind you. Those two Arabs you were running your mouth to, they're back there in that car. When we go downtown and squeeze their nuts a little bit what do you think they are going to tell us? Now you telling me you had a vision?"

Belachheb laughed a bit, smiled, and shrugged his shoulders as if to recognize his own folly.

"Well, I'm pretty drunk, you know," he added.

"You don't look drunk to me," Bill replied.

"Well, I was drunk when it happened," Belachheb insisted.

"When what happened?"

Belachheb got quiet.[24] Grandiosity did not work.

He stayed quiet as the unmarked car came closer to downtown. To this day there is a rumor, never confirmed nor denied by either officer, that Belachheb told Parker and Lachnitt that he wanted to kill himself. His victim mode failed to impress either officer; both had seen the senseless slaughter at Ianni's and the blood and brains on Belachheb's light gray pants. As the car raced south on Central Expressway at seventy miles an hour, one of the men is reported to have pointed to the door next to Belachheb and said, "That door is unlocked."[25]

Local television stations recorded Belachheb's entrance to the Dallas Police Department at about 3:30 A.M. Mohamed and Yanouri arrived as well, one of them saying to reporters, "It's not me." They were questioned, released and returned to Listi Street around 8 A.M.

The department organized a lineup, and one by one witnesses picked out Belachheb. As far as investigations go, it was as airtight as it was brief. Bill Parker did not need a damn thing, like a confession, from Belachheb. He had a murder weapon, a list of witnesses making positive identifications, three of Belachheb's friends signing affidavits that Belachheb admitted to the shootings, and blood and brains on the suspect's pants. Usually, when a suspect wants to talk, investigators jump at the chance, but before sunrise Bill Parker did not need or want to talk to Belachheb anymore.

"I like talking to you," Belachheb teased Bill.

"Yea, you'll like me less as time goes on," Bill replied coolly.[26]

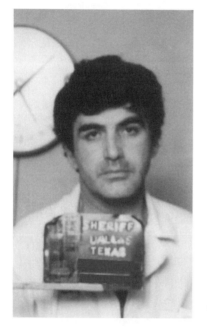

Mug shot of Abdelkrim Belachheb taken at the Dallas Police Department on June 29, 1984, approximately three hours after his arrest for the murders he committed at Ianni's Restaurant and Club. (Dallas County District Attorney Files)

[1] Terry Rippa quoted in *Texas v Belachheb*, 291st Judicial District, Cause no. F84-75078-SU, et. al., IV, 893-951; John McNeill quoted by Terry Rippa during interview; John McNeill.

[2] Barbara Watkins quoted in ABC News: *20/20*, August 22, 1985; Barbara Watkins; John McNeill; Dallas Police Department Files: *Affidavit in Any Fact*, by Barbara Watkins, June 29, 1984; Pam and dialogue with Barbara quoted in *Dallas Times Herald*, June 29, 1984.

[3] Dallas County District Attorney's Office: *Prosecution Report, Dallas Police Department*, by Robert B. Counts, June 29, 1984 and unidentified note; Terry Rippa quotes are from interview and *Dallas Morning News*, July 7, 1984; Richard Jones.

[4] Norman quoted in *Dallas Morning News*, June 30, 1984; Terry Rippa; Richard Jones; Dallas County District Attorney's Office: *Prosecution Report, Dallas Police Department*, by Robert B. Counts, June 29, 1984 and unidentified note dated June 30, 1984, unidentified and undated newspaper clipping; ABC News: *20/20*, August 22, 1985; *Texas v Belachheb*, 291st Judicial District, Cause no. F84-75078-SU, et. al., IV, 1012-62 and 1061-71.

[5] *Texas* v *Belachheb,* 291st Judicial District, Cause no. F84-75078-SU, et. al., IV, 1087-1108; Quotes are from the *Dallas Morning News,* December 24, 1984.

[6] Norman Kinne; Bill Parker quote from interview.

[7] *Texas* v *Belachheb,* 291st Judicial District, Cause no. F84-75078-SU, et. al., IV, 1109-1117; Dallas County District Attorney's Office: *Prosecution Report, Dallas Police Department,* by Robert B. Counts, June 29, 1984; Bill Parker.

[8] I have concluded that this was the route that Belachheb took because of the time of his arrival at Mohamed's house. He could not have gotten lost or taken an indirect route to be at the Listi Street house in the time frame outlined by witnesses.

[9] Dallas Police Department Files: *Investigative Supplement Report,* by G. W. King, June 29, 1984 and *Offense/Incident Report,* by T. Haney, June 29, 1984; *Texas* v *Belachheb,* 291st Judicial District, Cause no. F84-75078-SU, et. al., I, 3-13.

[10] Yanouri quoted in Dallas County District Attorney's Office: *Affidavit in Any Fact, Yanouri,* June 29, 1984, *Affidavit in Any Fact, Anne,* June 29, 1984; *Dallas Morning News,* June 30, 1984.

[11] Dallas County District Attorney's Office: *Affidavit in Any Fact, Mohamed,* June 29, 1984, *Affidavit in Any Fact, Anne,* June 29, 1984; Belachheb quoted by Mohamed in Texas v *Belachheb,* 291st Judicial District, Cause no. F84-75078-SU, et. al., VI, 1934-65.

[12] The conversation is a reconstruction from Mohamed's quotes in *Texas* v *Belachheb,* 291st Judicial District, Cause no. F84-75078-SU, et. al., VI, 1934-65 and Dallas County District Attorney's Office: *Affidavit in Any Fact, Mohamed,* June 29, 1984 and *Affidavit in Any Fact, Anne,* June 29, 1984.

[13] Anne quoted in *Dallas Morning News,* June 30, 1984; Norman Kinne quoted in interview; Dallas County District Attorney Files: *Prosecution Report, Dallas Police Department,* by Robert B. Counts, June 29, 1984.

[14] Dallas County District Attorney's Office: *Affidavit in Any Fact, Mohamed,* June 29, 1984; Dallas Police Department Files: Handwritten note from interview with Mohamed, June 29, 1984; Quotes are from *Texas* v *Belachheb,* 291st Judicial District, Cause no. F84-75078-SU, et. al., VI, 1934-65.

[15] Dialogue reconstructed from *Texas* v *Belachheb,* 291st Judicial District, Cause no. F84-75078-SU, et. al., VI, 1934-65; and *Affidavit in Any Fact, Yanouri,* June 29, 1984.

[16] Quotes are from *Dallas Morning News,* June 30, 1984.

[17] *Texas* v *Belachheb,* 291st Judicial District, Cause no. F84-75078-SU, et. al., I, 3-13 and IV, 1073-81; Dallas County District Attorney Files: *Prosecution Report,* by Robert B. Counts and *Investigative Supplement Report,* by G. W. King, June 29, 1984, and unidentified newspaper clippings.

[18] Bill Parker; Bill Parker quoted in *Dallas Morning News,* December 24, 1984; Dallas Police Department Files: Unidentified handwritten notes; Dallas County District Attorney Files: *Prosecution Report,* by Robert B. Counts and *Investigative Supplement Report,* by G. W. King, June 29, 1984; *Texas* v *Belachheb,* 291st Judicial District, Cause no. F84-75078-SU, et. al., I, 3-13, and IV, 1087-1108.

[19] Dialogue reconstructed from an interview with Bill Parker; Dallas Police Department Files: Unidentified handwritten notes.

[20] Quotes are from *Dallas Morning News,* June 30, 1984; Bill Parker; Dallas Police Department Files: Unidentified handwritten notes.

[21] Bill Parker quoted in interview; *Texas* v *Belachheb,* 291st Judicial District, Cause no. F84-75078-SU, et. al., IV, 1087-1108, and VI, 1934-1965; Dallas Police Department Files: Unidentified handwritten notes; Dallas County District Attorney Files: *Prosecution Report,* by Robert B. Counts, June 29, 1984.

[22] Bill Parker quote from interview; Dallas County District Attorney Files: *Affidavit in Any Fact, Yanouri,* June 29, 1984.

[23] Dallas County District Attorney Files: *Affidavit in Any Fact, Mohamed,* June 29, 1984; *Texas* v *Belachheb,* 291st Judicial District, Cause no. F84-75078-SU, et. al., V, 1225-36.

[24] Dialogue and quotes are from Bill Parker interview and his sworn testimony in *Texas* v *Belachheb,* 291st Judicial District, Cause no. F84-75078-SU, et. al., I, 13-22, VI, 1918-34, and

1966-86; Dallas County District Attorney Files: *Prosecution Report,* by Robert B. Counts, June 29, 1984.

[25] The story was related to me by Norman Kinne.

[26] Norman Kinne; Bill Parker; *Dallas Times Herald,* July 2, 1984; *Dallas Times Herald,* unidentified and undated clipping in the Dallas County District Attorney Files.

chapter nine

"A miracle from God"

> *"You gotta have some passion or you wouldn't be worth a shit over here."*
> —Jeff Shaw, Dallas County
> District Attorney Investigator

I

As he lay in a hospital bed in stable condition in the intensive care unit at the Dedman Medical Center in Farmer's Branch, Texas, John McNeill admitted that he "wouldn't have given ten cents for [his] life even when the ambulance people finally came in. [He] was in incredible pain." During the ambulance ride he tried to relax, believing that it might help him avoid bleeding to death. The attendants kept talking to him in an attempt to keep him conscious, but John wished they would just shut up and let him try to relax on his own. At the hospital he was able to talk to the physician. He told him that he had an uncle who was a doctor.

"Would you like to wait for him?" asked the surgeon.

"No. I don't think I have that much time," answered John.

So the Dedman staff immediately prepped him for emergency surgery. The diagonal path of the bullet, from lower back to upper chest, meant that he faced major exploratory surgery to determine exactly what the missile had done. The doctors would also have to repair the damage and stop any bleeding to assure his survival.

"When they put me on the operating table that night, they said, 'Is that the bullet?' I looked down and saw the bump under my skin and said 'Yeah.' I hadn't noticed it until then."

The fully jacketed 9-mm round had ended up in John's chest between the skin and the sternum. The hard, smooth missile had "neatly" sliced a path through his torso. Had he been shot with a hollow point, like most of the others, he would have died instantly.[1]

John McNeill was an extraordinarily lucky man.

II

On Friday, June 29, 1984, residents of the Dallas Metroplex woke up to stories about the Ianni's murders dominating the news. Newsreel footage showed Bill Parker escorting Belachheb through the hallways of the Dallas Police Department, in hand cuffs, on his way to be booked for murder. At Ianni's, the doors were locked and blinds covering the tinted windows were shut to prevent onlookers from watching workers clean up and replace the blood soaked carpet, the shattered smoked mirror, and the bullet-scarred woodwork and wallpaper. As though signaling an end to a bad horror movie, a thunderstorm moved into Dallas, adding humidity to an already considerably hot day.

Police questioned sixteen witnesses between 2:30 A.M. and daylight. Some of them were still in formal wear. Paul Lachnitt and Robert Counts showed them lineups; seven people positively identified Belachheb as the man who did the shooting.[2]

Dallas Police Chief Billy Prince called it the worst mass murder in the city's history. It was an occasion to remember other tragedies: outside of Dallas, in neighboring Grand Prairie, in August of 1982, John S. Parrish got angry over how much back pay he felt he was due when he opened fire on his supervisors. He killed six and wounded another four. In Dallas, in December of 1980, Thomas Ray Walker killed his wife and four children before he forced police officers to kill him outside of a supermarket in an act criminologists call "suicide by cop." Twenty-five years before that, in December 1955, Buford V. Calhoun of northeast Dallas killed his wife and three children. Then he phoned a relative to talk about what he had done before he killed himself.[3]

Like most business people in Dallas, Jim, Nick's partner and the businessman who had once hired Belachheb as a chauffeur, and had even been thinking about financing Belachheb's restaurant proposal, arrived to an office buzzing with talk of what had happened at Ianni's early that morning. Between 8:30 and 9:00 A.M., Jim took a call from Belachheb.

"Jim, have you heard I'm in trouble," Belachheb asked.

"No, I really haven't," replied Jim.

"Well, I need an attorney."

"Well, what's the matter?"

"I killed these people at Ianni's," Belachheb said.

"Well, I'll see what I can do."

During the conversation, Belachheb asked Jim to sign a bond for his release. Following a request from Jim, the comptroller of Jim's company confirmed that the person they knew as "Pierre" was actually Abdelkrim Belachheb—the shooter in Ianni's.

Knowing that his friend Linda Lowe was a frequent visitor to Ianni's, Jim then looked into whether she was one of the victims. "I finally got hold of Nick because Nick was out of pocket, and at that point, obviously, I didn't want anything to do with [Belachheb]." Shortly afterwards, Belachheb called again.

"Pierre, I'm not going to do anything. You killed my very good friend," Jim said sternly.

"I did Nick a favor," answered Belachheb curtly.

Jim didn't accept any more calls from Belachheb.[4]

Wade Thomas, Linda Lowe's brother, got to work, and as usual he and his boss walked over to the coffee machine.

"Did you hear about what happened in Dallas last night?" Wade asked.

"Yea, wasn't that terrible?" his boss replied.

"Yea, I'm a little worried because my sister lives in Dallas. That was a supper club type thing. I hope she's O.K.," Wade said as he started his work.

At 10:20 A.M. the Dallas Police Department contacted Wade's stepfather and told him that Linda had been murdered. He said he would break the news to Linda's mother. Shortly afterwards, the stepfather called Wade at work and said, "Son, you need to come home. Linda was killed last night."

Wade just sat there for a few minutes. He locked his desk and left—spaced out as he drove to his mother's home. Linda's daughter was already there, and two police officers arrived to let them know what had happened.[5]

"B. J."*, the wife of mechanic Joe Minasi, heard about the tragedy and was drawn to the restaurant. Her worst fears were confirmed when she located Joe's car—still parked next to Ianni's.[6]

Later that night, Cappuccino's was filled to capacity; and the talk was a strange mixture of money and murder—Ross Perot's sale of EDS (Electronic Data Systems, Inc.) to General Motors and the Belachheb murders across the parking lot in Ianni's.[7]

III

For many years, a triumvirate ran Dallas County. It was an alliance unlike any other. The first of the threesome was James Eric "Bill" Decker, the Sheriff. Elected in 1948, for the next twenty-two years no opponent ever challenged his re-election. He served until his death in 1970. Lew Sterrett was the County Judge who presided over the Commissioners' Court, a legislative body that controls the county budget. The third, and probably the most formidable, was Henry Wade, the District Attorney.

Observers understood that Wade called the shots. He graduated first in his class in 1938 from the University of Texas Law School, but he did not have an overpowering courtroom presence. He was politically astute and he knew how to run a District Attorney's Office. He had a gift for spotting talent—and hiring them. Once hired, it was a feather in the cap of any lawyer to have been one of Wade's assistants. He left them alone to do their job, and if they didn't, he fired them.[8]

By 1981, Wade had been the District Attorney for thirty-one years. His reputation was such that when a new District Court was created, the 291st Criminal District, Wade was influential in the interim appointment of its first Judge. Governor Bill Clements appointed Gerry Holden Meier to be the first female Criminal District Judge in Dallas County's history. At the time of her appointment in 1981, she was only thirty-two years old. Three years later she would preside over the trial of Abdelkrim Belachheb.

During her six years as one of Henry Wade's Assistant District Attorneys, Judge Meier had tried more than 300 cases. Her rise to the bench, however, was not without its frustrations and setbacks. She graduated from law school in 1974 with hopes of becoming a medical malpractice attorney. "There was not a law firm in Dallas that would hire me," she recalled years later, relating her "glass ceiling" experience.

In May of 1975, Henry Wade offered her a job she accepted even though she had no interest in criminal law. She began as a low-level misdemeanor prosecutor and quickly rose to the rank of Chief Felony Prosecutor; she was the first female in Dallas County history to hold that position.[9]

Judge Meier quickly fell in love with criminal law. Her love of the law and the majesty of the court were apparent through her by-the-book approach. Anyone who might have thought that the young, five-foot five-inches Judge Meier would have problems controlling her courtroom was in for a rude awakening.

From day one, she took control of her courtroom—and never let go. A seasoned prosecutor once observed, "She can put you in your place."

After only one year on the bench, she was dubbed the "Iron Maiden." She has "no earthly idea" where the nickname came from, but she hasn't let it affect her in the least.

Judge Meier has also been faced with a persistent rumor that she was sexually assaulted as a young woman and that it has tainted her objectivity, especially in rape cases. The rumor has even surfaced in motions and appellate briefs. In fact, she has never been a victim of sexual assault.

She has a distinctly Texan accent—but without the drawl. "There has never been a circus, or anything close to that, in a courtroom where I preside," she recently said, with piercing brown eyes. She allows no cameras in her courtroom, or anything else that can possibly alter the behavior of the lawyers or the jurors.[10]

Dallas County has sixteen categories of crimes assigned to courts. Once in a category, cases are assigned to one of fifteen criminal courts at random. In the spring of 1984, Judge Meier was returning to her courtroom following maternity leave. (In late April she had given birth to a son.) While still at home, her court coordinator called and told her the 291st had been assigned the Belachheb Case.[11]

At the District Attorney's Office, everyone knew Henry Wade was going to assign this case. Wade, of course, was at the top of the pecking order, followed by his First Assistant, who then had several Chief Felony Prosecutors who had the responsibility of trying the big cases—like capital murder. Wade pulled out his top gun for Belachheb.

Norman Kinne is from Brownsville in Texas' Rio Grande Valley. He is a solid, no nonsense Texas Aggie—Class of 1957. After graduation he spent two years in the United States Army before enrolling in the University of Houston Law School and graduating in 1963. Kinne felt that Dallas was the place to practice the law, which he did in private practice from his arrival there to 1971. That year, Kinne became an Assistant D.A. for Henry Wade. Kinne remained there for the next twenty-seven years.

Kinne's father once said, "[Norm] was no saint, but he never got into serious trouble either." His mother was a stay at home mom, and like her husband, she could not believe anyone could kill out of sheer meanness. Norm often saw them as a source of good, old-fashioned common sense he could bring into the courtroom.

Indeed, Norm Kinne is not a saint. He is equally comfortable arguing complicated legal principles in the sanctity of a courtroom, or telling a reporter something is "a bunch of crap." And he gets pissed off when people kill each other over a bottle of wine.[12]

In Corinthians II, the Bible says, "For ye suffer fools gladly... ." Not Norm. He barely tolerates stupid questions, and is a master at making an interviewer regret inquiries he finds offensive or does not want to answer directly. When asked if the Belachheb case was the biggest he had ever tried, he described a case he handled in which a young bride had been tied to a bed, raped, brutalized, and beaten to death. "That was a big case, but no one will ever write a book about her."[13]

In Napoleonic fashion, in court or during interviews, he successfully maneuvers opponents and others on to *his* battlefield—under *his* conditions—where *he* has the moral high ground. Defense attorneys find it difficult to recover from his effectively executed tactics.

Norman Kinne, the lead prosecutor in the Belachheb case. As a frustrated defense attorney once warned, while rubbing a glossy balustrade, "he's got a voice that'll take the varnish right off this rail." (Courtesy of Norman Kinne)

In the courtroom, his maneuvering is a gift. "He has a stare that looks right through you," said Jeff Shaw, his investigator for many years. That penetrating gaze is complemented by his "in your face" stentorian delivery. Predictably, his effectiveness brings with it many detractors; some call him a "screamer."

"There is no one that can put thunder in a courtroom like Norm Kinne," said a jurist not easily impressed by anyone, Judge Gerry Meier. He delivers drama, and juries believe him.

Bill Parker considers Norm the best prosecutor he has ever seen in action. Bill loves telling the story of a trial he attended where he saw Norm sit through all of the proceedings just to give the closing argument. The defense attorney, during his closing argument, wasted half of his time asking the jury not to listen to what Norm was about to tell them. "He's got a voice that will take the varnish right off this rail," the attorney said as he rubbed the balustrade in the courtroom. And Norm did not disappoint them.[14]

From the beginning, Norm knew where Belachheb's defense was headed. Belachheb could not say he was innocent; he could not say that what he had done was an accident; he could not say it was self-defense—that left insanity. "He wants to tell you about what a sad childhood he had and how everybody has been picking on him . . . I don't think this fellow is ignorant. When you go in and shoot down six people, you have to start thinking real quick. He came up with this insanity stuff real quick."[15] Kinne made that statement four days after the shooting; it was a prelude to the trial.

As a Chief Felony Prosecutor, Kinne had a number of attorneys on his team. He chose Rider Scott, a ten-year veteran in the D.A.'s office, to assist him in the prosecution of Abdelkrim Belachheb. Kinne and Scott complemented one another. If Kinne delivered the drama, Scott provided the meticulous, methodical, thoughtful legal foundation for the prosecution. He was also charged with impaneling the jury. "Mr. Kinne and Mr. Scott at the time were the best and the brightest in the D.A.'s office," remembered Judge Meier.[16]

As Assistant District Attorney for Dallas County, Rider Scott was one of the prosecutors of the Belachheb case. (Courtesy of Rider Scott)

Kinne's investigator was a United States Navy veteran named Jeff Shaw. He had graduated from the University of North Texas in nearby Denton with a degree in Marketing. He had hoped to make his fortune in Real Estate. Shaw's mother had encouraged him to apply for a job with Dallas County.

During his job search he met Henry Wade, who decided to give him a chance as an investigator. It was an unusual move on Wade's part; Jeff had no previous law enforcement experience. (Jeff was later to earn his Master's degree in Management.) But he loved his job. "You aren't worth a shit around here unless you have passion," he said recently. And indeed, his passion was the key to his success. (Today, he is the Chief Investigator for the Dallas County District Attorney.)[17]

Judge Meier's first action as presiding judge in the Belachheb case was to assign the task of defending Belachheb to the Public Defender's Office. The Chief Public Defender at the time was Ralph Taite, who had been appointed to that position a year earlier. The case was assigned to a staff attorney named Ted Calisi. Almost immediately, Calisi indicated that the trial was going to be a memorable one. "I can tell you there will be a lot of interesting revelations."[18]

On July 5, Calisi made public his intention to submit an insanity defense for Belachheb. "I think anyone accused of performing acts of such a heinous nature had to be insane," he said. "We're just talking about a sick person who had been sick for many years, and it just finally blew up."[19]

After Magistrate Tom A. Boardman arraigned Belachheb, a subsequent Grand Jury proceeding took only a page and a half of transcript. Bill Parker answered six questions about the incident itself. There was not much to say: They had a gun and seven people who positively identified Abdelkrim Belachheb as the man who did the shooting. He was indicted on July 17, 1984, on six counts of murder and one count of attempted murder.[20]

Almost immediately, Judge Meier appointed a psychiatrist to examine Belachheb. It was important to her to select a doctor with extensive experience examining patients accused of crimes. She chose Dr. Clay Griffith of Dallas who had been in private practice in psychiatry for twenty-five years and had interviewed over 6,000 people charged with felonies.

Griffith and Belachheb met for the first time on Sunday, July 1, 1984, for nearly three hours. Ted Calisi characterized the meeting as "for a very extensive and appropriate period of time." Belachheb's rights were read to him twice and he consented to the interview.

Griffith noted first that Belachheb had a normal gait and handshake. They were able to communicate effectively, unless Belachheb spoke fast, which Griffith thought, at times, was deliberate. In his report to Judge Meier, Griffith noted that, "[H]e does know what the charge is against him and when the alleged offense occurred. However, Mr. Belachheb was not able to talk to me specifically about the alleged offense, saying that he did not remember. He was, however, able to talk in detail, and did, about what happened on the day before the alleged offense, and what his emotions and thinking was, and what his behavior was prior to and up until the time of the alleged offense."

During Dr. Griffith's interview, Belachheb remembered when and how he was arrested and brought to jail. In addition, he was able to relate how he had come to be in Los Angeles in 1981 and to Dallas in 1982, as well as information about his marriage in 1983. Belachheb told Griffith he had never had any head injury in his life. Belachheb admitted that he had a drinking problem but denied ever taking drugs.

When Griffith asked him about his gun, Belachheb answered, "Well, I remember my gun. I had my gun in my car because some people I have fired want to kill me."

"And who are they?" Griffith asked.

"Places where I have been a head waiter," Belachheb responded.

"Do you remember firing the gun?"

"No."

"You do not remember at all firing the gun?" Griffith asked again.

"NO!" Belachheb said in a loud and angry voice.

The story he related to Griffith, the one he stuck to throughout the trial, was that he could not remember what he had done in Ianni's. The first thing he remembers after the killings was being at Mohamed's house and being arrested.

After denying any memory of the incident at Ianni's, Belachheb smiled and interjected: "I cannot hurt any creatures of God. I'm a Muslim—that's my religion."[21]

Dr. Griffith found no memory loss, or any " . . . evidence of any delusions or hallucinations at this time. I can find no evidence of any mental illness in the past, although he would not give me any specific information, except to say that he has had no serious illness, no head injury, no unconsciousness, and no seizures."

Dr. Griffith concluded that Abdelkrim Belachheb was of average intelligence and a person who could show anger and hostility when asked about certain subjects, and friendliness and jocularity when asked about others. His narcissism was apparent throughout the interview, and in the end, Dr. Griffith found him to be competent to participate in his own defense.

Belachheb's attempt to manipulate the seasoned psychiatrist failed completely. At the end of the examination, as the two men were walking out of the room, Belachheb turned to Griffith and said, "Doctor, if you can't help me, don't hurt me."[22]

There was little doubt in Dr. Griffith's mind that Abdelkrim Belachheb was a sociopath. A doctor who referred to his patient as a "moral imbecile" first described Sociopathic Personality Disorder in America in 1911.[23] Sociopaths do not meet the legal definition of insanity because they know the difference between right and wrong; they are aware of the pain and destruction they cause; they just don't care.

IV

Melinda Henneberger was a "Naturalized Texan" from southern Illinois and a Notre Dame graduate. While reporting for the *Dallas Morning News* was her first job, she could hardly be considered a "cub" reporter. Before moving to Dallas, she had lived in Europe and had gone to graduate school at the *Université catholique de Louvain* just outside Brussels. While in Europe, she was a free-lance reporter, but she understood that at some point she would have to get a full-time job. While visiting her sister Joan, a Southern Methodist University coed, she had decided to practice her job-interviewing skills by applying as a reporter for the *Morning News.*

Shortly after she returned to Brussels, the city editor called to offer her a job. It was during a rather loud party and she had trouble hearing him. "Come on over. We're having a party," she said, not realizing she was talking to a man offering her a job in Dallas. After the conversation, she announced to the revelers: "Guess what? I'm moving to Texas!"[24]

When Henneberger found out that Belachheb once lived in Brussels, she had been on the job at the *Dallas Morning News* for only six months covering the police beat in the wee hours of the morning. She knew this was her story.

First, she called Interpol in Belgium and in fluent French was able to confirm that Belgian authorities were looking for Belachheb and that he had an extensive criminal record. They didn't even know he was in America, much less that he had committed six murders.

Belgian authorities told Henneberger that Belachheb had a wife and two daughters in Belgium. She immediately went to the editors and argued to go to Brussels to retrace Belachheb's movements. They were hesitant at first, but later agreed to send her if she could first get an interview with Belachheb's American wife, Joanie. Joanie had not granted any interviews yet, and getting a story from her would have been quite a scoop. A DPD source showed her Joanie's picture, and she then "camped out" outside the jail every night waiting for her to arrive. Henneberger's persistence paid off. After declining a first request, Joanie asked Henneberger to follow her home.

The editors now agreed to send Henneberger to Belgium. The decision was made easier when she argued that she had friends she could stay with, and that one of them had confirmed where Belachheb's first wife, Jenny, lived.[25]

In 1984, Jenny was an executive secretary for an oil company. She had dropped the name "Belachheb" after her divorce and lived what Henneberger described as a "very lower middle class" life with her two daughters. Afraid that Jenny would refuse to see her, Henneberger did not call first. Instead, she went to Jenny's home and confronted her. Jenny was stunned, but she agreed to be interviewed at an outdoor café. As Henneberger described what Belachheb had done at Ianni's, Jenny grew more and more visibly upset.

"Nobody knows him like I do," Jenny said, as she launched into a long description of her frightful life with Abdelkrim Belachheb. Jenny told of how he couldn't keep a job, was a philanderer, and could not get along with anyone. Henneberger had the feeling that Jenny realized that she had been taken in "by this complete idiot."[26]

"He's not worried about those people. He hasn't got a conscience. He's worrying about whether he'll ever hold a woman again," Jenny said bitterly. "If he were a total stranger, I'd say give him the electric chair. Or better yet, cut him up into pieces."

During this interview, Jenny said that Belachheb "lies more than tells the truth." But she was also angry at Belgian authorities; they had done little or nothing to prevent this senseless tragedy.

After interviewing Jenny, Henneberger retraced Belachheb's visits to Brierbeek and Jean Titeca Hospitals and Foret and St. Giles Prison. She even located Dr. Yves Crochelet, who walked her to his office. She watched him pull out Belachheb's file, look it over and say, "I'm not surprised this happened." She never got the impression though that Crochelet thought Belachheb suffered from a medical condition causing uncontrollable behavior. More likely he was an ornery and disagreeable individual, constantly in trouble.[27]

Henneberger returned to Texas with a hell of an exclusive. Her feature article appeared in the Sunday, August 5, 1984, edition of the *Dallas Morning News*. It was more than just good reporting. Judging by how often it was quoted during Belachheb's trial, it became a major source of information for both the prosecution and the defense. As Henneberger looked back eighteen years later, she was stunned at how "both sides relied on a cub reporter for their information—to a large extent."

She was also surprised at the lack of international cooperation. American officials first found out about Belachheb's European criminal history, and Belgian officials and Jenny first found out about his American crimes from Henneberger.[28]

On the other hand, the prosecution had a gun, seven positive identifications, Belachheb's bloody clothes, six dead bodies, and one wounded man in Dedman Hospital just itching to testify against the "son-of-a-bitch" who shot him. Maybe it did not matter what Belachheb had done in Europe, or what Jenny, or Interpol, or Dr. Yves Crochelet had to say.

Ted Calisi, Belachheb's public defender, thought it mattered, and tried to secure public funding for a trip to Brussels to retrieve documents and take statements. According to his immediate supervisor, Ralph Taite, the Chief Public Defender at the time, Calisi tried to circumvent Taite to secure funding for the trip. The County Commissioners were not likely to approve such an expenditure anyway. As a result, Calisi resigned his position. According to Taite, Calisi called in sick on a Friday, and Taite found out about the resignation the following Monday, but only after contacting Calisi at home. The *Dallas Times Herald* later reported that Ted Calisi entered private practice after being upset over the "politics" being played over his proposed trip.[29]

Meanwhile, Joanie became involved in Belachheb's defense. Her closest family and friends urged her to have nothing further to do with him. Apparently forgetting that he was her third husband, and that only a few weeks before she had told him she would never see or speak to him again, she issued a statement that she was "not motivated by a great love affair. I feel responsible to Charlie and to God because of the vows I have made with them both." She also confirmed that she received death threats and that once the trial was over, she would move from Dallas. "I will not abandon Charlie," she insisted.[30]

Melinda Henneberger, the first reporter to do in depth interviews with both of Belachheb's wives, was stunned at how differently the two women reacted to what Belachheb had done. In Brussels, Jenny seemed more conservative and traditional. She wanted "a husband to be a husband." In Dallas, Joanie was more of a free spirit and very supportive and sympathetic. Joanie's comments to the press certainly illustrate the sympathy she had for her incarcerated husband.

Recalling Henneberger's reporting from Brussels, Joanie stated, "The doctor [Dr. Crochelet of Brussels] even said he was not surprised at the killings, and I'm wondering why they're doing nothing when there's obviously a serious mental problem." To another paper she elaborated that, "[t]hey are just really not qualified to handle the case. A case of this magnitude, they just don't have the staff to handle it. Frankly they have no interest in that little Berber." She also submitted a two-page typed statement to Dallas newspapers hoping to spin more sympathetic coverage of her husband during his murder trial.[31]

So, Joanie began to look for another defense attorney. Billable hours for a top-notch criminal defense lawyer, plus the fees necessary to hire experts to put on a successful insanity defense would easily run well beyond $100,000. The Belachheb cause looked hopeless. In early August, Joanie visited Frank Jackson, an attorney who had been identified by *D* magazine as one of "The Best Criminal Defense Lawyers in Dallas." He declined to take the case.

But the *D* article also inspired an August 9, 1984, *Dallas Times Herald* column by John Bloom. He had a few "suggestions" for the Belachheb trial, one of which was to "[f]ind a famous defense attorney, perhaps one known to specialize in insanity work, who will agree to take the case on a *pro bono publico* basis. . . . They're wealthy enough to write off a mission to Belgium and still reap lucrative publicity from a defense of the most hated man in Dallas."[32]

"John had piqued my conscience," Jackson said later. He called Joanie, they met again, and he agreed to take the case. Reports of Joanie mortgaging her houses to pay Jackson's fees were not accurate. While there was talk about possible book or movie royalties associated with the story, Frank knew that such income was only a very remote possibility. He took the case *pro bono* and decided to personally pay the substantial fees for the experts he anticipated hiring.

Officially, Frank Jackson became Belachheb's lawyer on August 14, 1984. "If you are not willing to step up and defend the most hated man, you should not call yourself a criminal defense lawyer," Frank said then and repeated years later.

Joanie could not have been more pleased: "This is a miracle from God," she said.[33]

Frank Jackson, Belachheb's defense attorney. The former professional football star agreed to defend "the most hated man in Dallas" as a matter of principle only a few days after he had been named by *D* Magazine as one of the "Top Ten Best Defense Lawyers" in Dallas. (Courtesy of Frank Jackson)

[1] John McNeill quoted in interview and in *Dallas Morning News,* July 7, 1984.

[2] *Texas* v *Belachheb,* Cause no. F84-75078-SU, et. al., Grand Jury B, July Term 1984, July 10, 1984; Dallas County District Attorney Files: Unidentified and undated newspaper clipping and *Prosecution Report,* by Robert B. Counts, June 29, 1984; *Dallas Times Herald,* June 30, 1984.

[3] Dallas District Attorney Files: Unidentified and undated newspaper clipping and *Prosecution Report,* by Robert B. Counts, June 29, 1984.

[4] Quotes and dialogue are reconstructed from Jim's sworn testimony in *Texas* v *Belachheb,* 291st Judicial District, Cause no. F84-75078-SU, et. al., VI, 1987-2015.

[5] Wade Thomas; Dallas Police Department Files: Unidentified handwritten note, June 29, 1984.

[6] *Fort Worth Star-Telegram,* June 30, 1984.

[7] Ibid.

[8] Norman Kinne; Jeff Shaw; The Honorable Judge Gerry Meier, interviewed by the author on July 23, 2002.

[9] *Dallas Times Herald,* October 28, 1984; Judge Gerry Meier quoted in interview; Norman Kinne.

[10] Judge Gerry Meier quoted in interview; Norman Kinne quoted in interview.

[11] Judge Gerry Meier.

[12] Norman Kinne; Judge Gerry Meier; Jeff Shaw; Bert Kinne quoted in *Dallas Morning News,* October 30, 1989; Norman Kinne quoted in *Dallas Times Herald,* October 28, 1984.

[13] Norman Kinne quoted in an interview.

[14] Judge Gerry Meier quoted in interview; Jeff Shaw quoted in interview; Defense attorney quoted by Bill Parker in interview.

[15] Norman Kinne quoted in *Dallas Times Herald*, July 2, 1984.

[16] Norman Kinne; Jeff Shaw; Judge Gerry Meier quoted in interview.

[17] Jeff Shaw quoted in interview.

[18] The Honorable Judge Ralph Taite, interviewed by the author on July 23, 2002; Ted Calisi quoted in *Fort Worth Star-Telegram*, July 2, 1984.

[19] Ted Calisi quoted in *Dallas Morning News*, July 7, 1984 and *Dallas Times Herald*, July 6, 1984.

[20] *Texas* v *Belachheb*, Cause no. F84-75078-SU, et. al., Grand Jury B, July Term 1984, July 10, 1984; *Fort Worth Star-Telegram*, June 30, 1984.

[21] Griffith's dialogue with Belachheb is reconstructed from his sworn testimony in *Texas* v *Belachheb*, 291st Judicial District, Cause no. F84-75078-SU, et. al., VII, 2198-2236 and Dallas County District Attorney Files: E. Clay Griffith, MD, to Judge Gerry Meier, July 3, 1984; Judge Gerry Meier; Ted Calisi quoted in *Dallas Times Herald*, July 2, 1984.

[22] Belachheb quoted by Dr. Clay Griffith in *Texas* v *Belachheb*, 291st Judicial District, Cause no. F84-75078-SU, et. al., VII, 2198-2236; Dallas County District Attorney Files: E. Clay Griffith, MD, to Judge Gerry Meier, July 3, 1984.

[23] *Texas* v *Belachheb*, 291st Judicial District, Cause no. F84-75078-SU, et. al., VII, 2198-2236.

[24] Melinda Henneberger quoted in interview.

[25] Ibid.

[26] Ibid.; *Dallas Morning News*, August 5, 1984.

[27] Ibid.

[28] Melinda Henneberger quoted in an interview.

[29] Judge Ralph Taite; *Dallas Times Herald*, July 9 and August 16, 1984.

[30] Joanie quoted in an undated *Dallas Times Herald* clipping in the Dallas County District Attorney's Files; *Dallas Morning News*, August 10, 1984; the fact that Belachheb was Joanie's third husband is confirmed by Joanie's sworn testimony in *Texas* v *Belachheb*, 291st Judicial District, Cause no. F84-75078-SU, et. al., V, 1237-1284.

[31] Melinda Henneberger; Joanie quoted in *Dallas Morning News*, August 10, 1984, and *Dallas Times Herald*, August 16, 1984.

[32] John Bloom quoted in his column appearing in the *Dallas Times Herald*, August 9, 1984.

[33] Frank Jackson quoted in interview; Joanie quoted in *Dallas Times Herald*, August 16, 1984.

chapter ten
_____

For the State

> *"It was not accidental; it's not self defense.*
> *What else can he say but 'I was crazy.'"*
> —Norman Kinne
> Assistant District Attorney

I

The genius of the American Constitution is that it was written to protect unpopular people and ideas. Freedom of the press protects *unpopular* print; freedom of speech protects *unpopular* speech. Popular ideas seldom need protection. So it is with individuals. Due process, search and seizure limitations, access to legal representation, the right to remain silent, and other rights are designed to assure that even the most reprehensible of American society, even those deemed unfit to live among us, have an opportunity to, at least nominally, defend themselves against the state. Like democracy, civil liberty, for only the few and the popular, is an oxymoron.

Defending Abdelkrim Belachheb was a defense of Constitutional rights *all* Americans enjoy. Forcing the state to answer an insanity plea, and thus prove guilt, assures caution and thoughtfulness by the state whenever it brings a defendant, even those clearly guilty of committing a heinous act, to trial.

"Defense lawyers have a bonded obligation to represent those accused of the most vicious, heinous crimes. If you can't do that, you don't deserve to be called a criminal defense attorney," Frank Jackson announced publicly when he agreed to take the case. It was no reflection on the Public Defender's Office, Jackson asserted, he just believed that his background in insanity defenses made him more qualified to present the Belachheb case before a jury.

By 1984, Jackson had presented three felony cases to juries using an insanity defense. Two were acquitted outright and the third ended in a hung jury. In the early '80s, Jackson defended Alfred Riccomi, a computer engineer prosecuted for the shooting deaths of his fifteen-year-old daughter and her friend. The verdict came in as not guilty by reason of insanity. Even more significant was the 1977 case of Gary Noble, an ex-Assistant District Attorney who had been charged with stealing more than 2,000 pills from a court's evidence room. The state presented two psychiatrists who testified to Noble's sanity, but Jackson brought in a doctor who convinced the jury that Noble was "mentally deficient" at the time of his arrest. It was the first not guilty by reason of insanity verdict in the history of Dallas County. The prosecutors of the Noble case were none other than Norman Kinne and Rider Scott.[1]

In 1984, Frank Jackson was a forty-four-year-old former football star from Southern Methodist University. He had played pro football for the Dallas Texans, Kansas City Chiefs, and the Miami Dolphins of the old American Football League. He had good looks and the build of a professional athlete. Terry Rippa thought of him as a "pretty boy attorney," and he was, as Judge Meier said, "very, very smooth." But, she was quick to add, in the Belachheb case his defense was " . . . creative and he did a good job. Most lawyers would have had nothing at all."[2]

The genesis of that "creative" defense came to Jackson during a convention of the National Association of Criminal Defense Lawyers (NACDL). While discussing the case with his friends, Dennis Roberts and Sandy Phelan, Jackson developed an insanity defense for Belachheb based on cultural maladaptation. They had been exploring cultural issues involving the "Black Rage" defenses in

San Francisco. (Roberts had been associated with William Kuntsler during the "Chicago Seven" trials.) "That discussion was the seed for my cultural insanity defense," Jackson recalled. The underlying precept was that the Moroccan culture relegated women to inferior positions. In America, the rejection of Belachheb's advances, in addition to brain damage brought about by head traumas, drove him into a state that was uncontrollable. It was a unique approach, even for an insanity plea. But, as Jackson was to admit later, "[t]here was really no other defense."[3]

Of course, the danger of the insanity route is that the defendant admits that he did, in fact, commit the act of which he is accused. In that regard, Belachheb had no choice; there was absolutely no doubt that he was the man who did the killing in Ianni's. Further, Jackson knew that the crime scene photos of five dead bodies (Marcell Ford had been taken to the hospital before crime scene photos were taken) would be used over and over again to reinforce the horror the jury felt. As Judge Meier has stated, with insanity "[the defense attorney has] to overcome the basic feeling we all have, or should have, that we are responsible for our actions."[4]

Compounding Jackson's challenge was a change in Texas law concerning insanity. State legislatures throughout the United States rushed to modify their insanity definitions after John Hinckley's attempted assassination of President Ronald Reagan in 1981. A storm of criticism followed Hinckley's "not guilty by reason of insanity" verdict. In Texas, before Hinckley, a jury had to believe that a defendant had a mental illness that prevented him from knowing right from wrong (the McNaughten Rule) *or* made him incapable of controlling his actions or conforming his conduct to the requirements of the law, what Jackson described in an interview as the "volitional prong" of the insanity defense. The new definition, which went into effect in August of 1983, eliminated the volitional prong.

The Legislature intended to narrow severely, but not eliminate entirely, the insanity defense in Texas. One of the authors of the new standard, Jim Spearly, who assisted Texas State Senator Ray Farabee in drafting the law, said, "... we want the jury to understand that not all mentally ill defendants are necessarily also legally insane.... A defendant can be judged crazy by the public but not insane by a jury."

There is a difference between being "crazy" and being "insane." By reducing insanity in Texas to the McNaughten Rule, the Legislature effectively disallowed an insanity option for anyone who engaged in preparation, execution, and flight during the criminal act.[5] That meant real trouble for Abdelkrim Belachheb—he had engaged in all three.

Yet, he was still entitled to a vigorous defense—no matter how far fetched.

II

On September 24, 1984, Abdelkrim Belachheb entered the 291st Criminal District Courtroom for the first time. Jeff Shaw remembers how utterly unimpressive Belachheb appeared. "There was nothing extraordinary about him. He was not an ogre or a monster," Shaw said. There was something incongruous about the monstrosity of the crime, and the "little Berber" (as Joanie had described him) before Judge Meier. Belachheb was dressed in prison-issued white overalls. While in jail he sometimes caused trouble because he refused to wear the jailhouse garb if it had the slightest stain, however small. He also meticulously organized and cleaned his cell to an extent that suggested, at least to untrained eyes of the guards, that he was compulsive.

Jeff also remembered that "[Judge Meier] was pretty well in charge of that courtroom. No doubt about it."

Before trial, Judge Meier met with the press and unambiguously enunciated rules and procedures she expected them to follow. She did not make motions available to the media and declined to clarify her rulings. She also forbade the taking of photographs, not only in the courtroom, but anywhere on the fifth floor of the courthouse.[6]

Of course, the press resented the restrictions; this was the biggest judicial event in Dallas since Jack Ruby's murder trial. The *Dallas Times Herald,* in a particularly sharp and personal editorial, described the trial as a "tight, formal proceeding presided over by the stern visage of Judge Gerry Meier, whose blunt cut hairstyle and clipped, stentorian delivery make her look like a robed Cleopatra presiding over Alexandria."[7] Judge Meier could not have cared less. She was far more attentive to the legal aspects of the case. "From a judicial standpoint, to be the presiding judge . . . was a privilege and a pleasure. There were good lawyers and good issues," she admitted.

Those good lawyers began sparring on September 24. Judge Meier granted Jackson's motion to require Kinne and Scott to refer to Belachheb only by name or "the defendant" or "the accused." (Kinne could not call him an "animal" and Scott could not refer to him as a "Murdering Moroccan," which was reportedly the label on the file he used during the trial.) She also granted Jackson's motion to prohibit the prosecution from revealing Belachheb's prior criminal history in Belgium. Although Jackson had every intention of bringing the information before the jury, he wanted to do so as part of his expert witness testimony thereby controlling its disclosure.[8]

But Frank Jackson did not get everything he wanted. He filed a discovery motion to gain access to a database District Attorney Henry Wade had been keeping on former jurors for nearly forty years. It reportedly contained data on over 100,000 former jurors. The motion was largely a protest against the practice, often filed routinely by criminal defense attorneys practicing in Dallas County, who knew it would be denied. Wade argued that the list was "work product" and not subject to disclosure rules or discovery.[9]

Several appeals court rulings have upheld Wade's position. But in an episode of uncharacteristic candor, which on its face seems to undercut his office's "work product" argument, Wade admitted that his interest in the list was political. "I figured if you tried a case before somebody and won it, they were prospective people to help you in a campaign," he admitted to the *Dallas Morning News*.[10]

Norm Kinne points out that "[defense attorneys] could do it as easily as we could if they just got organized."[11] The difference, of course, is that in the District Attorney's Office, county employees maintain the list and taxpayers fund the project—otherwise, it would not be "work product."

After pre-trial motions were ruled upon, Frank Jackson and Rider Scott matched wits during jury selection. Once Jackson filed the *Defendant's Notice of Intention to Raise Evidence of Insanity Defense,* he looked for what he called "twelve courageous jurors" for a "cerebral trial for intelligent people."

Rider Scott announced that he was looking for "well-informed, public-spirited people with common sense. Twelve people that can assess a ninety-nine-year sentence in a murder case."

Jury selection was often contentious as Jackson and Scott traded barbs. "I will not lecture you as Mr. Scott has done," Jackson said to a prospective juror. To which Scott objected to character assassination and backstabbing. And of course, Judge Meier did not allow that kind of exchange to go on for long.[12]

III

In the meantime, Abdelkrim Belachheb sat in a forty-square-foot cell in solitary confinement on the eighth floor of the Lew Sterrett Center. A glass wall allowed for constant surveillance by a guard standing only ten feet away. The lights were on twenty-four hours a day, and two guards checked Belachheb every fifteen minutes. An intercom inside the cell alerted the guards to any unusual noises. It was an umbrella of security not seen by any prisoner since Jack Ruby in 1964.

Belachheb was never allowed to mingle with anyone. When first brought to the center, he was calm and cooperative. When completing an information card, he indicated that he was an alcoholic and was suicidal at times. During that first night he asked for cigarettes but was told that the commissary was closed until the following Monday. Friendly guards slipped him a couple of cigarettes.

Less than two weeks later, on July 12, Belachheb began to cause trouble. At 7:15 A.M. a guard assigned to monitor Belachheb found him lying in his cell bunk staring at the ceiling. The guard also noticed a bloodstain on the sheets and blood dripping from his arm. Belachheb had managed to hide a disposable razor and had used it twice to slash his arm between the wrist and elbow. Although the cuts required eighteen stitches, the self-inflicted wound was nowhere near any major vein or artery.

"He didn't lose much blood and he was never in any life threatening situation. It did not appear to be a serious attempt," said Bob Knowles, the Commander in charge of the jail. Indeed, the cuts were estimated to be only about one-sixteenth of an inch deep. After Ted Calisi publicly asked why a prisoner, who had admitted he had suicidal tendencies, was allowed to keep a razor, the jailers were more careful. Belachheb was given a razor once a day, he was watched while he used it, and it was taken away from him once he finished shaving.[13]

"It was almost like he didn't think he was in jail. He really believed it was all going to work out for him," Lieutenant H. B. Sherman said from the jailhouse. He considered himself more of a guest with celebrity status than an accused and incarcerated felon. He demanded specially prepared milkshakes and refused to eat his meals because they were served on paper plates. After discovering that Frank Jackson had become his attorney, Belachheb confidently told the guards that he would be out in two months and that his life was certain to be chronicled in a book and movie. He had even decided how the royalties from these projects would be split: Jenny and his daughters in Belgium (fifty percent) and he and Joanie (twenty-five percent each).

And like an exposure-hungry movie star, he diligently scanned newspapers for stories about himself and Ianni's. (It is probably not a coincidence that his "attempted suicide" occurred at a time when coverage of the Ianni's massacre had finally begun to die down.) "His ego required a certain amount of maintenance and when he didn't get it he lashed back," Jeff Shaw remembered.

"He's got to have the limelight. He wants attention. He constantly tried to manipulate our system. He's good at it," Lieutenant Sherman said.[14]

Belachheb's attempts at manipulation also included performances for the parade of doctors, both court-appointed and for the defense, who visited him. He lied to every one of them. Judge Meier appointed the first, Dr. Clay Griffith, who visited on July 1, 1984. Dr. Kevin Karlson, a psychologist with a law degree, representing the defense, administered a battery of tests on September 14 and 15. Another court-appointed doctor, the controversial psychiatrist, Dr. James Grigson, visited on October 8. A session with Dr. Sheldon Zigelbaum, a psychiatrist for the defense, followed on October 27. The final visit was by two technicians from the staff of Dr. Homer Reed, a neuro-psychologist from Boston. The technicians saw fit to note that Belachheb was particularly perturbed to find out that they had not heard of his case in Boston. Additionally, they noted that they were "unsettled" by the way Belachheb stared at them. As they were preparing to leave, apparently they wondered aloud about a good place to eat in Dallas before returning to Boston. Belachheb volunteered a number of suggestions—one of them was Ianni's.[15]

IV

On the first day of the trial, Belachheb tried to fire Frank Jackson. By that time, Jackson had expended approximately $30,000 of his personal income on experts to develop a defense—not counting billable hours worth tens of thousands of dollars of *pro bono* work on his ungrateful client's behalf.

Judge Meier summarily denied Belachheb's attempt to dismiss Jackson. But from the beginning, one of the conditions Jackson made clear to Joanie and Belachheb was that he (Jackson) was to be in complete control of the defense. "[Belachheb] did what I told him to do . . . but the problem with Charlie was that he'd switch back and forth from lucid to goofy."

Belachheb sat quietly, appeared unconcerned, and almost never looked up to see the evidence Kinne introduced, which included horrific crime scene and autopsy photos, as well as portraits of each of the six victims. But his attempts at manipulation included complaints Jackson had to forward to Judge Meier. He complained about the food and the Judge at the same time and commenced a "hunger strike" over both. (It was not his first while in jail.) "I won't eat again until I have a new Judge," he was reported to have said. Judge Meier responded by formally ordering the Sheriff to serve Belachheb hot meals everyday during the trial.[16] He ate.

Jeff Shaw is convinced that Belachheb's crouched posture and downward gaze during trial was a ruse to reinforce the insanity defense. It is easier, the logic goes, to believe someone to be insane if they appear unfazed or unconcerned when confronted in public with the enormity of their crime.

But sometimes, during breaks and out of the sight of the jury, Belachheb would be taken to a hallway to use the restroom. On one of those occasions, during a chance encounter with Norm Kinne, Belachheb growled. Kinne recalled, "I've prosecuted many bad people, but I never had any of them *growl* at me. He sounded like an animal!" [17]

After months of pretrial motions, investigation and preparation, testimony for the guilt/innocence phase finally began on November 2, 1984. Kinne read the indictment to the jury, to which Frank Jackson replied, "Your honor, and ladies and gentlemen of the jury, the defendant pleads not guilty by reason of insanity."[18]

The first order of business was to establish that the victims were once real, living persons. To do that Kinne called a number of victims' relatives to the stand to identify photographs of the dead. Marcell Ford's sister, Joe Minasi's wife, Janice Smith's father, and Linda Lowe's mother appeared in quick succession. It was harder to get friends or relatives to identify Ligia Koslowski, who was from Chicago, and especially Frank Rance Parker, who was a pimp with an extensive criminal record. Parker had a surviving daughter who was happily married and had a family of her own. She begged Kinne to allow her to stay out of the trial because she did not want her children to know anything about their grandfather. Kinne, who had known of Frank Parker when he was alive, agreed.[19]

After completing her testimony, Mrs. Minasi stepped down from the stand, stopped in front of Belachheb, put her face in her hands, and began to cry. Belachheb continued to look at the floor. Marcell's sister knew better than to look directly at the defendant: "I didn't know how I would react if I did."[20]

The first to testify as to what had happened was John McNeill. He retraced his route from a business meeting to Farfallo's, where he sat next to Belachheb and saw him order a drink, to the fateful shooting at Ianni's. He also educated the jury about his wound, his trip to Dedman Hospital, and how he was extraordinarily lucky to be alive. Most importantly, he characterized Belachheb, while engaged in murder, as "deliberate."[21]

Terry Rippa followed with the most emphatic of the eyewitness testimony. He convincingly testified that since he was attracted to Linda Lowe's beauty, and wanted to ask her to dance, he paid particularly close attention to what was going on at the bar where she sat. He could not help but notice what was happening to Marcell, who was seated to Linda's immediate right. Unlike John McNeill, who was preoccupied with Barbara, Terry faced the bar and saw everything from beginning to end. He was an extraordinarily effective witness when it came to establishing the sequence of events.[22]

The owner of the Hines Boulevard Pawn Shop followed Rippa. He testified about Belachheb's June 2, 1983, purchase of the Smith and Wesson 9-mm semi-automatic pistol he used to commit the

Ianni's murders. Frank Jackson, however, objected to the submission as evidence of the ATF form the pawn shop had completed. Jackson said that certain entries appeared to have been retraced or overwritten with a pen in a different shade of ink. The owner testified that the document was authentic and it was admitted.[23]

Ata, the Iranian waiter employed by Ianni's, who was off-duty but drinking red wine on the opposite side of the bar and looking directly at Marcell Ford, testified to what he saw, which was essentially identical to Rippa's testimony. He added that Belachheb was "so cool, really cool, from the time he started until the moment he finished." He continued, "there was no reaction of anger, madness, or anything. His face was just nothing."[24]

The owner of the limousine service followed Ata to the stand. He spoke of meeting Ligia Koslowski and walking with her from Cappuccino's to Ianni's and of how he pulled Mary, the owner, and Sherlyn, the singer, to the floor as soon as he heard Belachheb pull back the slide on the pistol. He also testified to Belachheb's flight from Ianni's, indicating that Belachheb knew what he had done was wrong.[25]

Kinne's next witness was a paramedic with the Dallas Fire Department. He described how he and his partner set up a triage in an attempt to save whoever could be saved. They quickly determined that only Marcell Ford and John McNeill were alive. It was during this testimony that Kinne focused on the ghastly crime scene photos of the bodies on the dark blue carpet.

"The jury has a right to see exactly what happened," Kinne later related. He never worried that the photos might have the opposite effect of what he intended; that they might look at the photos and decide that only an insane person could inflict such terrible injuries and death.[26]

DPD Police Officers Thomas Haney and G. W. King described how they found and processed Belachheb's white station wagon on Bryson Street, after he ran it into a utility pole. They went into great detail about how the discovery of 9-mm bullets on the front seat alerted them that they might have been on the trail of the Ianni's murderer.[27]

A key prosecution witness, of course, was Bill Parker, who methodically walked the jury through his investigation and arrest of Belachheb in Mohamed's Listi Street home. He also described Belachheb's attempt to portray himself as intoxicated and amnesic.

Bill Parker's investigation, however, was not entirely without controversy. Less than two weeks after Belachheb had been arrested, on July 10, Bill Parker visited Belachheb and talked to him for about four and a half hours. Parker convinced Belachheb to remove his shirt to expose tattoos he had on his upper left arm. Parker took pictures and made a sketch of the faded blue ink. Almost immediately, Ted Calisi, Belachheb's public defender at the time, issued a strong complaint, causing Judge Meier to order that no investigator was to speak to Belachheb without informing her first. She issued her order on July 12; the same day Belachheb slashed his arms with a disposable razor.

Parker's July 10 meeting with Belachheb was never an issue at the trial because the state never attempted to introduce anything that came from it. Kinne wrote in a letter to Billy Prince, the Dallas Chief of Police, that Parker acted properly because there was never any intention to obtain a statement that could be used against the defendant. His intent, Kinne argued, was to obtain background information to determine if the tattoos had any terrorist significance. Finally, Belachheb had been read his rights and he did not indicate that he wanted his lawyer present. The Defense, of course, saw things differently.[28]

Four days after his initial testimony, Bill Parker returned to the witness stand. Jackson was interested in finding out why he had not written down Belachheb's comments as part of his report of his investigation. Why had he not transcribed his conversations with Belachheb at the time of arrest?[29] Parker answered with astonishing candor: It "causes complications in trial."[30]

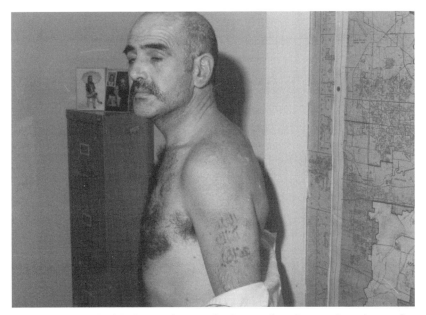

Because the Belachheb murders took place only a few weeks prior to the 1984 Republican National Convention in Dallas, law enforcement officials were concerned about possible connections to terrorists. Dallas Police were particularly troubled by the tattoos on Belachheb's left arm. (Dallas Police Department Files)

Bill Parker's first court appearance was followed shortly by heart-breaking descriptions of the causes of deaths from Dr. Nina Hollander of the Medical Examiner's Office. She used Norm Kinne as a model to illustrate the paths of bullets for each of the victims. Ronnie Ford, Marcell's brother, had to leave the courtroom when autopsy photos of his sister were displayed before the jury. Larry Fletcher of the Dallas County Institute for Forensic Sciences followed with ballistics evidence. No one was surprised when he testified that all the shells and rounds recovered from the victims and from the restaurant walls and floors could be positively linked to Belachheb's 9-mm semi-automatic.[31]

After a tactical police officer named Billy Joe Hill testified about how he was given the murder weapon by the occupants of the Listi

Street house, the prosecution rested its Case in Chief on November 7, 1984 at 9:50 A.M.[32]

Judge Meier turned to Frank Jackson and said, "What say the defense?"

---

[1] Frank Jackson quoted in *Dallas Times Herald*, August 16 and October 28, 1984; *Dallas Morning News*, August 16, 1984; Frank Jackson.

[2] Judge Gerry Meier and Terry Rippa quotes are from interviews; Jeff Shaw.

[3] Frank Jackson quoted in interview.

[4] Judge Meier quoted in interview; Frank Jackson; Norman Kinne.

[5] Jim Spearly quoted in *Dallas Times Herald*, October 28, 1984; Frank Jackson.

[6] Judge Gerry Meier and Jeff Shaw quoted in interviews; *Dallas Morning News*, September, 25, 1984; *Dallas Times Herald*, October 28, 1984.

[7] *Dallas Times Herald*, November 10, 1984.

[8] Judge Gerry Meier quoted in interview; Frank Jackson; *Dallas Morning News*, November 16, 1984; In a gesture of extraordinary cooperation, Judge Meier made her notes and court documents available to me for this book. It is hereafter cited as "Judge Gerry Meier Papers."

[9] The Dallas County District Attorney's Office is still extremely protective of its "work product." Requests by the author of this book to review internal memoranda were rejected by the District Attorney's Office even though the case has been fully adjudicated since the 291st received a mandate from the Court of Criminal Appeals on March 2, 1987—over fifteen years ago. The grounds for that rejection was that the communications were "work product," and thus, privileged. When asked to waive privilege, the District Attorney's Office declined to do so.

[10] Henry Wade quoted in *Dallas Morning News*, August 21, 1984; Judge Gerry Meier Papers.

[11] Norm Kinne quoted in interview.

[12] Rider Scott and Frank Jackson quoted in *Dallas Morning News*, October 30 and 31, 1984; *Texas v Belachheb*, 291st Judicial District, Cause no. F84-75078-SU, et. al., *Defendant's Notice of Intention to Raise Evidence of Insanity Defense*, October 16, 1984.

[13] Bob Knowles quoted in *Dallas Times Herald*, July 13, 1984; *Dallas Morning News*, July 1 and 13, 1984; *Fort Worth Star-Telegram*, July 13, 1984.

[14] Lieutenant H. B. Sherman quoted in *Dallas Times Herald*, November 11, 1984; Jeff Shaw quoted in interview; *Dallas Morning News*, November 13, 1984.

[15] *Texas v Belachheb*, 291st Judicial District, Cause no. F84-75078-SU, et. al., VII, 2290-2317 and 2384-2413.

[16] Judge Gerry Meier Papers; Abdelkrim Belachheb quoted in *Dallas Morning News*, October 28, 1981; Frank Jackson quoted in interview.

[17] Jeff Shaw; Norman Kinne quoted in interview.

[18] Frank Jackson quoted in *Texas v Belachheb*, 291st Judicial District, Cause no. F84-75078-SU, et. al., IV, 843-47.

[19] Ibid.; Norman Kinne.

[20] Marcell Ford's sister quoted in *Dallas Morning News*, November 3, 1984.

[21] *Texas v Belachheb*, 291st Judicial District, Cause no. F84-75078-SU, et. al., IV, 865-92.

[22] Ibid., 893-951.

[23] Ibid., 952-68.

[24] Ibid., Ata quoted on 969-1012.

[25] Ibid., 1013-61.

[26] Ibid., 1062-73; Norman Kinne quoted in interview; Jeff Shaw.

[27] *Texas v Belachheb*, 291st Judicial District, Cause no. F84-75078-SU, et. al., IV, 1073-86.

[28] Dallas County District Attorney Files: Norman Kinne to Billy Prince, July 26, 1984; *Dallas Morning News,* September 25, 1984; *Dallas Times Herald,* July 13, 1984. According to an FBI memo to Norman Kinne dated October, 1984, the tattoo on Belachheb's upper left arm is an Arabic inscription saying, "God save me from further torture." When I showed Bill Parker's drawing of the tattoos to Dr. Fatihah Hamitouche of the Center for Middle Eastern Studies of the University of Texas at Austin, she could only identify the word "God." Dr. Deborah Kapchan of the Anthropology Department of the same university recognizes the words "God Damn."

[29] There is no evidence whatsoever that any documents pertaining to the Belachheb Case were ever improperly withheld or destroyed by the Dallas Police Department, or that anyone ever acted improperly. That said, neither are there investigative reports which begin to document police activities during the investigation. They were never written, and Parker's sworn testimony seems to indicate that it was a systemic practice in 1984. Details of DPD activities were made public during sworn testimony only because the defense elected to go to trial.

[30] Bill Parker; Bill Parker quoted in *Texas* v *Belachheb,* 291st Judicial District, Cause no. F84-75078-SU, et. al., VI, 1966-86.

[31] *Texas* v *Belachheb,* 291st Judicial District, Cause no. F84-75078-SU, et. al., IV, 1122-1223.

[32] Ibid., V, 1225-33 and Judge Gerry Meier Papers.

chapter eleven

For the Defense

> *"What I believe of what he tells me is irrelevant. From a pure legal standpoint, if he tells me he did something for some reason, I am legally obligated to take that story and try to prove it to the best of my ability."*
>
> —Frank Jackson
> Abdelkrim Belachheb's Defense Attorney

I

"You now know what happened at Ianni's on June 29, 1984, and now the defense is going to tell you why it happened." So began the defense of Abdelkrim Belachheb.[1]

Belachheb's wife, Joanie, was Jackson's first witness. She began by describing how she and Belachheb first met and how they came to fall in love and marry. She described her husband as a Moroccan of the Berber Tribe and a Shiite Muslim. As she responded to Jackson's questions, she revealed the details of their unusual relationship—one where love and violence coexisted. She described her husband as "sick enough to kill." She said that she had told many of her friends that he was a time bomb waiting to explode. But she also said that he could be warm, loving, and sharing.

During her testimony, Joanie related the two most harrowing incidents of her life with Belachheb: the time he rammed her head against the back of her sofa and sent her to the hospital for three days, and the time he knocked her to the floor, knelt on her shoulders, placed a gun to her head, and threatened to kill her. Despite the horror she experienced, Joanie asserted that during those instances "he was in terror of me." She said that he was in an "altered state of consciousness" (a term she undoubtedly learned from his doctors) but that she could "see his eyes come back to a state of awareness." In spite of her fear, she kept returning to Charlie (Belachheb), she said, because she loved him.

Norman Kinne's cross-examination completely exposed Joanie and Belachheb's abnormal relationship and Joanie's co-dependency:

> Kinne: Now, let's see, you say that—how long had you been married before Charlie beat you up?
>
> Joanie: Oh, that happened before we got married.
>
> Kinne: Oh, before you got married he beat you up.
>
> Joanie: Uh-huh, that's right.
>
> Kinne: That was the first time he beat you up?
>
> Joanie: Yes.
>
> Kinne: All right. He put you in the hospital; is that the time he busted your skull across the sofa or whatever it was?
>
> Joanie: Yes.
>
> Kinne: Put you in the hospital?
>
> Joanie: Uh-huh.
>
> Kinne: All right. And you went ahead and married him anyway?
>
> Joanie: Yes, I did. When I moved in with him, I was married to him.
>
> Kinne: I beg your pardon?
>
> Joanie: When I moved in with him, I considered myself married to him.
>
> Kinne: All right. But you went ahead with the ceremonial marriage after he busted your skull across the sofa?
>
> Joanie: Yes.

Kinne next questioned her about the other incident she used to illustrate Belachheb's "mental lapse":

> Kinne: He has a gun to your head and *he* is frightened? [Italics added here and below]
> Joanie: Yeah, like he is protecting himself from something, and that's the way he looks.
> Kinne: *He* looks frightened?
> Joanie: Frightened.
> Kinne: Okay. *He* looked frightened when he put the gun to your head and threatened to kill you?
> Joanie: Yes.

Kinne also reminded her that, one week after the shootings, she had told DPD Officer Paul Lachnitt that, "He [Belachheb] is not crazy. He's a no-good revengeful son-of-a-bitch!"

"I deny that. I don't know him," she said of Lachnitt. "I don't know who you're talking about," she insisted as her voice rose. Then she added, "[B]ut I don't recall much of anything that week."

As the heated exchanges continued, Judge Meier had to warn Joanie on three occasions to answer Kinne's questions. After more of Kinne's relentless cross-examination, Joanie finally admitted, "my mind is in shock. It's hard for me to remember things."[2]

Frank Jackson's first expert witness was an anthropologist named Harrell Gill-King. Dr. Gill-King was the anchor of the "culture shock" portion of the defense strategy. "My particular interest in anthropology as it applies to this issue has to do with the effects of movement from one culture to another, especially when those cultures are very different and involve special considerations having to do with adaptation to the culture in which one arrives," he explained.[3]

After reviewing Belachheb's case over a period of fifty to sixty hours, Dr. Gill-King asserted that he had a factual understanding of what happened on June 29, 1984. He testified that, because Belachheb was in a dramatically different culture from his native Berber society, he lacked coping mechanisms and was in culture shock. "Maladaptation is when a person leaves one culture [and] moves to another culture for any length of time. I'm not talking about tourist travel here. I'm talking about becoming immersed in another culture. There is a period of time in which individuals seek the familiar," Dr. Gill-King explained.

Dr. Gill-King offered more specifics. "Now, the Berbers have been religious and political holdouts during the entire period of transition away from colonialism towards self-determination in Arabic culture and Morocco in particular." Belachheb, Dr. Gill-King explained, received a "particularly heavy dose of indoctrination," especially since he was raised by his grandfather—the Imam.

Dr. Gill-King said that the cultural difference between his native indoctrination and what he discovered in America was most apparent in relationships between men and women. He called it "dominance inversion." Belachheb found out during the early morning hours of July 29, that although surrounded by women, he was not the dominant party. "In his dealings with the various women involved . . . he felt, I think, that he was . . . in control of their behavior. He aspired membership in that group, he was flattered by the attentions of these people to some extent, but he felt that he was in control. This is very important to a self-determining Arabic person."

At times, the anthropologist seemed to be describing a computer program rather than a human being. Dr. Gill-King asserted that Belachheb " . . . simply responds to women according to the script, the code, the prescription, the values that his culture has given him regarding women."

Even before describing the nature of the dominance inversion explanation of Belachheb's maladaptation, Dr. Gill-King offered a preface: "First, my concern is not to justify anything that's happened. Here again, I'm here to understand it in the full context of what went on, and so I don't want to say anything that will impugn some of the other victims of this tragedy besides Mr. Belachheb."

It was equally clear, however, that the foundation of Dr. Gill-King's theories and conclusions were grounded nearly completely in what Belachheb told him. For example, when describing the events leading to the shooting itself, he detailed the impact of Marcell Ford's comment, "I can't believe I made love to a monkey like you," and Linda Lowe's pulling of Belachheb's hair. "That's a big 'no-no' in an Arab culture, where women are considered property," Dr. Gill-King explained.

It did not seem to matter to Dr. Gill-King, or to anyone on the defense, that Belachheb was the sole source for both instances. "What I believe of what he tells me is irrelevant," Frank Jackson was quick to accurately point out. "From a pure legal standpoint, if he tells me he did something for some reason, I am legally obligated to take that story and try to prove it to the best of my ability."[4]

While it is likely that Marcell said something highly insulting to Belachheb, which was consistent with her temperament, all of the witnesses of the events just before the shooting flatly reject the suggestion that Lowe pulled Belachheb's hair.

During two cross-examinations, Norm Kinne pounded on that dubious foundation, Belachheb as a sole source, underlying Dr. Gill-King's conclusions. Dr. Gill-King responded by identifying the media, Frank Jackson, Joanie, and psychiatrists for the defense as other sources.

> Kinne: In other words, the defendant tells you, tells his wife, tells his doctor all about his background as a child, but you have not attempted to verify that through any other source other than the defendant himself?
>
> Gill-King: I have not felt that it was necessary.
>
> Kinne: You assume he is telling you the truth?
>
> Gill-King: I do.
>
> Kinne: How many criminals have you dealt with, Doctor?

Dr. Gill-King further explained that, "Anthropologists have no way to proceed except by interviewing members of the cultures with which they are concerned."

After Dr. Gill-King alluded to Belachheb's Moroccan and European experiences, and his criminal record, the door opened for Kinne to pursue Belachheb's extensive criminal history. He asked about almost every crime Belachheb had been charged with in Morocco, Belgium, and Kuwait.

"Mr. Belachheb spent 1976-78 in a Kuwaiti prison for robbery. Was that some kind of Kuwaiti culture shock?" Kinne asked in a voice dripping with sarcasm.

Even if, from an anthropological standpoint, Dr. Gill-King provided expert witness testimony for the defense, the jury had to decide whether to accept his testimony as an excuse for what Abdelkrim Belachheb had done. "All of us here are victims of our values, whether we like it or not," Dr. Gill-King said from the witness stand. But then, some of the jurors must have wondered why Belachheb's wig did not come off of his head, if indeed, Linda Lowe had pulled his hair.

II

The next expert witness for the defense was Dr. Kevin Karlson, a person of impressive academic credentials. This was "the biggest and first case of [his] forensic psychology career."[5]

Dr. Karlson was a graduate of South Dakota State University who had earned a Master's degree in counseling psychology from Texas Christian University in Fort Worth. He had completed his Ph.D. program in clinical psychology from the University of Texas Southwestern Medical Center at Dallas in 1983 and only a year later had graduated with a juris doctor from Dedman School of Law at Southern Methodist University.

During his testimony, Dr. Karlson indicated he had training in sorting out the truth from self-serving lies that criminals can be counted on to tell. Out of about seventy hours he spent working on the case, Dr. Karlson spent about twelve to thirteen hours in direct interviews with Belachheb, during which he administered several tests. He estimated Belachheb's I.Q. to be about 76, but that was probably an underestimate since it was administered in English. Karlson's non-verbal portions of the batteries measured a 75, but more extensive tests administered by technicians for another defense doctor indicated that his I.Q. was closer to 85, or a level just short of the lower end of the average range.[6]

Belachheb's short-term memory was "reasonably decent," but Karlson found his long-term memory to be deficient. Belachheb was unable to discuss the shooting itself, but was able to discuss what had happened immediately before and after.

Dr. Karlson had Belachheb take two projective personality tests that were designed to identify what was psychologically important to the patient. The first was the Rorschach, ink blots to which the patient makes a response. When Karlson gave Belachheb the first card, he turned it around and looked at the back. Karlson interpreted that as a sign of paranoia. After rejecting three more cards, Belachheb gave twelve responses, few compared to the average of 17-25. Karlson testified that such a low rate was typical of an adult with organic brain disorders—and little ability to cope with stress.

The next test was the Thematic Apperception Test (TAT). In the TAT a person is given a series of pictures and asked to tell a story. For example, in one picture a girl is standing in the foreground, the father is pushing a plow in the background, and the mother is standing off to the side. Belachheb spoke of the scene in a "very wistful fashion." He described how this girl had her whole future ahead of her and how important it was for her to be educated, because if she could be educated then she could help her family to improve their position. Soon, he began to cry. Karlson testified that it was very rare for a patient to cry when talking about that picture.

The next test Dr. Karlson administered was the Minnesota Multiphasic Personality Inventory (MMPI). It was a personality in-

ventory using 550 true/false questions. The results indicated that
Belachheb was:

- Indignant and self-righteous
- In psychological distress (a score of 80+ meant psychotic, and
  his score was substantially above that)
- Overwhelmed, out of control, and unable to cope
- Suffering from bodily problems like sleep deprivation
- Severely depressed
- In a state of denial of his psychological difficulties (he was
  vehement about his not being crazy)
- Unable to conform to social expectations resulting in anger
  bordering on rage
- Very paranoid
- In a state of constant anxiety over the situation he is in
- In a state of schizophrenia
- Very egocentric, yet withdrawn

In short, Dr. Karlson found Belachheb to be psychotic and
grossly out of touch with reality.

Frank Jackson then introduced the second prong of the
Belachheb defense—organic brain damage:

> Jackson: Have you compared [the psychological testing with]
> the neuropsychological testing data you have received?
> Karlson: I have.
> Jackson: The combination [of] those factors and the diagnos-
> tic conferences with [other defense experts] and your own
> evaluations, I ask you, based upon those examinations and
> those criteria, do you have an opinion as to whether or not at
> the time of the shootings at Ianni's, Mr. Belachheb knew what
> he was doing was wrong?
> Karlson: I do have an opinion.
> Jackson: What is that opinion, please?
> Karlson: He did not; he could not have.

Karlson was the first at trial to assert that Belachheb was suffering from both organic brain damage and a personality disorder. The condition was "very severe"—even incapacitating.

During Dr. Karlson's examination, Belachheb voiced concerns about his parents back in Morocco. He did not want them contacted, he said, because there would be adverse consequences. During the same session, he told Dr. Karlson, "I am going to be the President of Morocco." [7]

"How could that be?" asked Karlson.

"I really don't know this but Allah knows," Belachheb said confidently.

Dr. Karlson attributed Belachheb's ability to function to a condition called dissociative phenomenon—a condition in which patients appear very impassive, can carry out a complex series of motor acts, and are expressionless.

Dr. Karlson believed that organic and clinical factors were preventing Abdelkrim Belachheb from exercising self-control—episodically. "His inability to control himself, as a result of the permanent damage to areas of his brain that are responsible for providing people with behavioral controls, is probably not ever going to change." Psychiatric hospitalization was Belachheb's only hope.

But under cross-examination Norman Kinne pointed out that Belachheb had not been violent while locked up at the Lew Sterrett Center for the past five months. Dr. Karlson replied that incarceration removed him from stressful situations. Dr. Karlson also reasserted that on June 29 Belachheb did not know the difference between right and wrong, although, he added, that he may know it now (i.e., November 8, 1984). The moral void could have been a "transient, short-term episode."

> Kinne: At what point in time that night did he cease knowing the difference between right and wrong?
> Karlson: It's difficult if not impossible to know exactly.

Shortly afterwards, Kinne illustrated, yet again, that Belachheb appeared to be the sole source of his doctor's information. Dr. Karlson elaborated: "Well, it's my opinion, based on what I know about the facts of this case, that Mr. Belachheb was engaged in conversation with Linda Lowe and Marcell Ford, and the contents of that conversation, as I understand it, are that Linda Lowe was asking him whether or not he had gotten what she asked him to get earlier in the day. He said no, he didn't."

Belachheb alleged that Linda Lowe had asked him to get her a supply of hashish and cocaine, and that they both were drug dealers. The *Dallas Times Herald* had published this tale on October 28, 1984. (The story had a grossly inadequate preamble that cautioned that Belachheb was the primary source of information and then proceeded to report the story as if it had been the product of responsible investigative reporting. This was also the story in which Belachheb spun stories of selling his body at age twelve or fourteen in the gutters of Casablanca, walking all the way to France, and being a revolutionary.) No other evidence ever indicated that Linda Lowe was ever involved in drug dealing, and those who knew her flatly reject the idea as utter nonsense. Neither is there evidence of Belachheb's drug dealing. Drug dealers, even small-time pushers hanging around middle schools, usually have money. Belachheb had none.

Dr. Karlson continued, "At that point Marcell Ford, who was sitting right next to him, said. 'I can't believe I ever made love to a monkey like you.' He apparently turned to walk away. Linda Lowe grabbed him by the back of the hair, as I understand it, and said, 'Leave this lady alone or it's all off with Nick,' which was the gentleman who was going to employ Mr. Belachheb as an exotic car importer. At that point Mr. Belachheb said that he was sure that everybody in the bar was laughing at him, which to me is classic symptoms of someone who is paranoid and psychotic . . . and at that point it is my opinion, that he lost touch with reality."

It was also Dr. Karlson's opinion that Belachheb regained his touch with reality when he rammed his car into a tree on the way to Mohamed's house.

Norman Kinne hammered at the idea of selective memory:

> Karlson: [Quoting Belachheb] "how could I have done what they say I did?" and he seemed very sorry.
>
> Kinne: Oh, he is telling you he doesn't remember what he did. Is that correct?
>
> Karlson: That's right.
>
> Kinne: And as a matter of fact, he never remembered any of those assaults that he has committed over the years?
>
> Karlson: That's right.
>
> Kinne: Assaulted eleven people in a period of about two years in Belgium and he doesn't remember any of them?
>
> Karlson: That's what he says.
>
> Kinne: Put his wife in the hospital over there with four fractured ribs and a broken hand and punctured lung. He doesn't remember that either?
>
> Karlson: Consistent with the clinical picture.
>
> Kinne: I see. Now, he does remember hitting himself in the head with an axe when he is ten?
>
> Karlson: What I suspect is that somebody told him what he did. I don't know that he remembers it, no, sir.
>
> Kinne: Well, what I suspect is that he remembers things that help him but doesn't remember things that hurt him. How does that fit?

III

While testifying for the defense, Dr. Kevin Karlson explained how he felt that there was more to Abdelkrim Belachheb's behavior than just psychosis. "As a result of our confusion [over whether] Mr. Belachheb was having organic problems or . . . suffering from psychosis that was not a result of organic disorder, we referred Mr.

Belachheb to a noted neuropsychologist, Dr. Homer Reed." Dr. Reed has been called the "Father of Neuropsychology."

During testimony, Dr. Reed explained the discipline of neuropsychology as that part of applied clinical psychology that focuses on brain-behavior relationships. Neuropsychologists study the impact of brain damage on behavior.[8] In 1984, there were only about seventy-five board-certified neuropsychologists in the United States.

Dr. Reed testified that he oversaw the administration of six to seven hours of continuous testing of Belachheb. "The test results demonstrated unambiguously that Mr. Belachheb has an injured brain."

During his testimony, Dr. Reed elaborated about his conclusions. "From a neurological point of view there is brain damage. It involves the whole brain, and we would say, then, that it is a diffuse kind of thing, but there are quite sharp gradations. There is an area of maximal involvement in the right temporal lobe," he said as he pointed to his own head to illustrate. "There is another area of maximal involvement in the left frontal parietal area . . . There is some degree of frontal lobe involvement and possibly some degree of subcortical involvement. By subcortical I mean involvement of the lower brain structures."

Dr. Reed added that the brain damage was not progressively disabling, but it was, nonetheless, ongoing in that there continued to be "misfiring" of the neurons—similar to seizures. When Frank Jackson asked him what brain damage does to a person, Dr. Reed answered that, in general, it hampers a person's problem solving abilities by limiting the application of common logic and wisdom others have who are not brain damaged. Brain damaged persons, like Belachheb, do not learn as well, and hence, do not benefit from experience. Dr. Reed then added a corollary: Belachheb was far more vulnerable to disrupting conditions of any kind, all types of stress, and even to things normal people would find innocuous, noise or common confusion. These patients "overload" easily and can handle only a limited amount of stimulation or information.

Otherwise, there is always a danger that everything "disintegrates" much more quickly than it would for a person with an undamaged brain.

> Jackson: Is it likely that a person with all of those problems might commit an act of violence, even a coordinated act of violence and not really know what he was doing at the time?
>
> Reed: Yes, that is a substantial possibility, in my opinion.

On the day of his testimony, November 8, 1984, Dr. Reed examined Belachheb's head. "He has got all sorts of bumps and indentations and scars that are consistent with what are obviously earlier injuries . . . They did not give me any additional information at all. I was, I guess, happy to find that he didn't have a perfectly formed head. I would not have been much put off if he had. You know, I don't put much emphasis on what you can feel with your hands."

During Norman Kinne's cross-examination, Dr. Reed admitted that he had first met Belachheb only that morning when he felt Belachheb's head. Technicians from his Boston office, in fact, had administered the tests he used as the bases for the conclusions he testified to.

Those technicians also provided notations Kinne used to establish that Belachheb had no remorse for what he had done and was far more concerned about whether he was getting any publicity. They noted that Belachheb was surprised, disappointed, and annoyed that they had never heard of him or the Ianni's murders in the Boston area.

Dr. Reed's technicians also noted that, "eye contact [with Belachheb] is <u>constant</u> and rather unsettling at times. He has no quarrels about meeting your gaze." His stare became unnerving, intense, and "unblinking." As they worked, they often looked up from their score sheets to find him staring. "This caused a good deal of internal stress [for] the examiners, which became very tiring, wearing after a long period of time."[9]

Kinne: Let me make a wild guess. Are your examiners female?

Reed: Uh-huh.

In spite of Belachheb's overbearing gaze, the technicians did manage to administer a number of tests. One was the Weschler Memory Scale. He scored a 60, compared to an average of 100. Approximately two-thirds of the population used as a representative sample to norm the instrument score between 85 and 115, which means Belachheb scored in the bottom one percent. In his report to Jackson, Dr. Reed wrote that Belachheb's assessment results "reflected severe impairment of memory functions. On measures of immediate memory, the patient's memory for spatial relationships appeared to be better than his memory for linguistic material. With thirty-minute and sixty-minute delayed recall trials, the patient demonstrated severely impaired memory for both visual and verbal material."[10]

They measured his intelligence as well, placing him in the bottom fifteen percent of the normative group.

All well and good, but Kinne got to the point that concerned him:

Kinne: Does the brain damage that you say he suffers from, did it blot out his conscience? He shows no remorse for what he has done. Is that part of the brain damage?

Reed: I can't answer that. I think it's outside my field of, you know, my expert competence.

Kinne [shortly afterwards]: You are not saying that his brain is damaged to the extent that he doesn't have a conscience any more, are you?

Reed: I am not qualified to comment on a person's conscience.

Kinne cross-examined Dr. Reed four times. Toward the end he injected a bit of Texas chauvinism: "But Mr. Jackson had to go all the way to Boston to bring you down here to Dallas to tell us Texans how the cow ate the cabbage in a case in our community. Is that right?"

"Whether or not he had to is not for me to say. He in fact did," Dr. Reed answered.

IV

Among the doctors retained by Frank Jackson, Dr. Sheldon Zigelbaum was the most influential in shaping the defense. Jackson and Dr. Zigelbaum had met two years earlier at a National Association of Criminal Defense Lawyers Association convention. In early September, Jackson contacted him and asked him to become involved in Belachheb's defense. Before agreeing to get involved, "Ziggy," as Jackson called him, outlined what had to be done, and Jackson saw to it. Dr. Zigelbaum's request for psychological tests is what led to the involvement of Dr. Kevin Karlson and the subsequent conclusion by the two of the existence of brain damage. That conclusion, in turn, led to the involvement of Dr. Homer Reed and his technicians.[11]

The *Dallas Times Herald* reported that Dr. Zigelbaum was one of the fathers of "post traumatic stress syndrome." They also noted that he was a source of fourteen *National Enquirer* stories in a five-year period (1979-84), which included titles such as "People who hate their cars are likely to crash," "How to choose TV shows that will relieve stress," and "How a married woman's signature reveals her personality."[12]

Dr. Zigelbaum essentially summarized the findings of the other doctors. "The significance for me," he said about Dr. Reed's report, "because the findings were so unequivocal that Mr. Belachheb has serious, serious brain damage in a diffuse area of his brain, the significance to me then was that it began to put the whole picture together—not a simple picture, a very complex picture." Belachheb, he continued, was plagued with "uncontrolled episodes of violence," which were totally out of his consciousness. When Jackson asked him to elaborate, he said, "Now these altered states of consciousness . . . sometimes called complex partial seizures with complex behavior that goes on during them . . . are not a straight

line. They don't begin and end. They begin and then consciousness comes back, and then one can go back into the altered state
again, and then consciousness comes back again." He compared it
to football players who have been known to play games and not
remember.

In Belachheb's case, it was the insults from females that brought
about the altered state of consciousness that blocked out his
memory. The insults should be considered in the context of his
cultural background, Dr. Zigelbaum insisted. He theorized that
Belachheb was in a "state of absent consciousness" during the shooting and that it was an incredibly disastrous experience. After it was
over, and Belachheb saw the victims lying on the floor, and he was
standing there with a gun in his hand, he possibly came out of his
altered state of consciousness and realized that it must have been
him who had just killed everyone—without really having any
memory of the experience itself. Only then did he flee Ianni's.

"At the time of that incident and as a result of both a severe
mental disease and mental defect, Mr. Belachheb could in no way
discriminate right from wrong," Dr. Zigelbaum said with confidence.
Elsewhere in the trial transcript he became even more emphatic:
"My opinion is, with a high level of medical certainty, based upon
all the information that we have gathered, that at the time of that
shooting that Mr. Belachheb was not conscious and therefore had
no capacity whatsoever to discriminate right from wrong."

But Dr. Zigelbaum was far less certain when it came to answering Norman Kinne's questions:

> Kinne: At what point in time did he become unconscious?
> Zigelbaum: That's very, very hard to pinpoint, and I can't—I
> don't know. It seems that he remembers everything up until
> the insult or the hair pulling experience with one of the
> women at the bar . . . "

But the most memorable part of Kinne's cross-examination, and
one of the oddest episodes of the entire trial, came when Dr.

Zigelbaum was answering Kinne's questions about the brain damage.

> Kinne: There is a depressed skull fracture on his head?
> Zigelbaum: Would you like for me to show it to you?
> Kinne: Well, you just going to point at it?
> Zigelbaum: No, no, no. You and I can feel it together if you like. I'll show you the other scars if you like.
> Kinne: All right, fine.

Prosecutors seldom, if ever, actually touch a defendant. As a matter of fact, Norm Kinne was more used to having defendants file motions that he not be allowed within three to five feet of them. He thought, "No, I don't want to touch his head!" Then he said to himself, "Why not?"

Kinne and Dr. Zigelbaum walked over to Belachheb, and the doctor placed Kinne's fingertips on the top right hand side of Belachheb's skull. "It was a depression on the top of his head," Kinne remembered, "Hell, I may have some." He also said to himself that, if this was the defense, "go for it, because it's not gonna sell to the jury."[13]

Norm Kinne saved the best question for last. It really summarized the issue facing the jury. He asked Dr. Zigelbaum if he had ever come across anyone who might be mean enough to do what Abdelkrim Belachheb did during the early morning hours of June 29, 1984—and not have some mental deficiency. Dr. Zigelbaum answered, "I have never come across one where mere meanness or the level of meanness is enough to carry out that kind of act."

At 2:55 P.M. on November 9, 1984, the defense rested.

---

[1] Frank Jackson quoted in *Texas* v *Belachheb,* 291st Judicial District, Cause no. F84-75078-SU, et. al., VI, 1234-36.

[2] Testimony is from *Texas* v *Belachheb,* 291st Judicial District, Cause no. F84-75078-SU, et. al., VI, 1237-84.

[3] For the rest of this chapter I intend to cover expert testimony as it was presented chronologically. Documentation of testimony by doctors called by both the prosecution and the defense can easily descend into pedantry. Henceforth, I will provide a citation for

the entire testimony of each individual. My coverage of Dr. Gill-King's contribution to the trial, including testimony and quotes, unless otherwise noted, is from *Texas* v *Belachheb*, 291st Judicial District, Cause no. F84-75078-SU, et. al., VI, 1284-1390.

[4] Frank Jackson quoted from interview; the strict legal obligation that the defense attorney has to vigorously pursue the defendant's version of events does not hold true for a psychiatrist or similar expert hired by the Defense Attorney. The expert is supposed to use professional judgment and opinion in making evaluations and can either accept or reject what the Defendant says. Developing opinions can be based on the facts examined, other information that is furnished the expert, the expert's experience and training, and relevant journals and treatises. I am indebted to Charles Butts, a defense attorney from San Antonio, for valuable advice and guidance on this issue.

[5] Quote is from an e-mail from Dr. Karlson to the author dated August 26, 2002.

[6] My coverage of Dr. Kevin Karlson's contribution to the trial, including testimony and quotes, unless otherwise noted, is from *Texas* v *Belachheb*, 291st Judicial District, Cause no. F84-75078-SU, et. al., VI, 1391-1567.

[7] Morocco has no President. It is a monarchy.

[8] Frank Jackson referred to Dr. Homer Reed as the "Father of Neuropsychology;" my coverage of Dr. Homer Reed's contribution to the trial, including testimony and quotes, unless otherwise noted, is from *Texas* v *Belachheb*, 291st Judicial District, Cause no. F84-75078-SU, et. al., VI, 1568-1621.

[9] The technician's handwritten notes are in *Texas* v *Belachheb*, 291st Judicial District, Cause no. F84-75078-SU, et. al., IX, it is State's Exhibit #90.

[10] New England Medical Center: *Neuropsychology—Test Report*, Abdelkrim Belachheb, October 31, 1984.

[11] My coverage of Dr. Sheldon Zigelbaum's contribution to the trial, including testimony and quotes, unless otherwise noted, is from *Texas* v *Belachheb*, 291st Judicial District, Cause no. F84-75078-SU, et. al., VI, 1628-1748.

[12] *Dallas Times Herald*, November 18, 1984.

[13] Norman Kinne quoted from interview.

chapter twelve

"An altered state of consciousness"

> *"Brain damage is fairly common."*
> —Dr. John Mullen
> an Assistant Professor of
> Neurological Surgery and Neurology

I

After the defense rested, Norman Kinne lined up witnesses who had dealings with Belachheb and were ready to testify that he was perfectly sane. Oh, he was *odd*, and in their minds maybe a little crazy, but he was certainly someone who had enough mental capacity to know the difference between right and wrong.

The first of the witnesses was Beth.[1] She was a secretary for a law firm and the person who had introduced Abdelkrim Belachheb to Joanie. She described Belachheb as a selfish schemer who readily admitted that he needed to marry a woman who had money—an American who could help him secure permanent residency in the United States. According to Beth, he seemed to have found what he wanted in Joanie, who spent large sums of her limited income on his expensive tastes. He had nice clothes, memberships in clubs, and drank to excess in plush bars and restaurants (not to mention his custom wig). Beth even testified that Belachheb shamelessly admitted to using Joanie's money to hunt rich women.

According to Beth's sworn testimony, Joanie had told her that Charlie beat her up so badly that he put her in the hospital. On December 31, 1983, during a New Year's Eve party, Beth asked Belachheb if that was true. "Yeah, I sure did. Bitch deserved it!" he answered.

Beth's testimony struck hard at the notion that Belachheb ever had any feelings of love or tenderness for Joanie, which went a long way towards discrediting Joanie's testimony characterizing Belachheb as sympathetic or sick. Beth was also the first in a line of witnesses to state categorically that during the time she knew him he was quite capable of controlling himself—and did.

During cross-examination, Frank Jackson brought out the point that throughout his interviews with Beth she never related her "bitch deserved it" conversation with Belachheb to him. He also reminded her that in the hallway, that very day, she had told him that she was "more convinced than ever" that Belachheb was crazy. The rest of her testimony consisted of discussions of what she meant by "crazy" and "irrational," with Kinne and Jackson arguing over context.

Kinne's next witness was an Ianni's customer named Stan,* a salesman for a sporting goods store.[2] He testified that on June 29 he and friends went to Ianni's for dinner following a golf game. While there, he had a nice chat with Linda Lowe, a friend of his for the past two years. While seated at one of the small round tables near a corner of the barroom, he observed Belachheb visiting up and down the bar at different spots. He noticed nothing unusual until the shooting started. After the shooting began, Stan described Belachheb's face as very calm. He testified that, while hiding behind furniture, he actually saw Belachheb put the gun to the victims' heads and shoot. "Take that, bitch!" he quoted Belachheb as saying, as the pistol fired missiles into the helpless victims.

After the first round of shooting, Stan went to the victims and saw that he could do nothing for them. When Belachheb returned and started to shoot again, Stan ran out of the back door. Stan's testimony was important because it illustrated that Belachheb's motive was revenge for a perceived wrong, which of course, required conscious thought.

Jackson's cross examination was rather odd in that he started by asking Stan if he had ever been a bookie or into drug dealing. Stan answered, "no" even after Jackson reminded him that lying under oath was perjury. But that line of inquiry did not last long as Jackson turned to questions about how Stan could quote Belachheb, who had a thick accent, and how he could characterize Belachheb's facial expression as angry, when he had never met or seen Belachheb until that night.

The next witness, Nick, Linda Lowe's boyfriend and the owner of a car dealership that had been considering hiring Belachheb to sell its expensive foreign imports, was particularly effective in establishing Belachheb's ability to think rationally.[3]

Nick described how he came to know Belachheb while the latter worked for Walker Limousine Service and how that had led him to suggest that Jim hire Belachheb as a limo driver for his investment firm. Nick said that he had come to believe that Belachheb was a "natural" at selling expensive foreign cars made by Mercedes, Rolls Royce, Ferrari, Porsche, and Lamborghini. Through Nick's testimony, the prosecution presented the jury with a successful businessman who was willing to trust and make an investment in Belachheb—hardly something he would have done for someone he considered paranoid, brain damaged, unstable or insane. Surely, he would not have made plans to have a man who did not know the difference between right and wrong greet customers wealthy enough to buy a Rolls Royce.

Nick also went into great detail about how Linda Lowe, at first charmed by Belachheb's harmless romantic Mediterranean gestures, developed a deep suspicion of him because of his constant gazes. He also flatly established that Lowe had absolutely no influence on who got hired or fired in his businesses. This made allegations of her threats to sabotage Belachheb's new job with Nick, which the defense had alleged was a precipitating factor in

Belachheb's descent into an "altered state of consciousness," most improbable.

Nick's son, John,* followed his father to the stand and testified about Belachheb's displaying a 9-mm semi-automatic pistol and threatening to use it on his employer at First American Investments if he did not get his last paycheck.[4]

After John, Ata, the off-duty bartender seated directly across from Marcell Ford during her altercation with Belachheb, returned to the stand.

> Kinne: Okay. When you saw Marcell push him back, you were watching closely?
> Ata: Yes.
> Kinne: All right. And when he turned to leave the bar, what did you say Linda Lowe was doing?
> Ata: Linda Lowe was lighting up a cigarette. She was not even looking towards the back.
> Kinne: All right. Did Linda Lowe or anybody else reach out and pull [Belachheb's] hair?
> Ata: Nobody.
> Kinne: Did Linda Lowe as much as turn around and even look at him as he walked by?
> Ata: No, never. After he was leaving towards the hallway, then they look at him when he is leaving.
> Kinne: After he is several feet away?
> Ata: Yes.
> Kinne: Okay. Did you see anybody, Linda Lowe or anybody else pull that man's hair or say anything to him?
> Ata: No.[5]

Ata's testimony related to the precipitating event that had supposedly led to Belachheb's "altered state of consciousness," the pulling of his hair—the event that Dr. Gill-King had identified as a "big no-no of Arabic culture," Dr. Karlson's probable point at which Belachheb lost touch with reality, Dr. Zigelbaum's probable point at which there was a loss of consciousness, the event that was an ultimate humiliation at the hands of an insolent American woman, an event powerful enough to bring about the cessation of knowing right from wrong—never happened.

Kinne's goal was to illustrate the ultimate flaw in Belachheb's entire defense: It was based nearly entirely on lies he told his lawyer and doctors—who were obligated (in Jackson's case) or left (in the doctors' cases) to use it to the best of their ability.

Kinne then brought out his own doctors. They were all from Texas, which throughout the trial seemed to matter to the prosecution. The first was Dr. John Mullen, an Assistant Professor of Neurological Surgery and Neurology at the University of Texas Health Science Center in Dallas.[6] Kinne called on him to discuss complex partial seizures where consciousness is altered. Dr. Mullen explained that there are many varieties of complex partial seizures. In one, a patient might "lose consciousness or awareness of their surroundings, begin picking behavior, walking in circles, sitting down, standing up." The many variations of that type of seizure usually last two to three minutes, at longest, and are usually followed by episodes of lethargy.

Kinne also zeroed in on the defense experts' use of different terms, like complex partial seizure and focal temporal lobe seizure, to refer to the same medical phenomena.

> Kinne: Doctor, if someone were to tell us that an individual was suffering from either a complex partial seizure or a focal temporal lobe seizure, they would be, in effect, telling us an epileptic seizure?
> Mullen: That's correct.

The jury, most of whom had probably never heard of "partial complex seizure" before the trial, undoubtedly recognized and understood the term "epilepsy." In 1984 about 1.1 million people had epilepsy in the United States alone and 71,000 of them lived in Texas. About eighty percent of patients with epilepsy can control their seizures and function fairly well.

Dr. Mullen testified that history is most important in the diagnosis of complex partial seizures and that a single seizure is not considered epilepsy. An electroencephalogram and/or CAT scan would be necessary to confirm a preliminary diagnosis, which should be done by a neurosurgeon. Dr. Mullen continued, "There is no stereotype form. Mainly the patients don't all have exactly the same type of pattern so I'll try to give you examples and give you our criteria. The patient can all of a sudden develop a blank stare, cry out, start repeating numbers, simple things like that. Start developing uncoordinated fragmentary, unsustained movements. These are words that we tend to use describing these things. Commonly they will pick at their clothes or flail their arms one way or the other, turning their head to one side or not. If they have something in their hand they may throw it, they may drop it. Picking at clothes is an extremely common form. Basically simple movements, but unaware of their surrounding during the seizure."

Dr. Mullen also helped to de-mystify the concept of brain damage. "Brain damage is fairly common," he said, and while neuropsychological tests can indicate brain damage, "no neuropsychological test can be used to diagnose any form of epilepsy."

After a long "hypothetical," which took four pages of trial transcript, in which he described the uncontested facts surrounding Abdelkrim Belachheb's movements and actions during the early morning hours of June 29, 1984, Kinne got to the heart of the matter.

> Kinne: Will you tell the jury what your opinion is with regards to whether or not the actions of this individual, whether those actions could have been a manifestation of a complex partial seizure?
>
> Mullen: No. I will categorically state no.

In Mullen's opinion, the time it took to prepare, execute, and flee Ianni's, by itself, eliminated any possibility of involuntary actions via complex partial seizure. Mullen pointed out that the average length of such a seizure was approximately twenty-nine seconds, and that movements during such episodes are "simple, uncoordinated, fragmentary and unsustaining."

Under cross examination, Frank Jackson focused on Dr. Mullen's lack of expertise in the area of behavioral medicine; he pointed out repeatedly that Mullen was not a psychiatrist.

> Jackson: No reflections on your credentials, Doctor, I know you are eminently qualified, and the EEG is a good diagnostic tool to determine brain damage?
> Mullen: It's helpful, yes.
> Jackson: And neuropsychology is a good tool?
> Mullen: With a cooperative patient, yes.

Dr. Mullen endured ten "direct" and "cross" examinations, largely due to Kinne and Jackson's sparring over whether Dr. Mullen was qualified to comment on behavior before, during, and after seizures. (He was qualified to comment on behavior *during* a complex partial seizure, which the defense argued Belachheb was having during the shooting.)

After Dr. Mullen, Kinne called a fairly quick succession of witnesses. Sara, the Ianni's patron that Belachheb had tried to pick up earlier that tragic evening, testified that he accepted, in stride, her rejection of his advances and he seemed in control of himself. DPD Investigator Paul Lachnitt testified that when he interviewed Joanie less than a week after the shootings, she said that "He [Belachheb] was a no-good, revengeful son-of-a-bitch," and that when he hit her head on the couch and sent her to the hospital it was because she objected to his going out and running around with other women.[7]

The most damaging testimony of the day, and probably the greatest setback of the trial (for the defense), was when Kinne called Mohamed to the stand.[8]

Mohamed testified that he had known Belachheb for about two years and that Belachheb had moved in with him in his Listi Street house when he first came to Dallas. After about four months, Mohamed asked him to move out, but he befriended Belachheb in other ways. On June 29, 1984, Belachheb owed Mohamed money, about $100. When Mohamed asked for his money back, Belachheb became enraged. On the night of the shooting, Belachheb "threw" his last paycheck from Augustus' Restaurant at Mohamed. (Mohamed ended up giving the check to Joanie.)

To a hushed courtroom, Mohamed described how Belachheb arrived at his home around 12:45 A.M. After describing how Belachheb pulled a gun on him, and how they wrestled in the front yard and ended up in one of the back bedrooms, Mohamed's testimony put to rest the question of whether Belachheb had any memory of what he had done a half hour earlier in Ianni's. Years later, Frank Jackson admitted "none of that looked good."[9]

According to Mohamed, Belachheb said that he had enough of this life. Then Belachheb admitted, "I have just shot some people, killed some people . . . a bunch of people." When Mohamed and Yanouri doubted him, he insisted that a radio be brought into the room so that they could all hear about it together on the news.

Mohamed also testified that Belachheb also admitted to wanting to kill from the moment he woke up that morning. Throughout the conversation, he continued to ask for the return of his gun, indicating to the jury that he was at least giving thought to using it again, long after his "altered state of consciousness" allegedly ended when he rammed his car into a utility pole on the 9200 block of Bryson. The best Frank Jackson could hope for was to remind Mohamed that, in an earlier conversation they had in Jackson's office, Mohamed had indicated that he could not remember the *exact words* of the exchange between him and Belachheb that night, and that there was a possibility that Belachheb might have said, "I *think* I may have killed a bunch of people on Midway," or something close to that.

DPD Sergeant Bill Parker also returned to the stand to reinforce Mohamed's theme that Belachheb knew exactly what he had done earlier that evening.[10] Parker spoke of his conversation with Belachheb, and how Belachheb navigated them through a labyrinth of northeast Dallas streets back to the police station. Parker volunteered the opinion that Belachheb was thinking of his defense—always.

After Bill Parker, Jim, the businessman who befriended Belachheb on a number of occasions, took the stand to testify about his relationship with Belachheb.[11] "I would say he was more a friend than an employee," the investment broker said. The jury must have wondered how such a polished and successful businessman could have been taken in by a guy like Belachheb. "I had no problem with the guy. He was always more than helpful with me. He was willing to do anything for me. Had I not had a rule within my company that I never hire a person that someone fires, I'd have hired him back."

Jim made no reference to seizures, fits of anger, delusions of grandeur, or any of the unpleasantries associated with Belachheb's defense. Indeed, in Jim's world, Belachheb was quite normal—even virtuous.

Kinne's next witness was easily the most controversial of the entire trial. Controversy always followed Dr. James P. Grigson, a Dallas-based medical doctor who specialized in psychiatry. Even in 1984, Dr. Grigson had been tagged "Dr. Death" by death penalty opponents who *hated* him. (Hated is not an exaggeration.) At times, death penalty opponents were not the only groups he angered. The *Dallas Times Herald* reported that Henry Wade, the District Attorney, was so livid with Dr. Grigson at one time, that Wade ordered his staff not to retain him as an expert ever again. (He later rescinded the order.) And in a gesture only Henry Wade could get away with, he allegedly asked the judges of Dallas County not to appoint him to cases either.

The occasion of Wade's wrath was Dr. Grigson's testimony on behalf of a Sheriff named Don Byrd, who had been brought to trial on a drunken driving charge in July 1983. At that trial Grigson testified that Byrd's car accident might have been caused by a mild stroke rather than intoxication. Byrd was acquitted.[12]

The inescapable fact is that Dr. James P. Grigson will be the enemy of *whomever* he is opposing in a court. Regardless of what one may think of his psychiatric worldview, he is an extraordinarily effective witness. [13]

"We *created* Dr. Grigson. We caused him to become Dr. Death. Then he became too hot and we couldn't use him anymore," Kinne observed in 2002. Prosecutors created "Dr. Death" because before a death sentence could be assessed in Texas, the jury had to agree on three issues regarding a convicted defendant:

- whether the defendant acted deliberately and reasonably expected that death would result
- whether the defendant would *probably* commit further criminal acts threatening society
- whether, in cases of provocation by the victim, the defendant acted unreasonably.[14]

The second of the trio of issues asks if there is a high probability that a convicted person "would constitute a continuing threat to society." It's called "future danger" and it requires predicting the behavior of an individual—which is an extraordinarily difficult science. Dr. Grigson had the reputation for being quite comfortable establishing future danger. By 1995, he had testified in approximately 150 capital murder trials—an average of five per year for the previous thirty years. Prosecutors liked his courtroom presence. Jeff Shaw recently said of him, "He makes a great witness."[15]

Defense attorneys have quite a different take on Dr. Grigson. "He has a reputation for rolling over lawyers with his folksy bullshit," said Frank Jackson, who added, "His approach to psychiatry has about as much efficacy as voodoo or rattling bones."[16]

The prosecution and the defense are equally passionate in their opposite views of Dr. Grigson—for the same reason: He is effective before a jury. Norman Kinne remembers a courtroom exchange he once had with Dr. Grigson:

> Kinne: Would you state your name, please?
> Grigson: James *Paul* Grigson

Kinne wondered—*Paul?* After the session ended Kinne walked up to him and asked, "James *Paul* Grigson? What's that all about?"

"Well, you look like you have a good group of Baptists on the jury so I thought I'd give them my full Biblical name," Grigson replied.[17]

In the Belachheb case, Dr. Grigson was not trying to predict future danger. It was not a capital murder trial, and he was not even retained by the state. Judge Meier appointed him. Her criterion was experience in criminal cases, and having been involved in over 11,000 criminal cases, over 5,000 of them major felonies, Dr. Grigson was probably the most experienced psychiatrist in the United States who had ever walked into a courtroom.

So, on November 9, Dr. James Paul Grigson walked into the courtroom to face two men: Norman Kinne, who believed that "[Grigson] is very impressive. He talks to a jury and they eat him up" and Frank Jackson, who expected "folksy bullshit."

In motions before Judge Meier, Jackson was ordered not to refer to Dr. Grigson as "Dr. Death." He was also instructed not to refer to Grigson's problems with Henry Wade or the Sheriff Byrd trial in any way.[18] (It was kind of a *quid pro quo*. "The State would not have wanted Grigson to be referred to as Dr. Death and the defense would not have wanted Kinne to refer to the defendant as an animal, which he was sometimes prone to do. Once it is said, it is impossible to have it unsaid," Judge Meier recalled.)

"There is a tremendous difference in evaluating a criminal and evaluating a person who walks off the street and asks to see a psychiatrist," Dr. Grigson began.[19] He had met with Belachheb on October 8, 1984, in the staff lounge of the county jail. In rather short order, Dr. Grigson had concluded that Abdelkrim Belachheb was a sociopath. He explained to the jury that sociopaths are not persons suffering from an illness. Instead, the term is used to describe people with certain characteristics: they do not have a conscience; they are interested only in their own self-gratification and pleasure; they break the rules; they manipulate and use other people; and they have a complete disregard for other people's lives. Belachheb was "at the very top. . . . You could not get any worse."

Kinne used Dr. Grigson to focus on the scores of psychological tests the defense doctors administered.

> Kinne: Are you familiar with the Rorschach test, the Minnesota Multiphasic battery of tests, some of these other tests for intelligence, etc.?
>
> Grigson: Yes, sir. I am.
>
> Kinne: You did not administer any of those to the defendant. Is that correct?
>
> Grigson: No, sir. They would be worthless. . . . They were not developed to evaluate people in a legal sense. They were developed in order to actually test people that are sick. It does not work in a legal setting because there is too much to gain from distorting the test—and they are easily distorted.

"Folksy bullshit" or not, the jury was eating it up. Dr. Grigson was getting through. Then he addressed organic personality syndrome: "He doesn't have any of the symptoms or characteristics of the organic brain syndrome. You would have mental changes, personality changes. He's been that way ever since he has been a kid. I mean, there is no change in his personality. There would be impairment in terms of his intellectual functioning, in terms of reasoning and judgment; there would be emotional ability with all the sudden unexplainable crying episodes, difficulty with concentration, difficulty with attention span, perhaps some type of motor paralysis. He has none of these."

Next Grigson responded to questions about paranoid personality disorder. "No. Because he is more socially involved with people, more actively involved, whereas the paranoid doesn't involve himself in social interaction. They are reclusive, usually withdrawn because they are distrustful, whereas Mr. Belachheb socializes, dances, goes to a bar which again, the paranoid personality would not do. They would be fearful of, you know, what might happen to them so they are reclusive, a whole lot more reserved."

Dr. Grigson next addressed the brain damage defense. "There is no significant degree of brain damage present that would show up or affect his thinking, his behavior, his feelings." During his examination, Belachheb displayed no motor paralysis, no cranial nerve deviations, his eyes focused normally, his tongue and speech worked, there was no facial paralysis, he was able to smoke and hold cigarettes, his coordination was normal, there were no sudden unexplained episodes like crying; he never rambled, there were no memory losses, except only those related to violence—it was completely selective, he never seemed confused. Grigson added that "the fact that they may have an ingrown toe nail doesn't necessarily affect the fact that they are competent or incompetent to stand trial, or that they are sane or insane."

Dr. Grigson concluded that Belachheb was a sociopath who chose to do wrong and got some satisfaction out of it that "the rest of us don't understand." Belachheb had no remorse. "His only regret was about being in jail."

On cross examination, Frank Jackson effectively pointed out that Dr. Grigson spent a total of one hour and forty minutes with Belachheb. He suggested strongly that Grigson had his mind made up that Belachheb was a sociopath even before the examination.

The next in the parade of doctors was Dr. Elliott Ross, an Associate Professor of neurology and psychiatry at the University of Texas Southwestern Medical School.[20] His testimony related to complex partial seizures. He began by stating that, unlike the doctors sponsored by the defense who preceded him to the stand, he would not testify under oath that a person could suffer from such seizures without first reviewing an electroencephalogram. He also challenged the notion that complex partial seizures could be diagnosed using psychological testing.

He then addressed the theory that Belachheb suffered from partial complex seizures while committing murder. Ross flatly rejected the notion: there was too much time involved; he made complex, serial decisions in a correct and logical sequence to accomplish a goal.

Ross also rejected the organic personality syndrome explanation. First, he asserted that a doctor would have to know what the patient's personality was before the injury to know if there was a change. Diffuse organic brain damage, from a neurological viewpoint, means severe brain damage that affects many, or almost all, structures of the brain. Usually these people are in the intensive care units on respirators.

Dr. Ross verbalized an opinion that thoughtful jurors must have been pondering all along: If Abdelkrim Belachheb suffered from diffuse brain damage, which was spread throughout his brain, why did it not manifest itself as some form of physical disability? What were the chances that such diffused damage could *only* affect his judgment and memory, and then *only* when he was violent?

Of all the doctors involved in the trial, only one was called for reasons other than a medical or psychological expertise. On November 10, Dr. Abraham Halpern took the stand for no other purpose than to discredit Dr. James Grigson.[21] It was a stunning tribute to Dr. Grigson's effectiveness as a witness.

At the time, Dr. Halpern was the President of the American Board of Forensic Psychiatry and the Director of Psychiatry at United Hospital of Porchester, New York.

> Jackson: Is his [Grigson's] reputation such—or do you have an opinion as to whether or not his reputation is such that it would entitle him to be believed under oath? Just yes, do you have an opinion?
> Halpern: I have an opinion.

Jackson: What is that opinion, sir?

Halpern: Well, his reputation is such that the conclusions that he verbalizes under oath are not considered objectively truthful and therefore are not to be believed.

Dr. Halpern's testimony might have been more effective had he not been made to admit that all but one of his sources of information from Dallas County were law partners or associates of Frank Jackson. The other source was someone he had spoken to on the phone for about ten minutes. He knew nothing of Dr. Grigson's examination of Belachheb, had never seen Belachheb himself, and had a working knowledge of the case that consisted of reading that morning's newspaper. Dr. Halpern was, however, able to supply an impressive list of forensic psychiatrists from throughout the country who, at meetings and conventions, had a shared disdain for Dr. Grigson's ubiquitous "future danger" testimony in capital murder trials. (But again, future danger was not an issue; Belachheb was not charged with capital murder.)

Kinne: And Dr. Halpern, they flew you all the way down here from New York just to tell this jury how bad a doctor's reputation in their community [i.e., Dallas County] is? Is that correct?

Halpern: That's correct. They felt—

Kinne: That's all. Thank you.

The last of the doctors to testify had been the first to see Abdelkrim Belachheb. Dr. Clay Griffith, a medical doctor specializing in psychiatry, had been appointed by Judge Meier to determine if Belachheb was capable of participating in his own defense.[22] Judge Meier's criterion, experience dealing with criminals, for appointing a psychiatrist had applied to Dr. Griffith as well. He had been in private practice in Psychiatry in Dallas for twenty-five years and had examined over 6,000 people charged with felonies.

"There is a vast difference between a person who schedules an appointment and evaluating someone who is charged with a felony,"

Dr. Griffith insisted. "Rarely does a patient spend their time lying to the doctor." He first interviewed Belachheb on July 1, 1984, to determine competency. On October 7, and again on October 27, Dr. Griffith tried to talk to Belachheb but he refused to come out of his cell.

The July 1 interview lasted two hours and forty-five minutes. Dr. Griffith was able to do enough to render an opinion as to Belachheb's sanity and competence. When asked why he did not administer a plethora of tests, as the defense had done, Griffith answered, "It was not necessary to administer any tests. Belachheb was verbal enough for the doctor to form an opinion. Those tests are not designed for persons who are charged with crimes . . . [They] are designed for persons who are really interested in learning more about themselves . . . No matter what's built into the test they still can be manipulated."

Dr. Griffith concluded that Belachheb was an alcoholic and a narcissistic sociopath. "I found that his intellectual functioning was really quite good. Certainly within the average range and maybe even a little above," he added. Belachheb felt very strongly that American women created all of the problems he had because they are so aggressive. But then, Griffith related, there was a long list of people who have caused him problems. He accepted no blame for any of his tribulations.

"It indicates to me that he is a real, full-blown, upper end of the scale sociopath."

On the Halstead-Reitan Test which indicated brain damage, Dr. Griffith said, "I wouldn't quarrel with it because it really has nothing to do as to whether he knew right from wrong or that he was killing people."

He added, "If he had brain damage, it had to be minimal. If he had we would have run EEG's and CAT scans—but there was no indication of it."

During his cross examination, Frank Jackson and Dr. Griffith sparred over whether Belachheb was a sociopath or whether he was paranoid and brain damaged. The sometimes-contentious exchanges also included a long debate over whether it was possible for a patient to intentionally deceive and invalidate test results. Dr. Griffith argued that psychological tests were designed for cooperative patients, genuinely motivated to improve their own mental health. He added that the length of the testing was irrelevant to its validity if the test-taker sought to manipulate the results.

> Jackson: You are saying a person accused of a crime can fake six hours of neuropsychological testing?
>
> Griffith: They can fake throughout the test, yes.
>
> Jackson: And you have testified about what some people might do if they have a paranoid personality disorder, but—Dr. Griffith, I'm through with you. I have no further questions.

Moments later the state and the defense rested.

II

Assistant District Attorney Rider Scott had been seated at the state's table throughout the trial. He was the member of the team who had methodically questioned each of the prospective jurors during *voir dire*. But during the guilt/innocence phase, he said little. Occasionally, he made objections, but for the most part, the case for the state was a Norman Kinne performance.

Closing arguments, however, entitled the prosecution to open, the defense to respond, and the prosecution to close. (It is an advantage rendered to the state because they have the burden of proving guilt beyond any reasonable doubt.) Rider Scott opened, probably sensing that the jury had tired of expert testimony. "There is nothing in the law that requires you to give any weight whatsoever to any of the expert testimony in this case . . . You can judge this just on your plain, common sense education and background."[23]

One by one, Scott listed Belachheb's crimes, from allegedly bombing a police station in Beni Ammar, Morocco, to more assaults in Brussels than the jury could possibly remember. He re-

minded them that Belachheb had spent two years in prison in Kuwait, that he had nearly killed his long-suffering wife in Belgium,
and that he had then decided to flee. Belachheb picked up in the
United States where he left off in Europe and nearly killed another long-suffering wife. "Culture shock for twenty-one years!"
Rider Scott said incredulously as his voice rose. He reminded the
jury of Belachheb's use of the word "bullshit." Ata, an eyewitness
seated about six feet away from Marcell Ford, remembered
Belachheb saying, "I'm tired of your bullshit!" as he pulled back
the slide on the pistol.

"Now let me ask you this: You are suffering from culture shock,
you are a Moroccan, you don't understand American customs, you
sure don't understand Texas because you have been out on the
West Coast with those California folks out there. Does he say, 'I
have had enough of your camel dung?'"

Scott also reminded them of how creepy Linda Lowe thought
Belachheb was. Scott quoted her: "He stares at me. Makes me feel
uneasy," she told Nick. It was possible that the last words she ever
heard were from Belachheb, "Take that, bitch!"

How could epilepsy be responsible for such a slaughter? "He
has the blood of six people on his hands and the remorse of no
one in his heart. He is a moral vacuum. . . . If this is a seizure, in the
history of the literature it is an historical first."

Then Frank Jackson rose.[24] He appealed to the jury to be enlightened. "It's a cerebral case for thinking individuals," he said,
speaking quietly in front of Kinne and Scott. He reminded the jury
of the definition of insanity: "Because of a severe mental disease or
defect the defendant, at the time of the offense, didn't know what
he was doing was wrong." Insanity, he reminded them required
only a preponderance (fifty-one percent) of the evidence.

"Insanity is not a medical term," Jackson continued. "Insanity,
by the testimony, is a legal definition for a complex psychiatric
phenomenon, and that's what we are dealing with. We are dealing
with a real . . . vital living concept in the law, and until it's taken out

of law, ladies and gentlemen, jurors like you, lawyers like myself and lawyers like Mr. Kinne and Mr. Scott are going to have to deal with it no matter how much they don't like it."

Frank Jackson then closed by challenging the jury, again. "It's a reasonable deduction from the evidence, ladies and gentlemen, that in the very outset of this particular episode it was apparent to any enlightened community that Abdelkrim Belachheb, at the time of the shootings at Ianni's, was crazy."

Long before the Belachheb trial, Norman Kinne had been tagged the "screamer" because, as Judge Meier observed, "he gets rather loud during final arguments."[25]

He did not ask the jury to be farsighted or enlightened. Like Rider Scott, he hoped they would use their common sense.

Kinne pointed out that the whole thrust of the defense—test results, behavior, background, sequence of events, cultural maladaptation, self-inflicted head trauma, beatings as a child, insults from American women, selective memory, dogmatic Islamic indoctrination—everything—had come from Belachheb. Kinne said that to believe the defense would be to believe Belachheb never lied or sought to manipulate tests and people to his own benefit. "I don't decide who you are going to believe and neither does Mr. Jackson. You decide," Kinne reminded them.

Slowly and methodically, in a volume that ranged from a whisper to a scream, he walked the jury through a minute-by-minute story of what happened on June 29, 1984. At each step, he sought to demonstrate the improbability of mental disease or defect. Meanwhile, Abdelkrim Belachheb sat passively, his legs crossed, throughout the oration.

It was all quite theatrical, which Judge Meier allowed. "I'm probably a little more tolerant on that when it comes to final arguments," she admitted, adding that she was once a prosecutor herself.[26]

If the trial had been reduced to closing arguments, the jury had a fairly simple choice. They could either be "enlightened" or have "common sense."

[1] My coverage of Beth's contribution to the trial, including testimony and quotes, unless otherwise noted, is from *Texas* v *Belachheb,* 291st Judicial District, Cause no. F84-75078-SU, et. al., VI, 1753-77.

[2] My coverage of Stan's contribution to the trial, including testimony and quotes, unless otherwise noted, is from *Texas* v *Belachheb,* 291st Judicial District, Cause no. F84-75078-SU, et. al., VI, 1777-91.

[3] My coverage of Nick's contribution to the trial, including testimony and quotes, unless otherwise noted, is from *Texas* v *Belachheb,* 291st Judicial District, Cause no. F84-75078-SU, et. al., VI, 1792-1841.

[4] *Texas* v *Belachheb,* 291st Judicial District, Cause no. F84-75078-SU, et. al., VI, 1841-45.

[5] Ibid., 1845-50.

[6] My coverage of Dr. John Mullen's contribution to the trial, including testimony and quotes, unless otherwise noted, is from *Texas* v *Belachheb,* 291st Judicial District, Cause no. F84-75078-SU, et. al., VI, 1850-97.

[7] Ibid., 1897-1907, Paul Lachnitt quoted Joanie, 1907-1918.

[8] My coverage of Mohamed's contribution to the trial, including testimony and quotes, unless otherwise noted, is from *Texas* v *Belachheb,* 291st Judicial District, Cause no. F84-75078-SU, et. al., VI, 1934-1966.

[9] Frank Jackson quote from interview.

[10] My coverage of Bill Parker's recall to the witness stand, including testimony and quotes, unless otherwise noted, is from *Texas* v *Belachheb,* 291st Judicial District, Cause no. F84-75078-SU, et. al., VI, 1966-87.

[11] My coverage of Jim's contribution to the trial, including testimony and quotes, unless otherwise noted, is from *Texas* v *Belachheb,* 291st Judicial District, Cause no. F84-75078-SU, et. al., VI, 1987-2015.

[12] *Dallas Times Herald,* November 13, 1984.

[13] During research for my two previous books, *A Sniper in the Tower,* and *Bad Boy from Rosebud,* as well as this book, and my untitled forthcoming book, my investigations included questions of insanity. As a result, I have analyzed the transcripts of five murder trials and interviewed several prosecutors, defense attorneys, and investigators. With the exception of the sole surviving officer of the court of McDuff's 1966 Tarrant County murder trial, Dr. Grigson's name came up as someone I needed to contact as a "valuable resource." I have not done so. With the exception of an e-mail exchange with Dr. Kevin Karlson, who no longer accepts forensic psychology cases, I have not contacted any of the expert witnesses for any of my books. I prefer analyzing their testimony at the time of trial.

[14] Texas House of Representatives: *House Study Group, Daily Floor Report,* March 11, 1985.

[15] Jeff Shaw quoted in interview.

[16] Frank Jackson quoted in interview.

[17] Quotes are from an interview with Norman Kinne.

[18] *Texas* v *Belachheb,* 291st Judicial District, Cause no. F84-75078-SU, et. al., Motion in Limine in Judge Meier Papers, November 12, 1984.

[19] My coverage of Dr. James Grigson's contribution to the trial, including testimony and quotes, unless otherwise noted, is from *Texas* v *Belachheb,* 291st Judicial District, Cause no. F84-75078-SU, et. al., VI, 2018-81.

[20] My coverage of Dr. Elliott Ross's contribution to the trial, including testimony and quotes, unless otherwise noted, is from *Texas* v *Belachheb,* 291st Judicial District, Cause no. F84-75078-SU, et. al., VI, 2105-58.

[21] My coverage of Dr. Abraham Halpern's contribution to the trial, including testimony and quotes, unless otherwise noted, is from *Texas* v *Belachheb,* 291st Judicial District, Cause no. F84-75078-SU, et. al., VI, 2163-97.

[22] My coverage of Dr. Clay Griffith's contribution to the trial, including testimony and quotes, unless otherwise noted, is from *Texas* v *Belachheb,* 291st Judicial District, Cause no. F84-75078-SU, et. al., VI, 2198-2236.

[23] Rider Scott's closing arguments are in *Texas* v *Belachheb,* 291st Judicial District, Cause no. F84-75078-SU, et. al., VI, 2290-2317.

[24] Frank Jackson's closing arguments are in *Texas* v *Belachheb,* 291st Judicial District, Cause no. F84-75078-SU, et. al., VI, 2318-83.

[25] Judge Meier quoted from interview; Norman Kinne's closing arguments are in *Texas* v *Belachheb,* 291st Judicial District, Cause no. F84-75078-SU, et. al., VI, 2384-2413.

[26] Judge Meier quote from interview.

chapter thirteen

For the Jury

> *"You are the exclusive judges of the facts proved, of the credibility of the witnesses, and of the weight to be given their testimony, but you are bound to receive the law from the Court, which is herein given to you, and be governed thereby."*
>
> —Judge Gerry Meier
> in her charge to the jury

I

From his arrest on June 29, 1984, to the end of the trial, his wife Joanie visited Abdelkrim Belachheb about once a week. During that time, he lost approximately thirty pounds and, since he no longer wore a black wig, his real, graying hair grew out on the sides of his bald head.[1]

In 1984, the 291st Criminal District Court was located in what was then called the Government Center. At the time of the trial, Judge Meier's courtroom was located on the "Civil Side" of the 5th floor, which meant it did not have direct access to the jail. Each day of his trial, Belachheb was escorted across the hall and through a stairwell. (Which was why Judge Meier prohibited cameras on the entire floor.) Because of death threats against Belachheb, Judge Meier arranged for a high level of security. Metal detectors, far less common in 1984 than today, were set up at the doors.[2]

On November 14, the jury began deliberating. Judge Meier informed them that all of their communications to her had to be in writing. She provided one of her personal notepads for the foreman to use.

Following lunch, the jury began deliberating at 1:28 P.M. About an hour later, the foreman requested some of the test results that Drs. Reed, Karlson, and Zigelbaum, all defense experts, had referred to in their testimony. They also asked for the exhibit list. A half hour later, they requested Dr. Reed's notes. By 4:06 P.M., they were requesting similar notes, but by the prosecution Doctors Griffith and Grigson, and all of the crime scene and autopsy photos. They also asked to see the gun. Judge Meier informed them that they had received all the doctors' notes that had been submitted into evidence. Ten minutes after their last request for doctors' notes, the foreman asked the court for coffee and tea, and offered to "trade" the beverages for pieces of cake someone brought into the jury room.[3]

It appeared that the jury was getting ready for serious and extended deliberations, which is often a bad sign for the prosecution. After dinner, the foreman sent another note to Judge Meier requesting a transcript of Norman Kinne's cross examination of Dr. Kevin Karlson. Judge Meier replied that the jury could only have the testimony read to them by the court reporter, and then only if there was a dispute among the jurors as to what the testimony was. They also asked for the "restaurant layouts" and the receipt of the purchase of Belachheb's 9-mm Smith and Wesson semi-automatic pistol.

By 10 P.M., the time set by Judge Meier as the time to retire for the evening, the jury had not reached a verdict. They were sent to a hotel.

The next day, November 15, 1984, the jury resumed deliberations at 9 A.M. At 10:10 A.M. the foreman knocked on the door and handed the bailiff a note torn from Judge Meier's pad:

To: Judge Gerry Meier

Your Honor, the jury has reached a unanimous decision

[Edward*]

Foreman

Shortly afterwards, Judge Meier held court. She looked over the crowded courtroom and gave one of her stern warnings: "I want no noise at all. If you feel you can't control yourself, leave now." Then she turned to the jury.

The Court: Mr. [Foreman] you may remain seated. I will ask you in each case whether the jury has reached a verdict. In Cause Number F84-75078-SU has the jury reached a verdict in that case?

Foreman: We have, your Honor.

Marcell's sister and Joe Minasi's wife, a friendship created out of tragedy, held hands. Linda Lowe's mother, Gloria Edge, clung to her husband's arm. Joanie nervously played with her hands and shook with anticipation.

The Court: I will read your verdict: "We, the jury, find the defendant guilty of the offense of murder, as charged in the indictment…"

Judge Meier did not refer to victims by name. The first verdict read was for Cause Number F84-75078-SU and was the indictment for the murder of Marcell Ford. Except for the officers of the court, no one knew which cause number was attached to which victim. Marcell Ford's brother, Ronnie, did not relax until all of the verdicts were read. Only then did he know for sure that his sister's murder had been avenged.

As Judge Meier read each verdict of guilty, victims' relatives began to relax and exchange bittersweet smiles. When the jury was excused, members of the tragic confraternity cried openly and hugged one another. "We got that [guy]," cried Gloria Edge.[4]

"When the jury says something, that's the way it is," Judge Meier said recently. They had listened to twenty-seven hours and forty minutes of testimony and deliberated five-and-one-half hours to reach their guilty verdicts. After being dismissed, the foreman admitted to the press that "it was hard for all of us" during the three week trial that usually saw a packed courtroom and intense scrutiny. He told the reporters gathered that Jackson was not able to prove the "severe mental defect or disease" requirement that rendered Belachheb incapable of knowing right from wrong. At first, according to the jurors willing to talk, they were split. The evidence they requested pretty well substantiates that claim; at first it was defense focused—then it was prosecution focused.

"I was fascinated. At times I felt rather sorry for him. Other times I didn't," added a twenty-seven-year-old female juror. Like many jurors in many cases, she indicated that she tended to believe what she saw with her own eyes—before accepting complicated psychiatric theories: "I couldn't pick up any real sign of human life [from Belachheb]. The only sign I got that he could even understand English was when the prosecution [Norman Kinne] was feeling scars on his head. He started to point to scars on his face and eyebrows, and that told me he knew what was going on."[5]

Common sense won over enlightenment. It usually does. Juries are never filled with academics out to impress one another with how visionary they are. Prosecutors will use their quota of preemptory challenges to disqualify such prospective jurors. Juries usually consist of people who have jobs, work hard, and behave themselves. Abdelkrim Belachheb asked a jury of common folk, each living lives with their own challenges, disappointments, and frustrations, to believe that being a Berber caused culture shock so profound that it brought about an act of mass murder. If true, common sense causes one to wonder why there aren't hundreds of Berber men murdering arrogant American women throughout the United States and other industrialized countries.

He asked the jury to believe that knocks on his head caused diffused damage throughout the brain that manifested itself, not in any observable physical handicap, but *only* in episodes of violence, and *only* then in bars, cafés, or at home with a defenseless wife.

He asked the jury to believe that an insult brought about an epileptic "fit" that lasted at least thirty to forty-five minutes, or nearly 100 times longer than an average seizure, and that he could not remember anything about what he had done. Most of the jurors, if not all of them, knew of epilepsy before entering the courtroom, and surely none of them has ever seen decision-making and coordination during a seizure the likes of which took place at Ianni's on June 29, 1984.

In Orwellian fashion, Abdelkrim Belachheb asked the jury to see him as suffering from paranoia while visiting nightclubs, dancing, and preying on women—sometimes successfully.

He asked the jury to believe he had no memory of committing murder or of his flight by driving a complicated route (at least eight to ten turns, including a parking lot, city streets, and a freeway with entrance and exit ramps).

He asked a jury—men and women who all knew of someone who at one time or another had banged his or her head, sometimes seriously during auto accidents, falls, or sporting events—to believe that what he had done at Ianni's was the result of a self-inflicted wound thirty years earlier when he was ten.

For the defense, the jury saw serious men of science trying to explain what happened at Ianni's by relying on their specialty as a solution. Psychiatrists saw disorders and mental illness; neurosurgeons saw diffuse brain damage; an anthropologist saw culture shock. Some of the jurors must have wondered if a CPA could have been brought in to find an accounting cause-effect relationship for the Belachheb murders. Even Frank Jackson commented on the resulting controversy on experts: "I had some [experts] who said to me, 'Sure, what do you want me to say?'"[6]

But the same holds true, of course, for the prosecution experts. By 1992, Dr. James Grigson had testified in 144 death penalty cases, 139 times for the prosecution, of which 131 of the defendants were sent to death row. By October of 2000, in a *Texas Defender Service Report,* the American Civil Liberties Union reported that he had testified in at least 390 capital cases in Texas alone.[7]

The Belachheb case was not a death penalty case calling for Dr. Grigson to predict "future danger." He was there to share his diagnosis of Belachheb as a sociopath, which he was qualified to do. Still, he illustrates how it is hard to believe that *anyone's* personal attitudes toward crime and punishment can be purged from the science they advocate in a court of law.

On the other side, Dr. Sheldon Zigelbaum stated unambiguously during trial that he had never seen anyone who could be so mean as to be a murderer. Presumably, since meanness is not an option, Dr. Zigelbaum can be counted on to find a psychiatric explanation for murder, and thus, he will never appear for the prosecution in a death penalty case. As Bill Parker says, rhetorically, "Anyone who says that [no one is mean enough to kill] does not understand murder."[8] Another interpretation of Dr. Zigelbaum's science, taken to the extreme, is that there is no such thing as murder.

Dr. Grigson has no problem giving scientific testimony he knows will result in the execution of another human being—and he is good at it—which is why he was sought after by so many and despised by as many others. "They have lost their right to live, or to freedom, because of what a terrible thing they have done," he has said about capital murderers.

Drs. Zigelbaum and Grigson are at opposite ends of a spectrum that has common sense as its center. In general, juries fall in the common sense center, and this is why, for all its faults, American justice works.

But those who despise Dr. Grigson, frustrated by his effectiveness as a witness and eager to neutralize him, resort to name-calling: to them he is "Dr. Death." The moniker has followed him for decades. On occasion, however, he has given his critics ammunition. The *Dallas Morning News* reported that Dr. Grigson was once asked by a judge to examine a defendant for competency who had cut off his penis and one of his testicles. "Dr. Grigson found the man sane" and presumably reported such to the court.

In 1980, the American Psychiatric Association (APA) reprimanded him for examining defendants for competency and then using that information for predicting future danger. Two years later, he was reprimanded again for allegedly testifying that he was able to predict future danger with 100% accuracy. The APA alleges that he claimed that impossible level of statistical competency without first having examined the defendant in whose trial he was testifying.[9]

A Florida professor of sociology and ethics has called Dr. Grigson a "charlatan masquerading politics under the guise of science."[10] In response, Dr. Grigson said, "There has been—there still is—a group that's opposed to the death penalty. They're not only trying to stop me from testifying, they're trying to stop psychiatrists from all over the state from testifying."[11]

A careful review of the Belachheb trial transcript shows defense experts that, at times, came close to being condescending toward the jury. After describing his academic qualifications, Dr. Harrel Gill-King, testified: "Let me try to say this delicately . . . in a case like this, no matter how hard the system of justice attempts to produce rational, intelligent peers, jurors, witnesses, and so forth, there is a sense in which because of the difference in cultures involved here, an individual probably cannot ever, by definition, be met by a jury of his peers."[12] Some of the jurors must have wondered if they were being told that they were not smart enough to understand what was going on—no matter how carefully they listened. The jury was also told by the same expert that unless they believed the defense "we can march backward into the dark ages."

Later, Frank Jackson told the jurors that accepting the arguments the defense presented would be a sign that they were accepting the "concepts that should prevail in an enlightened society." In essence, he implied that a guilty verdict could come only from unenlightened people.[13]

And so, much of the Belachheb trial was a parade of doctors lined up to do battle over the minds of the jurors. "They [the experts] all sound stupid when they disagree," an unidentified expert said just after the Belachheb trial. At least some jurors must have been haunted by the possibility that *none* of the experts really knew why Abdelkrim Belachheb did what he did on June 29, 1984.

Even before and certainly after the Belachheb trial, philosophically opposing "experts" pointed accusing fingers, called each other names, denigrated one another, cried "politics," and questioned each other's integrity. Common sense dictates that doctors, whether sponsored by the defense or the state, no matter how brilliant or enlightened, still cannot read minds. Until behavioral science reaches a reliable and measurable level of accuracy appropriate for challenges like predicting future danger, or explaining what criminals were thinking while gunning down innocent people, perhaps defendants must be judged on *what* they have done—not on a presumption of *why* they did it.

Resigned to the only loss he has ever suffered while presenting an insanity defense, in an interview for this book Frank Jackson admitted, "The reality of this case is that it was almost impossible to overcome six bodies."[14]

And maybe it should be. Doctors and lawyers do not define murder or insanity; the people of Texas do through their Legislature, and *they* are the ones who sit on juries.

II

As the tension died down after the guilty verdict on all six counts of murder and one count of attempted murder, Judge Meier and the officers of the court still had business to tend to. Texas has bifurcated criminal trials, which means there are separate proceedings or phases called "guilt/innocence" and "punishment."

The punishment phase of murder trials usually sees the state introducing a history of how the defendant is a habitually bad person. In this phase, the state can introduce extraneous offenses. In

Texas, for example, a death penalty cannot be assessed unless a jury is made to believe that a person convicted of capital murder is a "continuing threat" to society. The punishment phase calls for the prediction of an individual's future behavior, which is often as accurate as attempting to read minds. [15] It is also a time for the defense to bring on friends or relatives of the defendant to say nice things, to "humanize" the accused. In the Belachheb case, however, Jackson had a problem. "I couldn't come up with anybody that would say nice things about Charlie," Jackson said. Joanie would have, but as a witness during the guilt-innocence phase she was a near-disaster.[16]

In the Belachheb trial, the death penalty was not an option, and Frank Jackson had already opened the door to all of Belachheb's prior crimes in Morocco, Kuwait, and Belgium as part of the insanity defense; they were explored, in depth, during the guilt/innocence phase.

> Judge Meier: We are now at the point for the punishment hearing. What says the state on punishment?
> Kinne: State rests, your Honor.
> Judge Meier: What says the defense?
> Jackson: Defense rests, your Honor.
> Kinne: State closes.
> Judge Meier: Mr. Jackson.
> Jackson: Defense closes.[17]

That was it. All that was left were closing arguments for the punishment phase, the second round of jury deliberation, and Judge Meier's pronouncement of sentence.

After Judge Meier read the charge to the jury for the punishment phase, Rider Scott rose and said, "May it please the Court. Members of the jury, the State will waive its right to open argument. However, reserve the right to close by Mr. Kinne." Things were moving really fast.

Frank Jackson stood to deliver the final argument. "This verdict has gone a long way to invalidate the insanity defense in our society at any rate, because there is no question as to the quality of the expert testimony that you have heard," he said.

Then Jackson did a little predicting of his own. "Regardless of what verdict you reach, Abdelkrim Belachheb has been, will be assessed the death penalty, and that's the foregone conclusion. He won't survive. So what I was trying to get across to you, ladies and gentlemen, is the validity of—I was trying to ask you to tell me and the rest of this community what do you do with a person with a deranged mind? How do you treat them? What do you do with them? And if there is one person on this jury that doesn't think that Abdelkrim Belachheb has a deranged mind then you just have not listened to any of the testimony in this trial, especially from the defense side."

Frank Jackson had conducted a creative defense he had paid for out of his own pocket. Six people positively identified Abdelkrim Belachheb as the gunman; he was caught two hours after the crime with blood and brains on his clothes and the murder weapon was recovered. Yet it took the jury five and one-half hours to find him guilty.

After asserting that the jury must not have been listening to his experts, during the punishment phase of the trial, Jackson said that the trial was "one of the most fair trials" he had ever been a part of. Then he asked the jury to "search their hearts and consciences" but not to "second-guess" themselves. After only a few minutes, he thanked the jury and returned to his seat. Jackson was a good lawyer who saw the handwriting on the wall. He had not even made an attempt to tell them what to decide.[18]

Norman Kinne was quick to congratulate the jury on their verdict and praise them for the five-and-one-half hours they took to "thoroughly" consider all the evidence. Then he appealed to the jurors' sense of outrage. "Is there one person on this jury . . . who thinks that Abdelkrim Belachheb gives a damn about any of those people? If he is sitting here with his head bowed and he is feeling sorry, he is feeling sorry for himself."

Next, Kinne appealed to the jury's sense of fear. "If there is any one of you who would like to go into a restaurant in Dallas County and see Abdelkrim Belachheb chasing women there, then give him less [than the maximum penalty.]"

And finally, Kinne told the jury what he wanted them to do. "I'm going to ask you to assess his punishment at life plus a ten thousand dollar fine in each one of the cases wherein he is charged with murder, and for twenty years, a sentence of twenty years and a ten thousand dollar fine in the attempted murder case."[19]

It took the jury one hour and three minutes to reach a verdict. "We, the jury, having found the defendant guilty of the offense of murder, assess his punishment at confinement in the Texas Department of Corrections for life and assess a fine of ten thousand dollars." The same verdict was read six times, once for each cause. For the attempted murder of John McNeill, the jury sentenced him to twenty years and a fine of ten thousand dollars.[20]

As the prison terms and a total of $70,000 in fines were read, Belachheb lowered his head and rubbed his eyes. Legend has it that in some trials, when the time came to pronounce sentence from the bench, Judge Meier leaned across her desk and snapped at the defendant: "Get up!" She did not for this trial. "Would you stand, Mr. Belachheb," she said.

"Oooo, here it comes," thought Norman Kinne.

She assessed what the jury recommended, and "stacked" the sentences, meaning they were to be served consecutively, not concurrently. Belachheb got the maximum.

From the back of the courtroom Joanie tried to reach him but deputies kept her away. "You heard what they said. It's all over," Belachheb said as the bailiffs grabbed his arms and walked him towards the door.

The day before Joanie had walked out of the courtroom and said, "I think I am a victim, too. A victim of an indifferent society."[21] Prison records, though incomplete, indicate that she was to become the only person Abdelkrim Belachheb would ever have on his list of visitors. She remains a mystery. Why was she ever attracted to a man who had such utter disrespect, even contempt, for women? How could anyone be attracted to a man who genuinely believed that women did not want to be "treated nice"?

Frank Jackson has said of Belachheb, "He had some type of special lure for women." Jackson was also convinced that there was "little doubt" that Belachheb had relations with some of the victims. Belachheb's first wife, Jenny, said he was the only man who ever "turned her head." His second wife called him a "gift from God." Probably, as Frank Jackson remembered of Joanie, she was an "older lady who got enchanted by a foreigner's charm. She really loved him."[22]

Other, stronger women, saw him for what he was. "I think he *thought* he was [a ladies' man]," observed Judge Gerry Meier, one of few in the courtroom, the *Dallas Times Herald* reported, who could return his icy gaze and stare him down.

"I don't think he was so slick," added Melinda Henneberger, who admits today that she went into the case thinking he was insane. She still believes it was obvious that no well person could have done what he did. But, on the other hand, she feels that the defense not only failed to meet the legal definition of insanity, it would have been laughable in any other context. When it came to women, "He just knew who to pick." But unlike Jackson, Henneberger sees Joanie as a self-aware older woman who "knows that she got taken in by a younger guy. . . . She thought she was a fool for letting him take advantage of her," Henneberger remembered nearly twenty years later.[23]

Abdelkrim Belachheb looked harmless enough to most of the women he met, but soon they regretted ever having touched him. Some were first intrigued by his superficial good looks, his accent—and his grandiose lies. They saw Middle Eastern mystery—a rare chance to be attended to by an Omar Sharif-like character.

But Belachheb's visible demeanor was as fake as his hair. The more astute soon discovered that he was a parasite. Linda Lowe is a good example of that pattern. When she first met him, he kissed her hand and charmed her. It did not take her long to despise him. After many years of playing piano in hotels and nightspots she could spot his kind—and she wanted nothing whatever to do with him. Belachheb's reaction to her contempt, after he murdered her, was to claim to have had sex with her and call her a drug dealer. Norm Kinne called it "baloney," but Belachheb's vitriol was reported in one Dallas newspaper. Some still believe it today.[24]

III

It turns out that Belachheb's romantic persona was not the only thing about him that was fake. "He was very much a con man," remembered Frank Jackson. "I think he figured that he could con his way out of spending time in prison."[25] Jailers who had to monitor him twenty-four hours a day were anxious to get rid of him. Some of them saw, and others had read, about how Belachheb seemed so "out of it" in the courtroom. That was not the same person they saw constantly pulling stunts to get attention, vociferously searching newspapers for articles about what he had done, faking heart attacks, demanding milk shakes, and claiming hunger strikes. "We wanted to get him out of here as fast as we could so we could get back to normal operations. We had enough of him," said Bob Knowles, who ran the jail and arranged for an unmarked car to take Belachheb to the Texas Department of Corrections only two hours after he had been sentenced. (Under normal circumstances, convicted criminals were taken in groups to prison in buses that ran twice a week.)[26]

But before he could be sent away, Belachheb had to be sentenced by Judge Meier. He was led into the court on November 15, 1984, wearing prison garb he detested and shackled with waist, wrist, and leg irons. "If Moroccan eyes are the windows to the soul, his soul is a vast, expansive blackness," said Rider Scott, who carried his "Murdering Moroccan" file with him as he left the courtroom. "When they took him out, he fixed us with a stare that was ice cold."

By 4:30 P.M., Belachheb was led to the car Bob Knowles had waiting for him. Television cameras recorded a crying Belachheb, lips quivering and tears streaming down his cheeks, strutting in leg irons toward the exit. For two weeks, Belachheb had sought to portray himself as an out-of-touch, mentally ill and/or brain-damaged defendant unaware of what was going on as he stared at the floor. "All of a sudden he woke up!" remembered Jeff Shaw, who had been seated directly behind Kinne and Scott throughout the trial.[27]

"He was crying because of his own ass," remembered Norman Kinne.

And the tears did not last. "It wasn't long until he was his old self," Bob Knowles, Commander of the jail, told reporters the next day. "The car wasn't even out of Dallas and the tears dried up." One of the deputies who drove Belachheb to Huntsville said he was quiet and well-behaved.

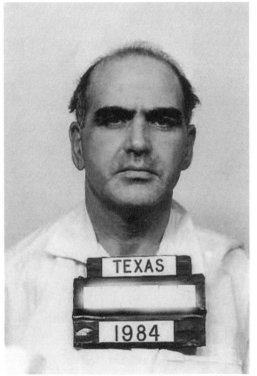

Mug shot of Abdelkrim Belachheb taken by the Texas Department of Corrections shortly after his arrival at the prison system in November of 1984. Unlike other convicted criminals in Dallas County, Belachheb was taken immediately to the prison only two hours after sentencing. "We had enough of him," said a Dallas County Jailer. (Texas Department of Criminal Justice)

"We had a flat tire and I talked to him while the other officer changed it," the deputy said. "He asked a lot of questions about where he was going and what would happen to him there. He asked me if they would hurt him there, and I assured him they wouldn't. He thanked me several times for answering his questions."[28]

On that day, prosecutors reminded reporters that because Abdelkrim Belachheb could not be brought to an execution chamber, he would be eligible for parole on June 29, 2004—the twentieth anniversary of the Ianni's Massacre.

IV

The verdicts brought about an occasion for debate over insanity, what it should be, and whether the American criminal justice system was working. Clouding the debate, however, was the memory of John Hinckley, Jr.'s March, 1981, attempt to kill President Ronald Reagan, who had just won re-election with one of the largest electoral majorities in American history. Hinckley pleaded not guilty by reason of insanity and was acquitted. Interestingly, Reagan himself was far more forgiving of his assailant than many who held the President's political worldview. Hinckley was confined to St. Elizabeth's Hospital in Washington, DC., where he underwent intensive psychiatric treatment.[29]

Much of the American public also remembered how San Francisco supervisor Dan White killed Mayor George Moscone and supervisor Harvey Milk in 1978, only to argue diminished mental capacity. White was convicted of voluntary manslaughter rather than murder because the jury accepted a diminished capacity defense based on testimony that White was suffering from untreated depression. A manifestation of that depression was the conversion of the health-conscious White, into a "junk food" junkie. It was offered as evidence of depression. Thus, the birth of the infamous "Twinkie Defense," which has come to symbolize the lengths to which defendants will go to avoid responsibility for what they do. And, right or wrong, it also shows how far lawyers and doctors are willing to go to assist them. White was sentenced to seven years in prison and was paroled in 1984, the same year as the Belachheb murders, after serving just five years. [30]

Less than three weeks after the Ianni's shooting, James Huberty murdered twenty-one people, including small boys on bicycles, in and around a McDonald's Restaurant in San Ysidro, California. Had that happened in Texas, many assumed, he would not have been eligible for the death penalty.

John DeLorean, an auto magnate and principal owner of the company that manufactured stainless steel "DeLorean" cars, was found not guilty of drug dealing, even though his illegal transactions were videotaped and shown to a jury. DeLorean's defense was government entrapment. Narcotics investigators, he argued, had taken advantage of the financial downfall of the DeLorean Company and enticed him to smuggle cocaine for badly needed cash.

High profile cases often give the public the illusion that criminals can make outlandish claims as a defense—and that it works. At the center of this illusion is the insanity defense. The reality is very different. In 1980, only four years before the Belachheb trial, over 80,000 criminal cases were heard in Texas, and only twenty resulted in not guilty by reason of insanity verdicts. (That is 2.5 one-hundredths of one percent.) [31]

"The people of Texas decide what's criminal and what's not and what's sane and what's insane," Norman Kinne has asserted. "They send legislators [to the capitol] to do that."

Two days after the trial ended, Rider Scott said, "It won't have any bearing at all on the insanity defense since in this case the defendant was not insane. But it could have an impact on capital murder legislation." And indeed, as the Texas State Legislature geared up for their 69th Regular Session in January 1985—less than two months away—capital crime bills were falling into the hopper. [32]

---

[1] Dallas County District Attorney Files: Undated newspaper clipping from the *Dallas Times Herald*.

² Judge Gerry Meier.

³ Judge Gerry Meier Papers

⁴ *Texas* v *Belachheb,* 291ˢᵗ Judicial District, Cause no. F84-75078-SU, et. al., VII, 2420-2425; *Dallas Morning News,* November 16, 1984.

⁵ Judge Meier quoted in interview; both jurors are quoted in *Dallas Morning News,* November 16, 1984.

⁶ Frank Jackson quoted in *Dallas Morning News,* November 18, 1984.

⁷ *Dallas Morning News,* February 16, 1992; the figure of 390 cases is taken from the American Civil Liberties Union: Freedom Network News, *Lawyers call for changes in death penalty in Texas,* which was posted on their website on July 4, 2002.

⁸ Bill Parker quoted in interview.

⁹ *Dallas Morning News,* February 16, 1992.

¹⁰ Florida professor quoted in *Dallas Morning News,* February 16, 1992.

¹¹ Dr. James Grigson quoted in *Dallas Morning News,* July 26, 1995.

¹² Dr. Harrell Gill-King quoted in *Texas* v *Belachheb,* 291ˢᵗ Judicial District, Cause no. F84-75078-SU, et. al., V, 1284-1390.

¹³ Dr. Harrell Gill-King and Frank Jackson quotes are from *Texas* v *Belachheb,* 291ˢᵗ Judicial District, Cause no. F84-75078-SU, et. al., V, 1284-1390, and VII, 2318-2383.

¹⁴ Frank Jackson quoted in interview.

¹⁵ Predicting an individual's future behavior is very difficult. Predicting the behavior of a group can be done much more accurately, and the larger the group the better. For example, auto insurance companies are generally good at predicting the accident rate of male, teenage drivers—it is quite high when compared to all other groups. But that does not necessarily mean that the male, teenage driver *next door* will get into an accident.

¹⁶ Ibid.; the "near-disaster" reference is my assessment of Joanie's testimony.

¹⁷ *Texas* v *Belachheb,* 291ˢᵗ Judicial District, Cause no. F84-75078-SU, et. al., VII, 2427.

¹⁸ Ibid., Frank Jackson quoted, 2429-33.

¹⁹ Ibid., Norman Kinne quoted, 2433-40.

²⁰ Ibid., 2440-43.

²¹ Ibid., 2440-50; Abdelkrim Belachheb quoted in *Dallas Morning News,* November 16, 1984; Norman Kinne quoted in interview; Joanie quoted in *Dallas Times Herald,* November 15, 1984.

²² Frank Jackson quoted in interview.

²³ Judge Gerry Meier and Melinda Henneberger quotes are from interviews.

²⁴ Confidential source.

²⁵ Frank Jackson quotes are from interview.

²⁶ Major Bob Knowles quoted in *Dallas Times Herald,* November 17, 1984.

²⁷ Rider Scott quoted in *Dallas Morning News,* November 16, 1984; Jeff Shaw quoted from interview.

²⁸ Norman Kinne quoted from interview; Bob Knowles quoted in *Dallas Times Herald,* November 17, 1984; the Deputy is quoted in *Dallas Morning News,* November 11, 1984.

²⁹ Hinckley shot Reagan in a pathetic attempt to impress movie actress Jodie Foster. He obsessed over her for many years after the attempted assassination. Finally, after eighteen years and reportedly significant progress in his psychiatric treatment, Hinckley was allowed to leave the hospital but only under close supervision. He eventually won the right to unsupervised furloughs, but after only one month, in May 2000, those privileges were revoked when guards found a book about Jodie Foster in his room. *American Experience,* www.pbs.org/wgbh/amex/reagan/peopleevents/ pande02.html, visited on September 7, 2002.

³⁰ On October 21, 1985, Dan White committed suicide by attaching a garden hose to the exhaust pipe of his car. He died of carbon monoxide poisoning.

³¹ *Dallas Times Herald,* October 28, 1984

³² Norman Kinne quoted from interview; Rider Scott quoted in *Dallas Morning News,* November 17, 1984.

chapter fourteen

"Dying by littles"

> *"The [capital murder] statute fairly well
> covered the field, but it doesn't cover this.
> . . . As far as I am concerned it ought to
> be."*
>
> —Norman Kinne
> Assistant District Attorney, Dallas County

I

Not long after Abdelkrim Belachheb shot and nearly killed
John McNeill, McNeill met with Norman Kinne as the latter
prepared for trial. McNeill fully expected that one day he was going to be able to witness Belachheb's execution. Kinne had the
task of telling McNeill that the crime Belachheb had committed
amounted to six counts of murder—not *capital* murder, meaning
no death penalty and certainly no execution. John became angry
and the best Kinne could do was assure him that the law was going
to be changed.[1]

"Charlie [Belachheb] got the maximum penalty under the law,
which is not enough," Kinne told the press immediately after trial.
"He should have gotten the death penalty."[2]

There was even some question as to whether Judge Meier had
the right to "stack" Belachheb's life sentences. In 1984, any sentence could be stacked, except for some instances of theft. Shortly
after she sentenced Belachheb, Frank Jackson called Judge Meier
at home and said he didn't think she could make the sentences

consecutive. He referred her to the statute mentioned above, which applied only to theft. "It is an odd turn of events that now he would be tried for death but his sentences, if he did not get death, could not be stacked," Judge Meier recently said. Had she not stacked his sentences, it is possible that Abdelkrim Belachheb could be on parole today, if he had behaved himself after his arrival there.[3] (More on this later.)

As soon as the verdict came in, State Representative Tony Polumbo, a Democrat from Houston, filed a bill with the Clerk of the Texas House of Representatives. It was numbered HB 8 (House Bill 8) and was later referred to Polumbo's Committee on Jurisprudence. Patricia Hill, a Republican from Dallas, signed on as co-sponsor. Two weeks after the Belachheb trial, the two legislators joined House Speaker Gib Lewis to announce that the Lewis "Crime Package," was going to include HB 8.

"The Penal Code tells me we think more harshly of robbery than a second murder," Polumbo said. "Had my bill been in effect, he [Belachheb] could have been sentenced for capital murder."[4] It was only the first echo to bounce off the walls of the Legislature during the next five months.

Polumbo's HB 8 sought to expand the list of capital murder offenses to include the murder of more than one person. The proposed "multiple murder" statute, included murders committed either during the "same criminal transaction" such as an act sometimes referred to as "simultaneous mass murder" like what Belachheb, Charles Whitman, or James Huberty did, or murders "pursuant to the same scheme or course of conduct," such as serial killing like Henry Lee Lucas and Kenneth Allen McDuff. It further proposed to make murder a capital offense if the defendant had a previous murder conviction.[5]

From the Committee on Jurisprudence, the bill was referred to a Subcommittee headed by Polumbo. The Subcommittee reported a re-written bill and submitted it as a "complete substitute." Four other bills in the Senate and two in the House expanded the capital murder umbrella, but HB 8 became part of the Speaker's package.[6]

Had it been introduced in the absence of the Belachheb murders, HB 8 might well have sailed through the Texas Legislature anyway. But the events of June 29, 1984, left no doubt about the eventual outcome; the Speaker candidly admitted that the publicity generated by the Belachheb trial would make it "easy" for the bill to pass.[7]

The source of the outrage was that despite the fact that Belachheb had gunned down six people, his life was spared because in 1984 the Texas Penal Code defined only five types of capital murder:

- the murder of an on-duty peace officer or firefighter
- murder in the course of kidnapping, burglary, robbery, aggravated sexual assault, or arson
- murder for hire
- murder while escaping a penal institution
- murder of a penal employee while incarcerated in a penal institution.

Abdelkrim Belachheb had done none of those things.

While the Belachheb case outraged most lawmakers, great care had to be taken to correct the "loophole" that saved him. Texas and federal courts had already found the statute, as it existed, constitutional. Significantly altering it might bring about judicial scrutiny and an unwelcome invalidation of the entire death penalty statute. It had happened before.

Before 1972, the Texas law (that had been ruled unconstitutional) had defined eight capital felonies—murder with malice, murder complemented with rape, armed robbery, treason, perjury resulting in the execution of an innocent person, the second conviction for transferring narcotics to a minor, kidnapping for extortion, and first degree lynching.

In 1972, the famous *Furman* v *Georgia* case had included appeals filed separately by two Texas death row inmates named Lucious Jackson, Jr. and Elmer Branch. They had been convicted of rape and sentenced to death.

In *Furman v. Georgia,* the Court ruled that the death penalty, as it was administered, i.e., giving juries near-unlimited discretion over sentences, was unconstitutional. But, the victory for anti-death penalty advocates was short-lived. Through *Furman,* the Supreme Court "taught" states how to make death penalty laws constitutional, and almost every state rushed to pass legislation assuring a more "equal" application—making executions far more, not less, common in the United States. At the time of the *Furman* ruling, nearly 600 men and women on death rows throughout the country, including 127 in Texas, had their death sentences commuted to life in prison.

The Legislature had to take care to write the new statute so that it could withstand judicial review.[8]

Opponents of the bill, and the death penalty in general, capitalized on the fear some had of a Supreme Court setting aside all death penalties handed down since *Furman.* In a vain attempt to derail the measure, opponents argued that the crimes of people like Belachheb were so rare that they did not merit the risk. Other opponents added, ignoring the trial jury's verdict, that Belachheb was deranged and that no statute would have prevented him from killing.

The opponents also added that the part of the bill that allowed for the death penalty for those who had already been convicted of murder also allowed for the possibility of a person being put to death, in part, because of a murder that may have been committed as long ago as decades earlier. Minority legislators voiced a concern about increasing the scope of a penalty used disproportionately against minority and indigent defendants—people seldom able to afford adequate legal counsel.[9]

HB 8 advocates saw it as the correction of "a glaring omission" in the capital-murder statute. "People who do not commit any of the crimes now defined as capital murder, yet do kill more than one person, cannot get the death penalty under current law." The most such criminals could receive, as the Abdelkrim Belachheb case showed (and was cited), was a life sentence as first-degree felons, with the possibility of parole in twenty years. "Such an outcome is an insult to the victims, their survivors, and society, because the statute placed a higher value on property than on human life."

Even opponents of capital punishment admitted that such a legal condition was odd. In an interview with the *Dallas Morning News,* George Dix, a University of Texas law professor admitted, "It seems obvious the statute is anomalous when it provides the death penalty for killing one person for fifty cents but not if you kill six people just because you hate them."[10]

Then came horrific scenarios: "The way the statute is written, some people could murder a whole family and yet not receive the death penalty unless they were also stealing the family's property or breaking into their home," one analysis of the bill read. HB 8 would eliminate this "illogical result." When addressing the Criminal Jurisprudence Committee, Representative Tony Polumbo pointed out that in 1984, a person could poison the drinking water of an entire city, killing all of its inhabitants, and still not be given the death penalty.

"Imagine a man walking into a bar and killing six people, most of them strangers," Polumbo told the Committee, referring of course, to Abdelkrim Belachheb.[11]

HB 8's sponsors also defended their proposal's constitutionality: "This bill would not jeopardize the constitutionality of the capital murder statute as opponents have argued. The US Supreme Court struck down previous statutes allowing for the death penalty because jurors had no individual discretion in deciding whether a convicted criminal deserved the death penalty. The current Texas statute contains provisions for the jury to decide the punishment in capital murder cases and it has been upheld by the Supreme Court."

It made no sense to argue, the sponsors asserted in debate, that it is not fair for someone who has committed a murder in the past to get the death penalty for committing another murder many years later. Such was conclusive evidence that those criminals have proven they are unreformed killers; *they* are the ones who deserved the death penalty.[12]

In which case, HB 8's sponsors sought to avoid a contentious debate on capital punishment, *per se*. The death penalty was already on the books, the Texas Legislature was not considering its abolition, and the Supreme Court had already upheld it. The bill, Representative Polumbo reminded everyone, merely sought to make a "fair and reasonable" extension of the capital murder statute by adding what was arguably the most heinous of all crimes—mass murder and serial killing.

Polumbo also reminded his colleagues that insanity was not an issue either; that statute was left untouched and defendants still had access to it as a defense.[13]

As she spoke before the Committee on Criminal Jurisprudence, Representative Patricia Hill, undoubtedly thinking of James Huberty and Abdelkrim Belachheb, also argued that the current death penalty statute had to be revised because "In 1973 when our death penalty law was passed, mass murder was an aberration. Since that time it has become a state and national disgrace."

The House committee held its first public hearings on February 11, 1985, less than two months after Belachheb's conviction. The Speaker of the House, Gib Lewis, started the discussion in the larger context of his "Crime Package."

The first of the witnesses was Rider Scott, one of the two men who prosecuted Abdelkrim Belachheb. He delivered background to the committee on Belachheb's long list of violent crimes over four different decades and on three continents. Then he displayed pictures of the victims and explained what happened at Ianni's on June 29, 1984. An Assistant District Attorney from Harris County (Houston, Texas) sat next to Scott and testified in favor of the measure as well, meaning that representatives from the two largest District Attorneys' offices in Texas delivered the same statement of support.

Rider Scott yielded the microphone to the President of the "Parents of Murdered Children" who warned the committee that "for capital murder offenses anything less than the death penalty is an insult to the victim and society."[14]

The first to testify against the measure was the Reverend Bob Breihan of the United Methodist Church of Austin, Texas. He represented a coalition of churches called Texas Impact, which concerned itself with human rights issues. In some of the most compelling and articulate testimony against capital punishment, the Reverend Breihan argued forcefully that the death penalty has never been shown to deter murder because murderers do not think or act in a reasonable or rational manner.[15]

Reverend Breihan did not use specific examples, but he could very well have reminded the Committee that of the three most infamous mass murderers of that era—Abdelkrim Belachheb, Charles Whitman, and James Huberty, two fully intended to die during their assault, and the third, Belachheb, went to his friend Mohamed's house believing he was going to be put into the electric chair. If any of the murderers bothered to think at all, their actions seemed to indicate that punishment, either "death" or "life," meant nothing to them as they loaded their guns.

The Methodist minister also addressed the question of vengeance. "An eye-for-an-eye is no longer appropriate—redemption is. . . . Our attitude should be the same as that of Christ's attitude toward the adulterous woman and the man on the cross," he said as he concluded his testimony.

Gara LaMarche, the Executive Director of the Texas Civil Liberties Union picked up the issue of deterrence, asserting that the Belachheb murders are exactly the kind of crimes least deterred by the death penalty. LaMarche decried the "catechism-like" quality of the death penalty debate. Then he added that, "Proponents of House Bill 8 claim that it is logical to include multiple murders in the death penalty statute as if logic played any part at all in the administration of the death penalty."[16]

Testimony from the opponents, however articulate, enunciated opposition to the use of the death penalty, which was not an issue before the Committee. The death penalty statute in Texas was not going anywhere. The only question was whether mass murderers and serial killers were going to be included, which was what HB 8 proposed. Two weeks later, on February 25, the Committee voted to recommend passage by the full House by a margin of 7-1.[17]

Shortly after the initial hearing, the Legislative Budget Board issued a *Fiscal Note,* which assessed the cost of implementing the bill. It read: "The fiscal implication to the State cannot be determined. It should be noted that the cap placed on the Texas prison population by the Prison Management Act will be reached in fiscal year 1986. The effect will be to shorten the length of stay on inmates already in custody. No fiscal implication to units of local government is anticipated."[18]

If so, the cost-neutral analysis for local governments had to be the result of the anticipated infrequency with which the statute was to be used. (Which was one of the reasons opponents said it was unnecessary.) There is little doubt that capital murder trials cost far more than non-capital cases. In a report by the Death Penalty Information Center, updated in 1994, a Duke University study was used to show how prosecuting capital murder differed from other murder trials. Capital murder trials resulted in:

- More pre-trial motions
- More questioning concerning individual jurors' views on capital punishment and more peremptory challenges to jurors at jury selection
- The appointment of two defense attorneys
- A longer and more complex trial
- A separate penalty phase conducted in front of a jury

- A more thorough review of the case on direct appeal
- More post-trial motions
- Greater likelihood that counsel will be appointed for a federal habeas corpus petition
- More preparation for, and a longer, clemency proceeding

(Undoubtedly, death penalty supporters would use the same list to illustrate the safeguards built into a system that assured justice.) The Death Penalty Information Center report also pointed out that in a capital murder trial there was virtually no likelihood of a guilty plea and a certainty that every avenue a defendant can take will be taken before that walk to the gurney in the death chamber. (And if the defendant doesn't explore every avenue, advocacy groups like the ACLU will—and properly so.)

In Texas, the average cost of a death penalty case was identified as $2.3 million, or about three times the cost of incarcerating an individual under the highest security for forty years. In a six-year period, Texas spent an estimated $183.2 million on the death penalty. No responsible public official can ignore the cost-benefit implications of such staggering amounts of money. Even Norman Kinne was quoted in the report: "Even though I'm a firm believer in the death penalty, I also understand what the cost is. If you can be satisfied with putting a person in the penitentiary for the rest of his life. . . . I think maybe we have to be satisfied with that as opposed to spending $1 million to try and get them executed."[19] (Today, Mr. Kinne does not remember making that statement.)

In all, HB 8, as a measure, received little debate. "Who is to take this life? I cannot do it and I cannot ask a state employee to do it," one legislator argued—in vain. All floor votes were voice votes. The Texas House of Representatives passed HB 8 on March 12, 1985. The Senate and the House adopted a Conference Committee Report on the Bill on April 16, 1985, and shortly thereafter, Democratic Governor Mark White signed it into law.

Today, in the Texas Penal Code, Title 5: Offenses Against the Person, Chapter 19: Criminal Homicide, §19.03 Capital murder reads:

19.03. Capital Murder

(a) *A person commits an offense if he commits murder as defined under Section 19.02(b)(1) and:*

    (1) *the person murders a peace officer or fireman who is acting in the lawful discharge of an official duty and who the person knows is a peace officer or fireman*

    (2) *the person intentionally commits the murder in the course of committing or attempting to commit kidnapping, burglary, robbery, aggravated sexual assault, arson, or obstruction or retaliation*

    (3) *the person commits the murder for remuneration or the promise of remuneration or employs another to commit the murder for remuneration or the promise of remuneration*

    (4) *the person commits the murder while escaping or attempting to escape from a penal institution*

    (5) *the person, while incarcerated in a penal institution, murders another:*

        (A) *who is employed in the operation of the penal institution*

        (B) *with the intent to establish, maintain, or participate in a combination or in the profits of a combination*

    (6) *the person:*

        (A) *while incarcerated for an offense under this section or Section 19.02, murders another*

        (B) *while serving a sentence of life imprisonment or a term of 99 years for an offense under Section 20.04, 22.021, or 29.03, murders another*

    (7) *the person murders more than one person:*

        (A) *during the same criminal transaction*

        (B) *during different criminal transactions but the murders are committed pursuant to the same scheme or course of conduct* [underline added]

    (8) the person murders an individual under six years of age.

    (b) An offense under this section is a capital felony

    (c) If the jury or, when authorized by law, the judge does not find
        beyond a reasonable doubt that the defendant is guilty of an of-
        fense under this section, he may be convicted of murder or of any
        other lesser included offense.

This—19.03(a)(7)(A-B) of the Texas Penal Code—is the legacy of Abdelkrim Belachheb.

II

Almost immediately after trial, Judge Meier appointed Frank Jackson to be Belachheb's appeals attorney. He filed an appeal based on five trial court errors. The first asserted that Judge Meier abused her discretion in appointing Dr. James Grigson as a disinterested expert. Jackson's characterization of Dr. Grigson was particularly harsh: "JAMES GRIGSON is a mendicant who utilizes procedures that have the efficacy of phrenology and astrology, but lack similar public acceptance. His appointment to a case guarantees the rubber stamp will be placed on the prosecution's desires. According to credible reputation evidence adduced at trial the stench of GRIGSON'S reputation has permeated the continental United States." The appeal continued, "In effect GRIGSON is the pariah of the medical community . . . [and] testifies on the basis reminiscent of the old water witches."[20]

Jackson argued that the defense was quick to object and that Dr. Grigson's reputation was so bad and his bias so obvious that any trial court which appoints him is guilty of an abuse of discretion. The appeals court pointed out that the defense's brief did not proffer proof to show why Dr. Grigson was not qualified as an expert.

In the second ground of error, Jackson argued that Judge Meier erred in refusing to allow him to inform the prospective jurors of the consequences of a verdict of not guilty by reason of insanity.

The Appeals Court cited portions of the Texas Criminal Code that specifically prohibited the jury from hearing those facts.

The third ground involved the testimony of Beth, the mutual friend of Belachheb and Joanie, and the person who introduced them. During the trial, Norman Kinne ran into a problem when he found out that Beth had been sitting in the courtroom listening to other witnesses testify. The "Rule" had been invoked by Judge Meier, which means that witnesses are not supposed to hear each other's testimony (to eliminate the possibility of one witness influencing the pending testimony of another).

Kinne wanted Beth to testify that Belachheb admitted to beating Joanie badly enough to put her in the hospital and was proud of it. She was there to rebut Joanie's earlier testimony. Kinne found out that she was in the courtroom only moments before he was to call her to the stand. The Appeals Court ruled that the enforcement of the Rule is within the discretion of the Trial Court, and a reversible error occurs only when there is a clear abuse of that discretion.

The fourth ground of error involved Judge Meier's denying a defense motion for mistrial when Jackson objected to Kinne's commenting on the weight of Dr. Grigson's testimony. It happened when Kinne asked Dr. Grigson if he (Kinne) had hired Grigson to see Belachheb. Jackson objected, "Your honor, I'm going to object to that. That's a direct comment on the weight of the evidence." Judge Meier sustained the objection and Jackson immediately asked that the Judge instruct the jury to disregard the statement—she did so. Jackson then asked for a mistrial and that motion was denied. The Appeals Court ruled that, even if damage had been done, it was rendered harmless by Judge Meier's subsequent instructions to the jury.

And finally, the defense contended that the trial court erred by refusing to submit a charge on the lesser offense of voluntary manslaughter. The charge was given in the cases involving Marcell Ford and Frank Parker. The defense asserted that it should have been given in all six murder cases. Voluntary manslaughter assumes that the behavior of the victim might have provoked the criminal act. Ford might have said something insulting to Belachheb, and Frank Parker was supposed to have tried to stop Belachheb. The Appeals Court ruled that there was no evidence that all six of those killed worked together to provoke Belachheb, and that Ford or Parker's alleged provocation could not be "transferred" to the others.[21]

On November 16, 1985, one year and one day after Judge Meier had sentenced Abdelkrim Belachheb to six consecutive life terms, the Court of Appeals affirmed his conviction. On March 2, 1987, Judge Meier received the Mandate, or the order from the Appeals Court, to carry out the sentence. Thus ended the appeals process for Abdelkrim Belachheb.[22]

III

The Dallas County deputies who delivered Belachheb to the Texas Department of Corrections first brought him to the Byrd Unit. It was, and still is, a diagnostic intake center located one mile north of Huntsville. Huntsville is the administrative center of the Texas prison system. He was placed in a single cell and was scheduled to stay there for a period of three to four weeks. He entered the facility with concerns about his safety. He had asked the deputies who drove him there if he was going to be hurt, so it is entirely possible that he was frightened enough to actually tell the truth while being processed.

The profile and resume he provided to the processor was vastly different from his earlier grandiose stories and job applications. He indicated that his past employment included cooking, welding, and being an electrician and a common laborer—no selling cars in Paris, no business employing dozens of people or contacts in the Middle East, and no formal education. Prison officials indicated that his I.Q. was about 66, but the test was administered in English. He admitted that he was an alcoholic and that he had psychiatric problems and had been admitted to hospitals in Belgium and Switzerland. He claimed to not have had any recent contact with his first wife, Jenny, and his two daughters. He also admitted fathering one illegitimate son—a boy he identified as "Smire."[23]

Interestingly, while being processed, Belachheb was inspected for identifying scars and marks; none of those listed were on his head. When asked to provide a rationale for the offense that brought him to the prison in the first place, he replied, "I don't know."

As a matter of routine, two weeks after his arrival prison officials at the Eastham Unit administered psychological tests prior to his unit assignment.

Within a month, Belachheb began to exhibit the same kinds of behavior patterns that caused the Dallas jailers to "get rid" of him as soon as possible. He complained constantly about the food. In mid-December, he told prison officials that he had been on a hunger strike for nearly two weeks. "He looked strong and fine, but he was put in the infirmary just in case," said Phil Guthrie, a prison spokesman. At the time, Belachheb ate with the other inmates in the cafeteria where no inmate's food intake was monitored. The infirmary he had been transferred to was located in the Huntsville Prison, also known as "The Walls." The Walls also housed the death chamber where all Texas executions are carried out. One of the many ironies of the Belachheb story is that he was at that particular unit to be cared for in an infirmary, not to be put to death. Some others convicted under the statute he inspired would not be so lucky.

Once in the infirmary—he ate.[24]

From the beginning, he did not get along well with the prison guards, and on occasion, he had to be "escorted" back to his cell, admitted prison Colonel D. D. Sanders. "He's having difficulty adjusting. Sometimes he interprets an officer doing his job as harassment. He takes pat searches as an insult."

Additionally, Belachheb made no attempt to become friendly with other prisoners. A Houston bank robber serving a seventy-five-year sentence tried once to befriend him only to give up. "He expects too much from everybody," the felon said. "He thinks we have to drop everything and think about [him] twenty-four hours a day . . . He has driven them all away."

Prison guards characterized him as a lethargic chain smoker sitting and brooding in an eight by ten foot cell. "He don't want anybody to bother him, and he don't bother nobody else," the Warden said.[25]

"[Belachheb] is just like every other prisoner," another official said. "Except he seems to go on a hunger strike fairly often."[26] By June of 1985, he had been on three hunger strikes. If they were designed to draw attention to himself, he must have been enormously gratified when his infamy resurfaced for the first anniversary of his murders. In an interview, Abdelkrim Belachheb answered questions about what he had done on June 29, 1984. But because he was allegedly in the fourth week of his third hunger strike, he had to be brought into the prison's visiting room in a wheelchair. "They say I don't have remorse, but I punish myself everyday," he said about what he called "the accident."

Maybe so, but he still blamed everyone but himself for that accident. Circumstances, family, friends, fate, his victims, women in general, brain damage, and cheap Spanish wine (which brought about his alcoholism) caused the Ianni's tragedy. He married Joanie, he said, to get his "citizenship papers" in the United States, all the while discarding her to look for " . . . a new life, looking for love."

His search for love did not include his family. "I won't write them until they write me," he said with complete indifference.[27]

The height of the attention directed at him was an August 22, 1985, broadcast of an ABC News newsmagazine *20/20* piece on the Ianni's murders. The twenty-minute segment, reported by former Dallas television newsman Bob Brown, chronicled Belachheb's criminal life in Morocco and Belgium. It included Belachheb's first televised interview. Brown also interviewed Belachheb's father, the aging Mohamed Belachheb in Morocco, who communicated through an interpreter. Jenny, Belachheb's still-bitter first wife, discussed their relationship and how he nearly killed her in November 1979. "He loves no one. He loves only himself," she said.

Meanwhile, Belachheb still obsessed over his looks. Earlier in the year the prison dentist had extracted some of his teeth. Belachheb postponed the interview until he could be fitted with dentures.

During his interview with Belachheb, Bob Brown pulled out a letter Mohamed Belachheb wrote to some family members of his son's victims. "It is with deep sorrow and regret that our family learned recently of the innocent people that have fallen victim at the hands of our son. It was a terrible act which time cannot heal. It caused our family to suffer like no other family can suffer."

As he listened to his father's words, his eyes watered and soon tears were streaming down his face.

"What would you tell your father," Brown asked.

"I don't know, I don't know . . . " wept Belachheb.

When asked what he thought of Belachheb's performance, Bob Brown said, "I don't think he was play acting. Generally, people I have met who have committed acts like that feel frustrated only because they have placed themselves in a position where they don't want to be. I didn't feel sorry for him."[28]

The major storyline of the *20/20* segment, however, was about how Belachheb was able to enter the United States using a tourist visa in spite of the fact that he was a fugitive from justice in Belgium. The broadcast was entitled *Passport for Murder*. It featured John McNeill, Barbara Watkins, Terry Rippa, Richard Jones, and Ata (all witnesses to the Belachheb murders.) It showed the barroom, pretty much as it looked on the evening of June 29, 1984. The barstools were recognizably the same used by the victims that night. Brown masterfully reported each step of Belachheb's deceptions to enter the United States—it was shockingly easy to do.

Abdelkrim Belachheb was a fugitive from justice, certainly in Belgium and probably in Morocco, when he secured a visa to enter the United States. His success in securing documentation was attributable to two factors: he lied, and State Department officials did not verify what he said on the application. But then, apparently no visa applications were checked in such a way back then. Another disturbing twist of the story is that even after it had been made clear that Belachheb had lied his way into the United States, government officials could not determine how he had done it.

"Obviously, fraud was involved. What form it took would be hard to say," said a State Department spokesman.

After minor sparring between the Immigration and Naturalization Service (INS), the FBI, the CIA, and the State Department, the latter finally admitted that "it is the responsibility of the applicant to provide correct information."[29]

In January 1985, an angry John McNeill stated, "We need to put some pressure on somebody, and we've go to do this together. I didn't appreciate getting blown away, and I think there was negligence there." John and relatives of four of the six people shot dead on June 29, 1984, joined together to institute a lawsuit against the INS. It never went far. But in many respects the litigants wanted only to draw attention to the problem.

"He should never have been in this country in the first place," John McNeill said.

"Asking him if he is a nice guy is not an adequate screening procedure," McNeill's attorney added.[30]

III

On the day of the guilty verdict that took Abdelkrim Belachheb away from her forever, Joanie told the press that, "He's [Belachheb] a victim, too. And he's ready to die. At least then he'll have some peace. I bought him a grave plot back in July. He'll die in prison. The death sentence would have been more merciful."

Seven months later, she still felt as if Belachheb's days were numbered: "I think part of him had already died—his spirit. I think he is looking to death as his only escape. There is no life for him. Even if he were free, he still knows that he has killed six people. He'll always have that prison of mind."

Joanie was not the only one making predictions about Belachheb. In a rare point of agreement, Dr. Sheldon Zigelbaum, Norman Kinne, and Dr. Clay Griffith all asserted confidently, but for different reasons, that Abdelkrim Belachheb could be counted on to be violent for the rest of his life. "If Mr. Belachheb is placed within an ordinary prison population, he will have one of those outbursts of violence, and the prison population will just kill him, as happens," Dr. Zigelbaum said.

"He's told you long ago what his behavior is going to be like and what it will continue to be like," Norm Kinne said in one of the last words he directed to the jury.

"You can expect that this man is going to commit assault no matter where he is. He is going to be dangerous," said Dr. Griffith during trial.

All three made the same observation: Dr. Zigelbaum saw a patient; Kinne and Griffith saw a heartless and brutal murderer. Few examples could be found to better describe the life of Abdelkrim Belachheb, or the quandary jurors are in when deciding life and death issues.[31]

And finally, except for those touched directly by what happened in Ianni's, after a year had passed and the first anniversary remembered, those curious enough to watch *20/20* turned off their televisions and forgot about Abdelkrim Belachheb.

"Now," Belachheb said, "I'm dying by littles. My life is stopping, shrinking."[32]

------

[1] John McNeill

[2] Norman Kinne quoted in *Dallas Morning News,* November 16, 1984.

[3] Judge Gerry Meier.

[4] The Texas Legislature: A Bill to be Enacted, HB 8, 69th Regular Session, 1985; Texas House of Representatives Committee on Criminal Jurisprudence: *Bill Analysis, HB 8,* 69th Legislature, Regular Session, 1985; Representative Tony Polumbo quoted in *Dallas Times Herald and Dallas Morning News,* November 29, 1984.

[5] Texas House of Representatives: *House Study Group, Daily Floor Report,* March 11, 1985, and Committee on Criminal Jurisprudence: *Bill Analysis, HB 8,* 69th Legislature, Regular Session, 1985.

[6] Ibid.

[7] *Dallas Morning News,* November 11, 1984.

[8] I cover the impact of *Furman* v *Georgia* in Texas in much more detail in Chapter 3 of *Bad Boy From Rosebud;* see also Texas House of Representatives Committee on Criminal Jurisprudence, Ibid.

[9] The irony in this case is that mass murderers and serial killers are almost always white males; Texas House of Representatives: *House Study Group, Daily Floor Report,* March 11, 1985, and Committee on Criminal Jurisprudence: *Bill Analysis, HB 8,* 69th Legislature, Regular Session, 1985.

[10] Ibid.; George Dix quoted in *Dallas Morning News,* November 16, 1984.

[11] Ibid.

[12] Ibid.; Tony Polumbo quoted in Texas House of Representatives Committee on Criminal Jurisprudence, 69th Regular Session, 1985, Committee hearings conducted on February 11, 1985.

[13] Ibid.

[14] Ibid.

[15] Ibid.

[16] Ibid.

[17] Texas House of Representatives Committee on Criminal Jurisprudence: *Committee Report, HB 8,* 69th Regular Session, February 25, 1985.

[18] Texas State Legislature: Legislative Budget Board: *Fiscal Note, in re: Committee Substitute for House Bill No. 8,* March 1, 1985.

[19] Death Penalty Information Center: *Millions Misspent: What Politicians Don't Say About the High Costs of the Death Penalty,* by Richard C. Dieter, Esq., Revised Fall 1994, www.deathpenaltyinfo.org/dpic/r08.html. A supreme irony of the Belachheb Case is that he is a good example of time and money saved by *not* pursuing the death penalty. Frank Jackson made a motion for a new trial that Judge Meier denied. The case was appealed to the Court of Criminal Appeals and only one year later the judgment of the trial court was affirmed and a year after that it was mandated. The adjudication ended there and neither Dallas County nor the State of Texas have had to dedicate any more time or money on Abdelkrim Belachheb. Except, of course, to keep him in prison, which is still a fraction of what it would have cost to exhaust all avenues of appeal through the state and federal courts before he would have been executed.

[20] Texas Court of Appeals, Second Supreme Judicial District: *Abdelkrim Belachheb v Texas,* Brief for the Appellant, No. 02-85-00029-CR, 3-4.

[21] Ibid.

[22] Ibid., *Mandate,* November 14, 1987.

[23] Texas Department of Criminal Justice: *Public Information Display Screen,* current as of April 10, 2002; Confidential sources.

[24] Confidential sources; Phil Guthrie quoted in *Dallas Morning News,* January 4, 1985.

[25] Quotes are from *Dallas Morning News,* June 23, 1985, and *Dallas Times Herald,* June 29, 1985; Confidential sources; *Houston Chronicle,* June 24, 1985.

[26] *Houston Chronicle,* June 24, 1985.

[27] Ibid., and *Dallas Morning News,* June 23, 1984.

[28] Quotes are from ABC News: *20/20,* August 22, 1985 and *Dallas Morning News,* June 23, 1984.

[29] *Dallas Morning News,* August 7, 1984; *Dallas Times Herald,* August 7, 12, 1984.

[30] Quotes are from *Dallas Morning News,* January 8, 1985.

[31] *Texas* v *Belachheb,* 291st Judicial District, Cause no. F84-75078-SU, et. al., VII, pgs. 1628-1748 (Zigelbaum), IX, 2433-40 (Kinne), VI, 2198-2236 (Griffith).

[32] Abdelkrim Belachheb quoted in *Dallas Morning News,* June 23, 1985.

chapter fifteen[1]

Ad Seg

> *"It is a place that robs a person of human-*
> *ity. The depression of the place hits you*
> *in the face. It is the most miserable place*
> *that you can imagine. If you want to*
> *punish someone, put them in there and*
> *forget about them."*
>
> —Dr. Keith Price
> Warden, William Clements Unit,
> Texas Department of Criminal Justice

I

The final "victim" of Abdelkrim Belachheb's murders was Ianni's Restaurant and Club. In some ways the establishment once typified the American Dream. Joe Ianni came to the United States from Italy as a toddler, was processed through Ellis Island, and by the age of eight was in Dallas. He and his wife Totsy worked hard all their lives to build a business, earn an honest living, and leave the results of that hard work to their daughter. In less than three or four minutes, Belachheb took two generations of hard work away from a family of good and decent people.

Like many other infamous crime scenes, Ianni's Restaurant and Club attracted a wide range of gawkers, from the merely curious to the disturbingly weird. The task of asking some of the stranger patrons to leave fell to the bartenders, like Richard Jones, or even

Mary, who performed those tasks carefully and as delicately as possible.

Ianni's bar business did not suffer, but the restaurant side was hurt badly. Infamy slowly eroded the business so that by May 1986 a fire became the occasion to close up once and for all. The space was later leased briefly as a Chinese restaurant, but it closed after a short time. In 1990 it opened again as a Mexican restaurant, which later failed as well. After five years of failed attempts to establish a business there, an employee of the property holding company that owned the building admitted that lingering notoriety made the space difficult to lease. "They should have made it a haunted house, huh?"[2]

During the summer of 2002, the space that was once Ianni's Restaurant and Club was empty. The interior has been gutted so completely that air conditioning ducts and telephone and electric wires hung like entrails from the skeletal remains of a false ceiling. Nothing inside indicates where the U-shaped bar once stood or where the Mike Harris Quartet played. The only remnant of that infamous night is a small square of hardwood tile in the foyer between the two front doors where Belachheb stood to unjam his gun between rounds of murder.

Next door, Cappuccino's is still in business today and its exterior still looks much like it did in 1984. But that area is not teeming with money as it once was. The north Dallas bubble burst in the late 1980s, and Dallasites have been living in a more realistic economic climate ever since. The large apartments, once considered upscale and plush, are beginning to show their age. The grounds are a little less perfectly manicured, and there is a sense that soon the area will need to be refurbished. There are rumors that the Harvest Hill Shopping Center, the home of Cappuccino's and Ianni's, will be leveled.

Melinda Henneberger, the cub reporter for the *Dallas Morning News* whose trip to Brussels broke the story of Belachheb's long criminal history in Europe, left Dallas after six years of reporting to write for New York's *Newsday*. By 1992, she had become a reporter for the *New York Times* and rose to the position of Rome Bureau Chief. In 2002, she resigned that position to write a book about a lost fresco by Leonardo da Vinci. "I knew she was going places," Norman Kinne said recently. Today, Melinda Henneberger is a reporter for *Newsweek*.

Richard Jones, the bartender who felt particles of gunpowder hit his face as Belachheb fired the first shot into Marcell Ford, had bad dreams and trouble sleeping for several years after that deadly night. He left Ianni's before the restaurant closed permanently in 1986. Today, he remains in the Dallas restaurant business as a manager of a well-known Italian restaurant.

John McNeill, the only survivor among those Abdelkrim Belachheb shot, is still a businessman in Dallas. The bullet that went through his torso shocked his spine and paralyzed him so that he could not walk for about three months. In all, Belachheb "took him out" for about a year. He continues to live with the staples surgeons put inside him during the early morning hours of June 29, 1984.

Terry Rippa, who waited patiently for a good song before asking Linda Lowe to dance, and thus became the most reliable witness at Belachheb's trial, is still a dancer. He is, in fact, a dance instructor, the Treasurer of the Dallas Push Club, and was inducted into the National Swing Dance Hall of Fame.

Linda Lowe's brother, Wade Thomas, lives in Fort Worth and is an official with a large aircraft company. "There is no closure for me. I think about my sister every day—no matter what I am doing," he said during a recent interview. Gloria Edge, Linda's mother, never recovered fully from the loss of her daughter, and it took Wade over a decade to listen to any of Linda's music, which he has in the form of her demo tape recordings. "I never knew what hate was before," Wade said, referring to Abdelkrim Belachheb, but with a hint of sadness.

Frank Jackson is still a top-notch criminal defense attorney in Dallas. The Belachheb case remains, to this day, the only insanity defense he has ever brought before a jury that ended in conviction. After more than three decades in criminal law he reflects: "[Norm Kinne] and I started work in the District Attorney's office the same day. Norm found a home. I got out as soon as I became saturated with the same thing day after day and realized the challenges were truly on the defense side."[3]

Dr. Sheldon Zigelbaum, the architect of Belachheb's medical and psychiatric defense, later became the Director of the New Center for Psychotherapies in Boston. In May of 1989, the Massachusetts Board of Registration in Medicine filed sexual misconduct charges against him for allegedly having sex with two patients he was treating during the late 1970s and '80s. During the hearings, six women (four others came forward after the charges were made public) testified that Dr. Zigelbaum had sexually abused them; at least three of the six added that he had encouraged them to use illegal drugs with him. Each testified that he had initiated sex with them while they were in "vulnerable emotional states" due to serious personal problems they had brought to him in his capacity as their therapist. "The charges are being totally denied and are untrue," Dr. Zigelbaum said when asked to comment.[4] In addition to the sexual misconduct charges, he denied allegations of illegal drug use. After one of the women testified that he asked her to secure cocaine, he claimed never to have seen the white powder, much less ever snorted it. He lost much credibility, however, when a former live-in babysitter to his children testified that she witnessed him using the illegal drug regularly. After two years of contentious hearings, the Board voted unanimously to strip Dr. Zigelbaum of his medical license on January 22, 1992, as a result of "gross misconduct in the practice of medicine, malpractice, practicing medicine with gross incompetence and gross negligence."[5]

Today, a physician search of the Massachusetts Board of Registration in Medicine website shows Dr. Zigelbaum's license status as "revoked." A phone call to the Board confirmed that the revocation was permanent as of January 22, 1992, but the *Boston Globe* reported as early as October 4, 1994, that he continued to advertise himself in the 1993-94 *Yellow Pages* under the "Physician's Guide" listing for psychiatry. Apparently the loss of his license prohibited him from writing prescriptions, admitting patients to hospitals, or treating illnesses, but Massachusetts had no law prohibiting him from seeing patients as a psychotherapist.[6]

Jeff Shaw, Norm Kinne's investigator, rose to the position of Chief Investigator for the Dallas County District Attorney's Office, a position he holds today.

Rider Scott later became the First Assistant District Attorney for Dallas County and then the Chief of Staff and Chief Counsel for Texas Governor Bill Clements from 1987-91. He is now a partner of the law firm Thompson Coe of Dallas and is one of the most prominent attorneys in Dallas. (Mr. Scott agreed to an interview for this book, and we had a number of very helpful and pleasant telephone conversations, but we were never able to reconcile our schedules for an appointment for a formal interview.)

Only one month after the conclusion of the Belachheb trial, the *Dallas Morning News* ran a feature entitled "Hanging it up." After twenty years as a Dallas Police officer, seventeen of them as an investigator, Bill Parker announced that he was going to formally submit his resignation as a peace officer on January 3, 1985. He was called a "blood from a stone" interrogator whose skills, at times, seemed to border on the miraculous. "It just isn't fun anymore," he said, frustrated by what he called tighter restrictions and larger bureaucracies.[7]

Today, Bill Parker is the owner of Parker-Jones, Inc., a private investigative group. (He does not take defense cases.) On June 22, 2002, in his office's kitchenette, Bill leaned back in a chair, put his feet up on the table and puffed on a cigar. Belachheb was a relatively simple case; from an investigative point of view, it was all over in two hours. "Do you know how many people got killed in the St. Valentine's Day Massacre?" he asked.

"Seven," the interviewer answered quickly and correctly.

"The difference is that we *solved* our case," Bill said as he took a long puff and spun that cigar in his mouth.

On July 23, 2002, on the seventh floor of the Frank Crowley Courts Building, Judge Gerry Meier still presides over the 291st Criminal District Court, and she is still in complete control. She still has to contend with an occasional 11.07 Writ Of Habeas Corpus that accuses her of not being an impartial judge because she was once sexually assaulted.[8] "I have never been sexually assaulted," she says emphatically.

When an interviewer once hesitated to ask her about being called the "Iron Maiden," she knew what was coming and said, "Go ahead, I can take it." Indeed, she can. Male judges controlling their courts as she does are surely more likely to be considered strong and decisive. Instead, she has had to deal with ridiculous sexism and being called the "Iron Maiden." During an interview for this book, she answered every question without hesitation—hiding nothing. She is matter-of-fact and by-the-book in everything—and will surely be that way until she leaves the bench. Maybe she will leave with a few regrets or second thoughts, but they will not be apparent.

Judge Gerry Meier retired at the end of 2002, after twenty-one years on the bench and six and one-half years as a prosecutor before that. She admits that the past twenty-seven years have "taken their toll," but she will return, occasionally, as a senior visiting judge.

After twenty-seven years with the Dallas County District Attorney's Office, Norman Kinne retired at the end of 1998. Today, he lives near the shores of Lake Whitney, where he plays a lot of golf. He frequently serves as a Marshal on the course there. He has had numerous opportunities to practice law or otherwise become involved in cases—but he turns them down. He has seen his share of controversy; when he retired he meant it.

At the dining room table of his home several miles outside of Whitney, Texas, he sat for an interview, openly wondering whether it was possible to write an entire book on Abdelkrim Belachheb. The case was open and shut. During an interview, toward the end of the afternoon, he pulled out a couple of bottles of cold Miller Genuine Draft for him and an interviewer to battle the June afternoon heat. His voice is still resonant, still having the force of his famous courtroom orations.

II

It happened more than once: A prison official looks at a computer monitor, wrinkles his forehead, leans forward and says, "Whaaat?" Then they punch in more code to call up different mainframe screens to verify what they have just seen.

The information available about Belachheb is nearly unbelievable. "He doesn't play well with the other children," one official said metaphorically. Indeed, after eighteen years in the Texas Prison System, an inmate who behaves moderately well should have between 3,000-4,000 days of "good time" earned. Abdelkrim Belachheb has *none*.

After first going through routine diagnostics at the Byrd Unit in Huntsville, Belachheb was assigned to the Eastham Unit. Within five weeks, he made enough enemies to require him to be reassigned to the Ellis II Unit.

While at Ellis II, on March 25, 1985, the Immigration and Naturalization Service (INS) placed a "detainer" on him. A detainer is an order that a government office, like the INS or a sheriff's office, be contacted before a prisoner is released or paroled. Because he obtained a visa, travel authorization, and permanent resident status through fraud, it is almost certain that if Abdelkrim Belachheb ever gets paroled, he will be deported immediately.

His prison record hauntingly resembles his criminal record in Europe. On December 6, 1985, he threatened harm to another inmate; on December 23, 1985, and January 6, 1986, he refused the orders of guards and was assigned to the highest level of security in the prison system—Administrative Segregation, also known as "Ad Seg." The list goes on—a total of almost fifty disciplinary infractions ranging from minor incidents, such as refusing to work or obey orders, to more serious crimes, like assaults causing injuries.

He has made enemies and created disturbances wherever he has been assigned. At Ellis II he threatened to harm inmates and struck at least one guard. He was assigned to Ad Seg there. History repeated itself at the Wynne Unit.

He never got along well with African American or Hispanic prisoners or guards, and by 1993, he had managed to make enemies of other Muslims.

In 1995, he had to be assigned to the Connally Unit, where he eventually made it to Ad Seg again. On September 7, 1999, he was assigned to the Clements Unit in Amarillo, where he is today.

Eight days after his arrival in the Clements Unit, Belachheb, then fifty-five years old, got into a fight in a vocational education shop with a six-foot six-inch, twenty-three-year-old Hispanic serving a five-year sentence for car theft. Belachheb apparently surprise-attacked the younger and stronger inmate with a three-foot long, "two by four" piece of lumber. Very quickly the young man grabbed a weapon of his own. As about fifteen other prisoners looked on, the instructor ordered both of the men to stop, but they did not until guards arrived. Both were sent to the infirmary for injuries. Belachheb had cuts and bruises; his opponent required eleven stitches near his left ear and four on his top lip.

On January 9, 2001, Belachheb caused a disruption serious enough to require the movement of other inmates from the immediate area. Apparently a prison lieutenant, who was African American, told him to carry certain personal items and move on to another location. Belachheb, who pled not guilty to causing the disturbance during a hearing one week later, claimed that he told the officer that he was on medical restriction and could not do so. At the same hearing, the lieutenant testified that he told Belachheb to leave the gear for buggy transport. Nevertheless, he said that Belachheb threatened to "kick said officer's black ass" and clinched his fist in an aggressive manner. Belachheb was found guilty of the disturbance and fined a loss of forty-five days of recreation, commissary, and property.

On July 21, 2001, Belachheb assaulted another Hispanic inmate nicknamed "Paco." At the time, Paco was thirty-six years old and had a history of robbery and assault. Belachheb attacked him with a five-and-one-half inch razor blade handle with six razors glued to the end. He struck Paco on the head and body causing injuries "requiring treatment beyond first aid." Belachheb required similar treatment as well. On July 25, 2001, he pled guilty to all of the charges leveled against him, and was shortly thereafter assigned to high security Ad Seg—which is where Abdelkrim Belachheb is to be found as of September 15, 2002.

III

In Texas, requests for interviews with prison inmates must be made through the Office of Public Information of the Texas Department of Criminal Justice (TDCJ). From there, a prison official forwards the request to the inmate, who has an absolute right to accept or reject the request. On May 22, 2002, my request for such an interview was forwarded to Abdelkrim Belachheb; by May 28, 2002, he had rejected that request. Prison officials do allow prisoners to receive mail and Belachheb received another request for an interview that way. My letter asked him to reconsider. I included a self-addressed stamped envelope, which he used to reply: [9]

"Courtesy and admiration has motivated me to answer your letter . . . "

The physical appearance of the letter is stunning—almost pleasing to the eye. His penmanship is close to elegant; each curve and loop is almost identical in size and shape. Undoubtedly, great time and care went into this communication. The bottom of every letter touches the light blue lines on the white pages almost perfectly. There are no erasures or scratch-outs. "From BELACHHEB ABDELKRIM #387133" is neatly underlined twice with a straight edge, and the two lines are perfectly parallel.

He continues, " . . . please, allow me to bring to your good attention on the fact that my complexioned life story before and since June 29, 1984, demands much more than few pages." It would be impossible, he wrote, for any American to have a "fair-comprehensive understanding" of his life experiences in a few pages in a book. "Sir; as a matter of fact, without my full cooperation and determination, there is no writer could be able to write all my life story accurately and successfully because there will be many essential facts missing that had occurred in my life." Adequately chronicling the life of Abdelkrim Belachheb, he said, is "practically impossible" since one interview in a "<u>cage</u>" could never capture the complexity of his story.

Grandiosity again. After eighteen years in prison Abdelkrim Belachheb has not changed at all. Predictably, in a few lines the mode switched to victimhood.

"[I]f my living conditions were different then they are actually, I may be delighted to meet . . . for an interview, and work something out. Unfortunately, the circumstances under which I am living leave me no other alternative but to decline your request to meet me because I do not wish to subject myself to possible retaliations for speaking to you—as well as constance harassments."

Then he described High Security Ad Seg in the Clements Unit: "I am confined in the Clements Unit High Security Segregation in windowless cell, dead-locked-up 24 hours a day never get out, and the noise is excessive, totally deprived from natural light and fresh air. Daily mental abuses, and the food is used as a means of punishment." His words are hauntingly similar to complaints he made about the Dallas County Jail eighteen years earlier to Judge Meier.

Grandiosity returned in the next paragraph. He indicated that any project about his life in which he cooperated "would be composed of two books from which probably a successful movie."

Then, in a postscript, the role of victim returned: "High Security Segregation is a living HELL, inhuman and extremely cruel. Has been build by a very vicious mind with the goals to torture prisoners!!" Like his right to a fair trial and vigorous defense, the words, even though they are from Abdelkrim Belachheb, warrant an investigation.

Amarillo, Texas, is in the center of the Texas panhandle. The area is a confluence of great plains, magnificent red canyons, and foothills that eventually blend into the Rocky Mountains. From Amarillo, it is easier to drive to Denver than to Austin.

Early in the morning of September 13, 2002, I drive east on 24th Street toward the Clements Unit where Abdelkrim Belachheb now lives. The sunrise turns the sky into a massive orange inferno, but the ground, as far as the eye can see, is colorless—almost without life. The area has no trees for relief from relentless Texas summers. Inmates planted what trees there are on the grounds. Some of them lean to the north, made that way by prevailing southerly winds.

Clements is high security, which means there is a double fence around the entire perimeter. The warden there, Keith Price, has a Ph.D. in criminal justice. He readily explains that the Clements Unit has a "prison within a prison" called High Security Ad Seg.

The inmates are there because of their behavior *while inside* the prison walls. As Richard Duffy, the Major in charge of that section of the prison said, "You could have a person here who had been convicted of a minor offense. But because they are trouble in prison, they are sent here." High Security Ad Seg is not visible from the front gates of the prison, where visitors enter on the south side. It is back in the northwest corner. To get there, visitors and employees alike—even Major Duffy and Warden Price—must show IDs at least five times before reaching Belachheb's cellblock, which is called a "pod."

A long hallway connects several pods. Down one hall, a nurse is on duty. In another room, an inmate sits in a dentist chair and is having his teeth cleaned. Not far off is the kitchen where meals are prepared for everyone in the area. The guards usually eat the same meals as the inmates (but they do admit to adding seasoning). Meals are served to inmates three times a day from carts holding dozens of trays (each with identical portions of food,) designed to keep food warmed at 140 degrees. Abdelkrim Belachheb is served three hot meals each day, which he takes in his cell. The meals at the Clements Unit are hardly punishment.

His address indicates that he is located in Pod "F," cell 108. Those pods are surreal places. "It is a place that robs a person of humanity. The depression of the place hits you in the face. It is the most miserable place that you can imagine. If you want to punish someone, put them in there and forget about them," admitted Warden Price.

Gang members, white supremacists, and other extraordinarily dangerous men populate Ad Seg. Because of the violence they have directed toward other inmates or guards, these men are in their cells a minimum of twenty-three hours a day. They have their own shower so that they can clean themselves without leaving. During their daily hour of recreation, they are taken outside, alone, to large cages that have a basketball hoop and a chin-up bar. Sources

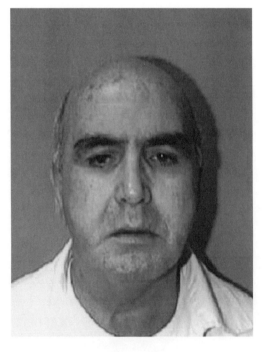

Abdelkrim Belachheb as he appeared in 2002. (Texas Department of Criminal Justice)

inside the prison indicate that Belachheb seldom, if ever, takes advantage of the opportunity to leave his cell. He apparently does not want the fresh air and sunshine he claims to crave.

At least one of the guards believes that Belachheb has successfully manipulated the system and is, in fact, where he wants to be—apart from blacks and Hispanics and in a cell by himself. If he is ever sent back to the general population, this guard believes, he'll attack someone or cause enough trouble until he is sent back to Ad Seg.

While walking through Pod F, there is an overwhelming sense of sadness. First, there is sadness because men such as Belachheb, who care nothing about the swath of destruction they caused, exist. And second, there is sadness because society must resort to a place like Pod F to control such creatures. There are no bars there. The heavy white doors have long, narrow vertical windows with reinforced Plexiglas panes; the cells look more like large refrigerators than jails. As guards and visitors walk through the center of the pod, the inhabitants, every one of them, peer through their narrow windows as if they are seeing something they have never seen before. Some of them do not appear to be wearing clothes.

Common decency requires our wondering if anything could possibly be done to rehabilitate these men, to reintroduce them into the human family. But the truth is that if they are placed anywhere else, and treated any differently, they will kill someone—and that is not a Grigson-like prediction—most of them have already tried.

Abdelkrim Belachheb will be eligible for parole on June 29, 2004—the twentieth anniversary of the Ianni's Massacre. According to his prison datasheet, however, his projected release date is "99 99 9999," TDCJ computer code for "never," which means it is highly unlikely that he will ever get out. Since November 15, 1984, he has lost 3,495 days of good time, and it is inconceivable that anyone would offer to "sponsor" his release.

IV

In spite of the law he brought about, Abdelkrim Belachheb is a poster boy, not for capital punishment, but for life in prison. Some death penalty opponents argue that life in prison is a harsher punishment than lethal injection. In this case, that notion is true. In cell 108 of Pod F, at the High Security Section of Ad Seg of the Clements Unit in Amarillo, sits a man who wallows in self-pity and finds something to complain about nearly every moment of his life. He believes everyone is out to pick on him, he hates the food, and believes he is being harassed and even tortured. Every day he awakens in the same miserable surroundings knowing why he is there. For a man who believes that his life can only be chronicled by *two books and a major motion picture*, surely such an existence is worse than death.

---

[1] Unless otherwise noted, this chapter is largely based on confidential sources and my field research.

[2] Richard Jones; Employee quoted in *Dallas Times Herald*, October 20, 1991.

[3] Frank Jackson quote from an e-mail to the author on October 8, 2002.

[4] Dr. Sheldon Zigelbaum quoted in *Boston Globe*, June 6, 1989 and January 23, 1992. One of Dr. Zigelbaum's accusers alleged that he approached her for sex when her father was undergoing brain surgery. Another, a psychiatric nurse, said he came on to her after she asked for help with depression and suicidal feelings.

[5] Ibid., January 23, 1992.

[6] Ibid., July 6, 1993 and October 4, 1994; The Massachusetts Board of Registration in Medicine physician search can be found at http://www.docboard.org/ma/df/name.html As of October 8, 2002, Dr. Zigelbaum is still listed on *Lycos Yellow Pages* under "Physicians and Surgeons."

[7] Bill Parker quote from *Dallas Morning News*, December 24, 1985.

[8] An "11.07" is a post conviction writ of habeas corpus. It can be filed only after a conviction is final, that is, after being affirmed on appeal and a mandate issued. It states that the person is being held illegally because of some error. It is much like an appeal except the allegations in an 11.07 cannot be the same issues that were raised on appeal. They most often allege ineffective assistance of trial and/or appellate counsel, newly discovered evidence, or error in computation of time served.

[9] Belachheb's written words are as he wrote them—*[sic]* is not used.

Notes on Sources

In the course of writing this book, I amassed several thousand pages of information and conducted several interviews. It would be pedantic to list all of the sources of information already cited in the endnotes, which is as much a bibliography. Here I will describe only the largest and richest of those sources.

Interviews

In May of 2002, I asked the Office of Public Information of the Texas Department of Criminal Justice to contact Abdelkrim Belachheb and relay my desire to interview him for this book. Inmates of the Texas prison system have an absolute right to grant or deny interviews. Mr. Belachheb declined. I then made a direct appeal to Mr. Belachheb by letter. In his reply, he cordially declined my request and volunteered his opinions and observations about the high security Administrative Segregation section he lives in at the Clements Unit in Amarillo, Texas. (See Chapter 15.) In order to investigate Belachheb's claims, and describe the Clements Unit and how he is treated, I toured the prison on September 13, 2002. The Warden assigned a Major to give me complete access to the entire facility, including high security Ad Seg, the health facilities, and the kitchen that prepares meals served to the inmates in that part of the prison. Prison officials offered Mr. Belachheb an opportunity to be interviewed by me at that time, and he declined again.

In an attempt to be as sensitive as possible, and not wishing to "ambush" anyone who may still be troubled by the Belachheb murders, I wrote letters to nearly every person mentioned in this book who is still alive and who could be located. Some of the more important characters, including "Joanie" received a follow-up. In the letters I sought permission to make contact by phone to schedule an interview. Civilians granting an interview included Ronnie Ford, the brother of Marcell Ford; Wade Thomas, the brother of

Linda Lowe; Terry Rippa; Barbara Watkins and Richard Jones, eye-witnesses to the shootings; and John McNeill, the lone survivor among Belachheb's victims. I also interviewed Melinda Henneberger, former reporter for the *Dallas Morning News* and Rome Bureau Chief of the *New York Times*.

Officers of the Court agreeing to be interviewed included Norman Kinne, the lead prosecutor; the Honorable Gerry Holden Meier, the presiding judge; the Honorable Ralph Taite, former Chief Public Defender and presently a County Court Judge in Dallas County; Frank Jackson, Belachheb's Defense Attorney; Jeff Shaw, an investigator for the Dallas County District Attorney; and Bill Parker, formerly of the Dallas Police Department. I also engaged in short conversations and limited e-mail exchanges with Rider Scott, former prosecutor. Unfortunately, we were never able to reconcile our schedules for a formal interview.

Primary Sources

This book is almost completely based on contemporaneous primary documents. As is the case with any adjudicated crime, the richest source of reliable information is the trial transcript. In Texas, it is called the *Statement of Facts*. I secured a copy of *Texas* v. *Belachheb* from the Texas Court of Appeals, Second Supreme District, in Fort Worth, including some exhibits introduced by both the state and the defense. The Belachheb transcript was particularly valuable because of the quality of the direct and cross examination of expert witnesses by very talented lawyers.

In an extraordinary gesture of cooperation, the Honorable Judge Gerry Meier made available her court documents and hand-written notes on *Texas* v. *Belachheb*. They were invaluable.

I also secured access to open records case files of the Dallas County District Attorney. The District Attorney's Office, however, exerted "privilege" over the release of individual memoranda and staff notes collectively known as "work product." They were sustained by a Texas Attorney General's opinion. When I requested a voluntary waiver of privilege, the District Attorney's Office declined. The open records from this source included affidavits, official reports from the Dallas Police Department, and redacted documents from the United States Department of Justice, the State Department, Interpol, and the Immigration and Naturalization Service. My access to crime scene photos was from this source.

The Dallas Police Department provided copies of their affidavits and official reports. Copies of some of Belachheb's personal papers, such as his job applications and resumes, were included in this body of materials. Since the Belachheb Case was so "open and shut," there was little in the way of incident reports to document the investigation (which for all practical purposes lasted only two hours). The most valuable of the documents were the hand written notes taken by officers while interviewing eyewitnesses and other persons connected to the case.

The Texas Department of Criminal Justice's Office of Public Information provided data sheets on Abdelkrim Belachheb, much of which is available on its website.

The Legislative Reference Library in the Texas State Capitol has all of the documents relating to the passage of HB 8 of the 69th Regular Session (1985) of The Texas Legislature. Especially helpful were tape recordings of the proceedings of the Committee on Criminal Jurisprudence, the *Bill Analysis, HB 8*, 69th Legislature, Regular Session, 1985, the Texas House of Representatives: *House Study Group, Daily Floor Report*, March 11, 1985; and the subsequent *Committee Report, HB 8*, 69th Regular Session, dated February 25, 1985. Also noteworthy is the Texas State Legislature: Legislative Budget Board: *Fiscal Note, in re: Committee Substitute for House Bill No. 8*, March 1, 1985.

Secondary Sources

No other book has ever been written about the Ianni's murders. At the time of the Belachheb murders, the Dallas Metroplex was served by three major daily newspapers: the *Dallas Morning News*, the *Dallas Times-Herald,* and the *Fort Worth Star-Telegram.* Competition between the *Morning News* and the *Times-Herald* produced first-rate reporting, including Melinda Henneberger's trip to Belgium to retrace Belachheb's European criminal career. Generally, the *Morning News* provided more accurate and responsible reporting. However, as the endnotes suggest, my use of newspapers was almost always verified by interviews or primary documents.

Good books on the history and geography of Morocco include Thomas K. Park, *Historical Dictionary of Morocco* (London, 1996), and Moshe Gershovich, *French Military Rule in Morocco: Colonialism and Its Consequences* (London, 2000). Also, Mark Ellingham, Don Grisbrook, and Sharen McVeigh, *Morocco* (New York, 2001) provides simple yet vivid descriptions of places of interest in the Fes/Meknes area.

Good Internet sources about the different areas of Morocco include www.cia.gov and www.arab.net/morocco. My use of those sites is current as of July 4, 2002.

The Perry-Casteñada Library of the University of Texas at Austin has a large collection of maps developed shortly after World War II that are ideal for describing the Meknes/Fes region because they were developed while Abdelkrim Belachheb grew up in the area.

It should be noted, however, that this book addresses Moroccan history and culture *only* insofar as it relates to Belachheb's defense; my study is limited to that context and is not intended to be a reference in this area. The authoritative study of the Brotherhood of the Hamadsha remains Vincent Crapanzano's, *The Hamadsha: A Study in Moroccan Ethnopsychiatry* (Berkeley, 1973). David M. Hart is a prolific writer and the authority on tribes and society in Morocco.

Recognizing my limitations when it came to Moroccan history and culture, I consulted with Dr. Deborah Kapchan, a former resident of Morocco and presently an Associate Professor of Anthropology, the University of Texas at Austin, and Dr. Fatihah

Hamitouche, a Berber and a visiting Fulbright Scholar of the Center for Middle Eastern Studies at the University of Texas at Austin. Both very generously provided valuable suggestions most of which I accepted and incorporated into my work; but of course, the responsibility for veracity is mine alone.

Bob Brown's report for ABC News' *20/20* from Morocco and Belgium is a valuable source about the only witness to Belachheb's childhood who has ever spoken publicly—his father, Mohamed Belachheb. It was first broadcast on August 22, 1985.

Index

Belachheb's crimes in, 30-
31,153, 169, 211, 234-35;
Belachheb fugitive from, 45;
divorce petition granted, 50;
Belachheb's work history in,
63-64; Belachheb's psychiatric
visits in, 73; Melinda
Henneberger in, 142-43
Beni Ammar, Morocco, 14, 16,
18, 21-22, 24, 26, 63, 198
Berbers, 14; history, 15, 18, 20-22,
24, 26, 146, 152, 164, 167, 206
Beth (Belachheb acquaintance),
50, 54-55, trial testimony, 182-
83, 231
Black Rage (defense), 150
Bloom, John (columnist), 146
Blum, Michael (policeman), 103-
4
BMW, 64
Boardman, Tom A. (Magistrate),
140
Bobby (Linda Lowe's first
husband), 69
Boston Globe, 242-43
Boston, Massachusetts, 156, 176-
77, 242
Branch, Elmer (death row
inmate), 223
Breihan, Reverend Bob (death
penalty opponent), 226
Bremond, Texas, 68
Brierbeek (psychiatric hospital),
34-35, 144
British Empire, 14
Brotherhood of the Hamadsha,
17, 19
Brown, Bob (Journalist), 10, 16,
234
Brumel Hotel (Luzanne,
Switzerland), 63
Brussels, Belgium, Belachheb's
crimes in, 29-31; 198;
cosmopolitan nature of, 30-31,
34-37; 54, 57, 63-64, 142-43,

145, 240
Busy Bee Grill (Dallas), 84
Byrd Unit (Prison), 232, 245
Byrd, Don (former Sheriff), 190-
92
Byzantines, 14

C

Café des Ours (Brussels café), 33
C Jam Blues, 95
Calhoun, Buford V. (murder),
133
California, 44-47, 199
Calisi, Ted (public defender),
139-40, 144-45, 155, 160
Canada, 38
capital punishment, 8, 9, 191,
211, 217-18; debated in the
Texas Legislature, 220-28; 252
Cappuccino's Restaurant and
Club, location, 1-2, 62; Marcell
Ford at, 86-87; Barbara
Watkins at, 89; Belachheb's car
at, 97; call to police from, 113;
Bill Parker's car at, 116; talk of
murders, 134; Ligia Koslowski
at, 159; still in business, 240
Carol (waitress), 99
Carthaginians, 14
Casablanca, Morocco, 13, 22-23,
29, 36, 38, 42, 173
Center for the English Language,
47
Central Intelligence Agency
(CIA), 11, 41, 236
Chevrolet, 64
Chicago Seven Trial, 151
Chicago, Illinois, 46, 86, 158
Christianity, 15
Citrogen, 64
Clements Unit (prison), 239, 246,
248-49, 252
Clements, Bill (Governor), 135,
243
Cleopatra, 153

Belachheb's crimes in, 198-99, 211, 234-35
Moscone, George (Mayor of San Francisco), 217
Moulay Idriss (Islamic leader), 19
Mullen, Dr. John (prosecution expert), 182; trial testimony, 186-88

N
National Association of Criminal Defense Lawyers, 150, 178
National Enquirer, 178
National Swing Dance Hall of Fame, 241
Nazis, 14, 15, 20-21
Nelson, Willie, 69
Netherlands, 29, 38
neuropsychology, 175
New Age Refrigeration, 88
New Center for Psychotherapies, 242
New York City, NY, 41, 46, 196
New York Times, 241
Newsday, 241
Nick (Dallas businessman), 70-73, 76-78, 96, 133, 184-85, 199
Noble, Gary (former Jackson client), 150
Norman (musician), 95, 114
North Dallas Bank Building, 80
Nzala Beni Ammar. *See* Beni Ammar

O
Oak Cliff (Dallas), 114
organic personality syndrome, 193
Oswald, Lee Harvey, 4

P
Paco (prison inmate), 247
Padre Island, Texas, 81
Paganism, 15
Pam (bartender), 113

paranoid personality disorder, 193-94, 198, 207
Parents of Murdered Children, 226
Paris, France, 23, 63, 232
Park, Thomas K. (author), 15
Parker, Bill (detective), at crime scene, 1-5; background of, 114-17; arrests Belachheb, 124-28, 132; regarding Norman Kinne, 138; at Grand Jury, 140; testimony of, 160-61; returns to stand, 189-90; regarding death penalty, 208; today, 243-44
Parker, Frank Rance (victim), background of, 89-90; *89,* at Ianni's, 92, 105; murdered, 108-9; 115, 117; family of, 158; voluntary manslaughter, 231-32
Parker-Jones, Inc. (private detective agency), 243
Parkland Hospital (Dallas), 4, 114
Parrish, John S. (murderer), 132
Passport for Murder (20/20 episode), 235
Patton, General George S, Jr. (US Army), 20
Perot, Ross (businessman), 134
Pete (restaurant owner), 76-78
Peugeot, 64
Phelan, Sandy (lawyer), 150
Phoenix, Arizona, 91
Polumbo, Tony (legislator), 221, 224-25
Porsche, 70, 184
post traumatic stress syndrome, 178
Price, Dr. Keith (warden), 239, 249-50
Prince, Billy (chief of police), 132, 160
Pyrenees Mountains, 23